Playing Dirty

PLAYING DIRTY

Sexuality and Waste in Early Modern Comedy

WILL STOCKTON

University of Minnesota Press
Minneapolis
London

A version of chapter 2 appeared previously as "'I am made an ass': Falstaff and the Scatology of Windsor's Polity," *Texas Studies in Literature and Language* 49, no. 4 (2007): 340–60; copyright 2007 by the University of Texas Press; all rights reserved. A version of chapter 5 appeared previously as "Cynicism and the Anal Erotics of Chaucer's Pardoner," *Exemplaria* 20, no. 2 (Summer 2008): 143–64; copyright 2008 by Maney Publishing, www.maney.co.uk/journals/exm and http://www.ingentaconnect.com/content/maney/exm.

Published by the University of Minnesota Press
111 Third Avenue South, Suite 290
Minneapolis, MN 55401-2520
http://www.upress.umn.edu

Library of Congress Cataloging-in-Publication Data

Stockton, Will.
    Playing dirty: sexuality and waste in early modern comedy / Will Stockton.
        p.   cm.
    Includes bibliographical references and index.
    ISBN 978-0-8166-7459-6 (hc: alk. paper) — ISBN 978-0-8166-6607-2 (pb: alk. paper)
    1. English literature — Early modern, 1500–1700 — History and criticism.   2. English drama (Comedy) — History and criticism.   3. Sex in literature.   4. Human body in literature.   5. Sodomy in literature.   6. Feces in literature.   7. Anus (Psychology).
8. Psychoanalysis and literature.   I. Title.
    PR428.S48S76 2011
    822'.0523093538   2010032608

Printed in the United States of America on acid-free paper

The University of Minnesota is an equal-opportunity educator and employer.

18 17 16 15 14 13 12 11   10 9 8 7 6 5 4 3 2 1

Contents

eAcknowledgments

THIS BOOK IS QUITE DIRTY, AND NOT ONLY BECAUSE IT IS about scatological comedy and thus full of dirty jokes. If dirt is "matter out of place," as Mary Douglas famously defines it, this book is also structurally dirty — or what I call "playful." Most first books are more tightly organized, their geography more uniform, than this one. Thus my first acknowledgments go to those people who first helped me theorize and market such an unclean project: Linda Charnes, Karma Lochrie, Ellen MacKay, and Shane Vogel. Ellen deserves special thanks for being a most generous friend, and for repeatedly reminding me to play nice.

Vin Nardizzi and Jim Bromley are friends who have inspired this book over the course of many conversations, and both have also commented on various parts of the manuscript. Stephen Guy-Bray, Noreen Giffney, Michael O'Rourke, Goran Stanivuković, Scott Herring, and Joan Pong Linton are among those who have supported this project more generally, providing at times crucial advice and encouragement. Clare Kinney and Elizabeth Fowler fostered my interest in Renaissance literature when I was an undergraduate. I would also be severely remiss if I did not thank Jeff Peeples and Robert Spiotta, who taught me how to write about literature when I was entertaining misguided aspirations of being a horror novelist.

Two of this book's chapters have appeared in earlier forms as essays in *Texas Studies in Literature and Language* and *Exemplaria*. I am grateful to the editorial staff and anonymous readers at both journals, and especially to R. A. Shoaf at the latter, for shepherding these essays into print. At the University of Minnesota Press, Richard Morrison, Adam Brunner, Kristian Tvedten, Rachel Moeller, and Mike Stoffel have been equally beneficent shepherds. Christopher Pye and a second, anonymous reader reviewed this manuscript for the Press, and both offered invaluable advice for its improvement. Sallie Steele compiled the thorough index.

My colleagues at Ball State University and Clemson University have made my transitions — from graduate student to assistant professor, and then from one assistant professorship to another — remarkably painless. I am particularly grateful to Adam Beach, Pat Collier, Jonathan Beecher Field, Bob Habich, Susan Hilligoss, Joyce Huff, Michael LeMahieu, Kecia McBride, Debbie Mix, Lee Morrissey, Barton Palmer, Catherine Paul, Rai Peterson, and Elizabeth Rivlin, as well as the many students who have made teaching so enjoyable. I also appreciate Ball State for graciously supplying me with funds to secure reproduction rights for previously published material in this book.

I hope my parents, Anne and Chip Stockton, are not so embarrassed by such a dirty book. I love them dearly, and their support forms the backbone of my career. Thanks as well to the rest of my family, my friend Dennis Brito, and my current and late canine companions — Mao, Tojo, Min, and Hobbes — who offered their own breed of support by frequently sacrificing room on the couch for me to read.

Finally, I will not pretend that I can adequately acknowledge my gratitude to my partner, Howard Anderson. Despite his strong aversion to most things grotesque, Howard has built a life with someone who, for the past six years, has thought almost obsessively about the relationship between eroticism and excrementality. Howard has also endured my terribly ornery writing moods, many of them prompted by a certain relic-peddling pilgrim. I have promised him that the content of my next project will not be so filthy. At this moment, however, I can think of no better way to express how happy Howard makes me, and how much I owe him, than to dedicate this book to him against his wishes.

Introduction

My lord, as I was sewing in my chamber,
Lord Hamlet, with his doublet all unbraced,
No hat upon his head, his stockings fouled,
Ungartered, and down-gyvèd to his ankle,
Pale as his shirt, his knees knocking each other,
And with a look so piteous in purport
As if he had been loosèd out of hell
To speak of horrors, he comes before me.
— Ophelia, *Hamlet,* 2.1.78–85

I N A FAMILIAR SCENE FROM ONE OF SHAKESPEARE'S MOST FAMIL-
iar plays, there remains a detail not often discussed. Having just
met with the ghost of his father, Hamlet appears to Ophelia without a hat, with his doublet unfastened, and, as Ophelia reports to her
father, with "his stockings fouled / Ungartered, and down-gyvèd to his
ankle[.]" For the most part, the sumptuary aspects of Hamlet's appearance have not roused much critical or editorial interest. Taken together,
they construct the image of a disheveled and ragged prince that testifies readily enough to the fact that Hamlet has been traumatized by his
encounter with his father's ghost. Yet here at the beginning of this book,
I would like to pause over this third detail — the fouled stockings — to
ask after their unique import in the construction of this image. Specifically, I would like to ask what Ophelia means when she says that Hamlet's
stockings are fouled. Has Hamlet dragged his stockings on the ground,
or, just perhaps, has Hamlet soiled himself?

Depending on one's critical orientation toward filth, one can probably come up with several, or no, reasons for asking this question. (I have not encountered any discussion of this question in print, though several fellow scholars claim to me that they "heard it somewhere.") Leaning toward psychoanalytic criticism, and thus tending to find filth "symptomatic," I ask this question because it provides a useful way back into Jacques Lacan's famous reading of the play, "Desire and the Interpretation of Desire in *Hamlet*." In this series of lectures from his sixth seminar, Lacan translates Freud's analysis of Hamlet's Oedipal paralysis into an account of a man who has not simply "lost the way of his desire," but who has more precisely lost the phallus.[1] Hamlet's rejection of Ophelia evinces this loss: she becomes the phallic "symbol signifying life," whom Hamlet calls a "breeder of sinners" (3.1.122–23).[2] Lacan does not elaborate on his diagnosis in these terms, but Hamlet's loss of the phallus also suggests the prince's "regression" to the anal stage of psychosocial development. To allow a scatological translation of *fouled* is to allow that Hamlet's struggle with bowel control symptomatizes this loss. It is in this "anal" capacity too that Hamlet becomes one of Shakespeare's clowns: he "proceeds basically by way of ambiguity, of metaphor, puns, conceits, mannered speech," or the playful "substitution of signifiers."[3] All words are unmoored, vulnerable to manipulation, until he meets with the phallus again in death. According to Lacan, "I'll be your foil" (5.2.192) is the prince's most telling pun, for it signals Hamlet's perception of the phallus in the sword wielded by his double — his *foil* — Laertes. Both Ophelia's brother and the sword materialize the phallus as Hamlet's lost object in this tragedy of the "punster's annihilation."[4]

I leave it to the reader to judge the persuasiveness of this revised Lacanian reading of *Hamlet.* Perhaps the reading works within the terms Lacanian psychoanalysis sets out for itself, but even so I do not think a scatological translation of *fouled* — which I would allow but which I cannot prove anymore than one can disprove it — should necessarily serve to reinforce the centrality of the phallus in Hamlet's psychic life. I also think that Lacan focuses too much on making sense of Hamlet's misogyny and his participation in the duel to realize the consequences of his own quasi-deconstructive suggestion regarding Hamlet's clowning:

It is in this playfulness, which is not merely a play of disguises but the play of signifiers in the dimension of meaning, that the very spirit of the play resides.

Everything that Hamlet says, and at the same time the reactions of those around him, constitute as many problems in which the audience is constantly losing its bearings. This is the source of the scope and import of the play.[5]

If the "sprit of the play" lies in the "play of signifiers," Lacan admits into his own phallocentric interpretation of the play's "dimension of meaning" none of the "problems" that cause the audience to lose its bearings. More specifically, in conflating the play with its protagonist, he does not allow the play of signifiers to take place outside the playground of the phallus.[6] Like Polonius, Lacan approaches Hamlet with a desire to uncover the true cause of his "antic disposition" (1.5.173), reducing him and the play to a confirmation of what the psychoanalyst already knows: that everyone desires the phallus. And while his approach holds considerable explanatory potential, it also makes sense of Hamlet's madness at the expense of its own identification of the play's antihermeneutic impulse — what many critics have likewise identified as the play's metacritical resistance to interpretation.[7]

The Body of the Time

If my reader will forgive me for so predictably opening a book on psychoanalysis and early modern literary studies with a discussion of *Hamlet,* the curious case of Hamlet's stockings does bring into focus a number of issues with which this book is concerned. One of these issues, although almost entirely implicit rather than explicit in the chapters themselves, is the status of psychoanalysis as a hermeneutic. In both analytic practice and literary studies, psychoanalysis has long functioned as what Paul Ricouer first described as a hermeneutic of suspicion, a paranoid mode of critical interpretation that treats all symptoms as manifestations of the kind of "complex" truths long detected in Hamlet's psyche.[8] By contrast, this book puts into literary critical practice several aspects of Jean Laplanche's antihermeneutic practice of psychoanalysis — a practice based in, though not reducible to, Freud's early theory that the cause of hysteria lies in the subject's seduction as an infant.

Freud abandoned seduction theory in part because it led him to the conclusion that an improbably large number of children were subject to sexual abuse, and in part because the reality of seduction proved difficult to establish. Yet Laplanche redefines seduction as a child's reception of "enigmatic signifiers": not just real physical abuse, but, more "innocently," verbal and nonverbal messages freighted with untranslatable content. According to Laplanche, a child represses what does not make sense about these messages into his or her unconscious. This understanding of the unconscious as an individual reservoir of nonsense chafes against Freud's later understanding of the unconscious as a reservoir of universally shared desires. The latter constitutes psychoanalysis as a hermeneutic of suspicion, but through the former Laplanche revitalizes Freud's original practice of psychoanalysis as a method of *detranslation*— a way of making sense of ciphered messages, or symptoms, through the technique of free association, and without immediate recourse to "preestablished codes."[9]

This book is not about seduction theory, but it affirms that free-associative detranslation can function as a psychoanalytic method, and consequently that psychoanalysis can function as what Eve Sedgwick calls a method of "reparative reading." This way of reading challenges methodological conventions, even those of psychoanalysis (which is not a monolith), by respecting the difference between works of art and the critical theories devised to make sense of them. In her critique of "paranoid reading," Sedgwick represents the psychoanalytic hermeneut as Lacan (and Judith Butler in Lacanian mode) "asserting the inexorable, irreducible, uncircumnavigable, omnipresent centrality, at *every* psychic juncture, of the facts (however facetious) of 'sexual difference' and the 'phallus.'"[10] This same Lacan insists that the truth of Hamlet's madness lies in his loss of the phallus. Practicing psychoanalysis as free-associative detranslation does not mean that "preestablished codes" like "sexual difference" or "the phallus" (or "repression," "lack," and "castration") are never germane; as my own readings attest, these codes are variously useful in various contexts. But these codes are also always open for reconfiguration, for theoretical expansion, through engagement with individual texts. Furthermore, antihermeneutic psychoanalysis allows the signifier to play, to freely associate, outside of what other texts or readers have already established as translative paths, and in doing so it establishes new, rather than rediscovers old, syntheses between signifiers. Crucially, antihermeneutic psychoanalysis is not synonymous with an inattention to "depth," or with a rejection of the unconscious, but rather with an attention to gaps, omissions, and slippages that avoids the immediate identification of these as evidence of psychoanalytic dogmas. As practiced here, antihermeneutic psychoanalysis avoids the totalizing tendency of other psychoanalytic reading practices and allows early modern texts to inform, rather than simply be subject to, psychoanalytic theories of anal eroticism and comedy.

Practicing psychoanalysis as an antihermeneutic also requires a queer orientation toward time — queer because it resists what Jonathan Goldberg and Madhavi Menon have described as a heteronormative "capitulation to teleology" that maps time only along a *straight* line.[11] Heterotemporality neglects the ways in which messages — in texts or as whole texts — are, as Laplanche says, "retranslated . . . following a temporal progression which is, in alternative fashion, by turns retrogressive and progressive."[12] Other early modernists have argued that in its capacity as a historiography, psychoanalysis is uniquely equipped to resist this capitulation. While distinguishing queer historiography by its "willful perversion of notions of temporal propriety and the reproductive order of things," Carla Freccero defends psychoanalysis as "a historical method" that "argues for an eccentric relation between events and their effects" and "challenges the empiricism of what qualifies as an event itself."[13] Graham Hammill has also made queer use of psychoanalysis to explore the Christian civilizing process's temporal consolidation of the body and its "unhistorical" residue, the Pauline flesh.[14] Freccero's and Hammill's work contributes to a larger defense of psychoanalysis against the blunt charge of ahistoricism — the charge that psychoanalysis simply ignores historical difference. As Carla Mazzio and Douglas Trevor write, "psychoanalysis really *is* history: a method of interpretation organized around generating narratives of the past."[15] This truth notwithstanding, I maintain that the antihermeneutic psychoanalytic method can be most accurately described as (a)historical — at once ahistorical and historical, where history is understood as a sequential narrative of messages (or Freccero's "events"). Antihermeneutic psychoanalysis attends simultaneously to the construction and derogation of historical narratives by focusing on messages that signify in excess of both their historicity and received psychoanalytic notions. History arranges itself through the translation of these messages and rearranges itself as these elements are subject to retranslation and detranslation.

With this (a)historical and antihermeneutic calibration of the psychoanalytic method, this book analyzes both early modern and psychoanalytic constructions of the anus as a dually erotic and excretory orifice. Again, it does not do so in order to assert (often prescriptively, as such arguments go) the supremacy of the phallus as the object of desire, or the insusceptibility of sexual difference to deconstruction. Quite the opposite, it argues that sexual difference is something that anal eroticism, which often has nothing at all to do with the phallus, does deconstruct. Psychoanalytic theories of anal eroticism also do not figure explicitly in each chapter, but the construction of the anus that I am analyzing throughout has its Freudian origins in the stage theory of maturation: the theory that around the age of two children become subject to the repressive demands of an "external world" that tells them the pleasures they derive from defecation are shameful, and that defecation itself is "improper and must be kept secret."[16] Of course, the extensive psychological, anthropological, and historical critiques of Freud's narrative of psychosocial development render claims for the universality of this childhood experience untenable, at least as Freud describes it.[17] Equally untenable are claims that certain personality traits such as cleanliness and thriftiness necessarily derive from a subject's pronounced infantile struggle with bowel control. My claim here is only that psychoanalysis, as variably practiced by Freud, Lacan, Laplanche, and others (the analysts I prefer reading, but hardly the only ones who have anything to say about anal eroticism), develops historically antecedent ways of thinking about the anus, its pleasures, and their subjection to civilizing injunctions. Justified critiques of psychoanalytic universalism should not foreclose the ability to establish these historical continuities, nor should they prevent us from acknowledging that, in certain cases, psychoanalytic theories seem quite appropriate to the "puzzle" at issue. A historicist disregard for psychoanalysis leaves the impression that psychoanalytic theories are thoroughly ahistorical, without their own history in medical and social thought. At the same time, it renders inaudible the ways in which literature can speak back to psychoanalysis, not simply as the subject of its reading but as part of its past and future.[18]

The case of Hamlet's stockings further illustrates how the detranslation of early modern scatological symptoms requires carefully attending to relationships between signifiers whose resonance is not solely psychoanalytic. Here the strange repetition of King Hamlet's appearance to his son in Hamlet's appearance to Ophelia solicits a connection between the prince's fouled stockings and the "foul crimes" (1.5.12) for which the king is "confined to fast in fires" (1.5.11) until they are "burnt and purged away" (1.5.13). Considering the scatological resonance of purgatory, one might posit that the father's purgation of the flesh manifests in the prince's loosening of his bowels. (Hamlet appears "*loosèd* out of hell / To speak of horrors" [2.1.84–85, emphasis added].) When the king's ghost later reappears to Hamlet in Gertrude's chamber, Gertrude exclaims that Hamlet's hair "like life in excrements / Start up and stand on end." (3.4.112–13). Hair is one of the many excremental products of the humoral body, so Gertrude does not exactly mean that her son's head is covered in animated dung. Yet if psychoanalytic physiologies are proleptically sensible within early modern humoralism — as David Hillman, Cynthia Marshall, and Michael Schoenfeldt have argued — Lacan's notion of the play of the signifier may connect these excremental referents despite their construction under an earlier discourse of the body.[19] Schoenfeldt writes that the psychoanalytic emphasis on catharsis derives from Galen, the difference being that Galen "imagines humoral excess as the source of illness, [whereas] psychoanalysis locates dangerous excess on the plane of the verbal, the imaginary and the mnemonic."[20] *Hamlet,* I would argue, effects a translation between these and other understandings of excess: anatomical, linguistic, and religious, early modern and psychoanalytic. This book in turn explores the scatological manifestations of such purgative logics, more than once placing humoral physiology in relation to psychoanalytic physiology as two discursive regimes whose differences, if overstated, can render inaudible the ways they resonate with one another.

This exploration itself builds on many of the works that collectively make up the field of "waste studies." As Susan Signe Morrison defines this field in her book on late medieval excrementality, waste studies is "focused on filth, rubbish, garbage, and litter."[21] The most influential works in this field include Norbert Elias's *Civilizing Process*, the classic sociohistorical account of the formation of the bourgeois bodily habitus; Mary Douglas's *Purity and Danger*, an anthropological study of taboo and "dirt"; Mikhail Bakhtin's *Rabelais and His World*, a formalist analysis of the carnivalesque celebration of the "lower bodily stratum"; Julia Kristeva's *Powers of Horror*, a psychoanalytic study of abjection; and, most recently, Martha Nussbaum's *Hiding From Humanity*, an examination of the politics of disgust.[22] Navigating the analytical terrain mapped by these works, a growing number of medieval and early modern scholars have worked to situate the excremental body historically by studying changes in waste management regulations, the emphasis on purgation in medical (again, especially humoral) discourse, the delineation of private and public space in both urban and rural environments, excremental aesthetics, and the relationship between the sacred and the profane in religious cultures.[23] This book ultimately seeks, however, to pressure what Hamlet calls, in his instruction to the players, the "body of the time" (3.2.21–22) — to pressure, that is, the body's historicity by pressuring the joints between sexuality and waste, especially scatological waste. Hamlet's instruction that the players show precisely this body's "form and pressure" (3.2.22) cannot but sound ironic in a play in which time is so famously out of joint. The joints on which I focus in this book connect different vocabularies of anal eroticism. These vocabularies are not simply early modern and psychoanalytic, but more specifically "fundamentalist" and death driven.

To invoke these vocabularies is to invoke two essays known to most scholars of early modern sexuality: Leo Bersani's "Is the Rectum a Grave?" and Jeffrey Masten's "Is the Fundament a Grave?" Bersani answers his titular question in the affirmative: consequent to the AIDS pandemic, the rectum has become a grave, a symbol of devastating, infectious passivity, and the mortal end of "the masculine ideal . . . of proud subjectivity."[24] In this respect, the gay man's immediate ancestor is the syphilitic Victorian prostitute: "The realities of syphilis in the nineteenth century and of AIDS today 'legitimate' a fantasy of sexuality as intrinsically diseased. . . .

Women and gay men spread their legs with an unquenchable appetite for destruction."[25] Looking further into the past, Masten points to Jonathan Goldberg's and Patricia Parker's work on sodomy and the preposterous (*hysteron proteron*) as an "utterly convincing" demonstration of the link between the grave and rectum — or in period terms, the *fundament* — in the Renaissance.[26] But Masten also crucially reopens Bersani's titular question to suggest that the fundament's etymological relation to *foundation* vanishes in a translation of *fundament* to *rectum:*

> The fundament is not always necessarily imagined in this cultural context as a passive recipient or receptacle of dominating penetration. Instead, it is a "grounde, a foundation, a building," — "it hath *or is* a grounde or foundation." Or, as Florio also translates, "Also an offspring, beginning, or groundworke." This is not a language of passivity; in fact, it seems largely outside or unengaged with an active/passive binary. At the same time, the fundament is imagined as originary: an offspring, beginning — and thus at some distance from the preposterous ends of other anal rhetorics.[27]

Citing examples from John Florio, Thomas Elyot, James I, Andreas Vesalius, Phineas Fletcher, Christopher Marlowe, and Shakespeare, Masten excavates the cultural sarcophagus of this foundational anal rhetoric. In the process, he situates the rhetoric of fundamentalism alongside and in opposition to the coterminous rhetoric of the preposterous.

I quibble with Masten only insofar as he disallows the same coexistence of anal rhetorics within psychoanalysis when he turns to address fundamentalism's queer potential. Appealing to Guy Hocquenghem's 1972 anti-Oedipal manifesto *Homosexual Desire,* Masten pits the fundamentalist body against the Freudian one:

> [M]y hypothesis is also a historicist attempt to address Guy Hocquenghem's theorization of the anus as the seat of privately owned subjectivity: "[I]t forms," he says, activating the etymologies at the base of my argument, "the subsoil of the individual, his 'fundamental' core." To think this way might be to emerge from within the Freudian model that Hocquenghem's text itself works to resist, in which (he argues) "the homosexual can only be a degenerate, for he does not generate — he is only an artistic end to the species." The fundament — if not, in

Hocquenghem's terms, "the homosexual" — might be said to found, to generate, to merge in a (to us) strangely active-passive, object-subject position.[28]

Masten later qualifies this claim by noting that fundamentalism "may hold no great liberatory erotic potential," especially in texts where it seems activated without any "sodomitical or homosexual valence."[29] Nonetheless, he leaves us to assume that the Freudian body is irredeemably homophobic — that the homosexual, in Hocquenghem's interpretation of Freud, "can only be a degenerate, . . . an artistic end to the species."

No doubt heterosexist practices of psychoanalysis warrant such a critique, as Hocquenghem well knew. But psychoanalysis is not an irredeemably heterosexist leviathan, and its own fundamentals are not entirely purged of the anal rhetoric of fundamentalism.[30] Lacan offers, for example, the following explanation for the title of his seminar *The Four Fundamental Concepts of Psychoanalysis:*

> [F]*undamentum* has more than one meaning, and I do not need to remind you that in the Kabbala it designates one of the modes of divine manifestation, which, in this register, is strictly identified with the *pudendum*. All the same, it would be extraordinary if, in analytic discourse, we were to stop at the *pudendum*. In this context, no doubt, the fundamentals would take the form of the *bottom* parts, were it not that those parts were already to some extent exposed.[31]

Linking the fundamental concepts of psychoanalysis to the pudendum (and the pudendum to divinity — a connection informing my reading in chapter 5), Lacan describes the psychoanalytic method as a probe of the dually genital and anal "bottom" of the subject — "the subsoil of the individual, his [or now her] 'fundamental' core." Lacan thereby activates, like Hocquenghem, the etymologies at the base of Masten's argument. Furthermore, he illustrates Celia Daileader's important corrective to Masten's philology. In her essay on Renaissance gynosodomy (a term she uses specifically to reference men's anal sex with women), Daileader points out that Renaissance anatomists' frequent figuration of the female reproductive system as scatologically grotesque means that "any figuration of the anus-as-foundational is bound to draw its power from analogy with the womb."[32] I would now quibble with Daileader's totalizing assessment of this analogy, but the fundament does frequently figure in Renaissance and psychoanalytic morphologies as a feminine seat of generation, a seat that is also potentially a threat to life, or a grave.

Chapters 3 and 4 of this book look to both morphologies to expand the study of sodomy beyond male homoerotic relations. Though Foucault identified sodomy as an "utterly confused category," with the potential to code nongay but otherwise transgressive sexual relations, the study of early modern sodomitical discourse has been largely restricted to the study of male sexuality.[33] Daileader's work on gynosodomy has helped loosen this restriction, as has Valerie Traub's work on the tribade.[34] Here I am less interested in specific kinds of female sodomites or sexual practices, however, than I am in the ways the discourse of sodomy conflates and confuses the anus and the vagina, female and male bodies, and threatens sexual difference.[35] My approach to sodomy is both (a)historical and antihermeneutic: rather than seek to clarify what sodomy means, or restrict its relation to certain bodies or orifices, I allow sodomy to queer opposite-sex relations predicted on genital and orificial clarity, thereby exacerbating a crisis in contemporary understandings of heterosexuality that were not yet formed in the early modern period. This approach allows us to gauge how heterosexuality is more than simply an anachronism when used to discuss early modern sexual relations. It is also a questionable clarification of more complex, messier erotics.

This book more broadly explores the queerness of bodies situated within psychoanalytic and early modern morphologies of fundamentalism. These include female bodies (chapters 1 through 4), aristocratic bodies (chapters 1 through 3), fat bodies (chapter 2), Jewish bodies (chapter 4), and homosexual bodies (chapters 3 and 5). I call these bodies queer because they bear the burden of ahistoricity and excrementality within straight or linear narratives of history and the civilizing process. We might well substitute *queer* for *dirt* in Mary Douglas's classic observation: "Dirt offends against order. Eliminating it is not a negative movement, but a positive effort to organize the environment."[36] Queer bodies are often degenerate and wasteful by definition, differentiated from the reproductive telos of both historical and contemporary body politics, and produced by the purgative movements of a heteronormative social order. One value of queer criticism, for many critics including myself, lies in its ability to explore the way certain figures both manage and exacerbate personal and cultural anxieties about impurity. Yet the utility of psychoanalysis with respect to a queer theory and history of anal eroticism remains in question. Working within psychoanalysis, Leo Bersani urges the political embrace of the same image of degenerate homosexuality from which Jeffrey Masten argues historicism affords "a way out." I hope to cut a path between these two perspectives. I seek to demonstrate that psychoanalysis can lead us back into the foundations of history and toward a queer recalibration of time, identity, and sociality.

An Invitation to Play

This queer recalibration of time, identity, and sociality also works through a series of psychoanalytic ideas about comedy deriving in large part from Freud's work in *Jokes and Their Relation to the Unconscious*. Although Freud focuses almost exclusively on jokes, I extend Freud's ideas to multiple exercises of wit — the *Witz* of Freud's German title — in early modern comedy, including jests, tricks, wordplay, and the rhetorical skills praised by Renaissance humanists. I am particularly interested in Freud's arguments regarding the constitutive role of repression in the generation of wit and wit's role in helping to negotiate boundaries of individual and communal identity. Furthermore, by developing Freud's ideas in light of Lacan's translation of Freud, I use the term *comedy* to circumscribe a "play of the signifier" that one finds even in a tragic text like *Hamlet*. As a frame for my own analyses, comedy is not dramatic form (the usual meaning of *comedy* in early modern studies) but a synonym for playfulness that cuts across the boundaries of genre.[37]

The chapters in this book are additionally playful in the sense of being analytically promiscuous. They branch out in a number of different directions: toward humanist poetics, the "butt" of jokes, sexual conversion narratives, the anti-Semitism of Christian fundamentalism, and ideology critique, among other topics. I have tried in this introduction to map out the shared terrain — the playground — on which these chapters play, but like essays in a collection, the chapters themselves rarely return in any direct way to the arguments I have so far made. The chapters do not share or develop a single, overarching thesis, nor have I arranged them in the chronological order of their early modern primary texts. Such "lack of focus" may frustrate some readers, but I did not conceive this book in monogamous fidelity to a single big idea. Rather, I conceived it while flirting with ideas that were sometimes interconnected — ideas that only came together as a monograph because I allowed myself to entertain the implications of the queer critique of teleology and chronology for the standard scholarly monograph that usually presents arguments more historically and theoretically bounded, more narrowly focused and cumulative. This book is accordingly full of promiscuous shifts in attention. And while its promiscuity may well benefit those who read a book's chapters out of order (and the many more still who do not read books in their entirety), my more serious hope is that it also works to relate a wide array of analytical concerns often separated by disciplinary barriers around historicism, psychoanalysis, queer theory, early modern studies, and medieval studies.

Chapter 1 sets out to reclaim psychoanalytic concepts of neurosis and repression for the study of comedy and sexuality. Revisiting Edmund Wilson's infamous diagnosis of Ben Jonson as an anal erotic, I argue that repression does have a role to play in the civilizing process and that this role is rather foundational in the genesis of Jonsonian comedy. This chapter also addresses what Dominique Laporte has identified as the interrelation of two reformations in the English Renaissance: the humanist reformation of language and the legal reformation of waste management systems. Through a reading of Jonson's poem "On the Famous Voyage" and Sir John Harington's *Metamorphosis of Ajax,* I theorize what I call humanist "homopoetics," a poetics of male linguistic facility opposed to feminine forms of rhetorical waste. I argue that homopoetic efforts to sanitize language falter on the exercise of wit as a dually erudite and dirty manipulation of meaning.

Chapter 2 turns to the comic "butt" and specifically to the somatic relation of the butt to Falstaff as the comic "ass" in *The Merry Wives of Windsor.* Because claims for a pun on *ass* and *arse* in Renaissance English are debatable, I posit that Falstaff's admonition he has been "made an ass" in Windsor Forest amounts to an (a)historical pun. My detranslation of Falstaff's line attends to the manner in which the play's incessant wordplay translates the fat knight into the butt of a communal joke and the butt/arse of the Windsor body politic. In this capacity, Falstaff becomes the semiotic dumping ground for the excesses of gender, national, and class differences that otherwise fracture the Windsor community. This chapter summarily illustrates how Shakespeare uses the figure of the comic ass to trope a fundamental position in the body politic.

As a pair, chapters 3 and 4 both grapple with the ways in which the discourse of sodomy conflates the anus and the vagina. Both chapters also explore correlations between narrative and somatic foundations, or "ends," in texts that express profound anxiety about the happiness of their own conclusions. In chapter 3, I read Shakespeare's *All's Well That Ends Well* in light of the ideology of the ex-gay movement — as a sexual and spiritual conversion narrative about turning men's "sick desires" from anal, dead ends to vaginal, procreative ends. All ends well, I argue, only because the play cuts away from two "sex scenes": Helen's cure of the king's fistula and the bed trick. I maintain that the anus tropes the eroticism of both scenes, and that both scenes demystify the work of heterosexual healing they are supposed to effect. Overly insistent on its own happy ending, *All's Well* demonstrates how the intractable perversity of fantasy life upsets the teleology of conversion.

Linda Williams's influential study of hard-core pornography's "frenzied" attempt to spectacularize female pleasure informs chapter 4's reading of Thomas Nashe's *The Unfortunate Traveller.* Whereas Williams associates pornography with twentieth-century developments in photographic technology, I contend that visual frenzies are first and foremost effects of signifiers that structure the visual field. Beginning more or less at the gruesome end of *The Unfortunate Traveller* and working backward to its beginning as a trickster tale, I argue that Nashe pornographically revises the Freudian primal scene of the obscene joke in which one man verbally exposes a woman to another man to satisfy his own frustrated libido. For Nashe, this exposure amounts to a sodomitical rape that collapses the anus and vagina into an undifferentiated cloaca. My reading of *The Unfortunate Traveller* also analyzes the text's anti-Semitism in terms of its comic fashioning of a Christian male body. I conclude by suggesting that Nashe's own philosophical skepticism might usefully orient a critical reaction to this anti-Semitism.

The final chapter of this book looks to the pilgrims in Chaucer's *Canterbury Tales* for a model of queer sociality and argues against the critical tendency to view the Pardoner as a kind of queer hero. It begins by situating Chaucer's Pardoner within the context of modern cynicism, or what Peter Sloterdijk calls "enlightened false consciousness." Although the Pardoner admits that his relics are fraudulent, he encourages the pilgrims' belief in their power. I read the Host's scatological rebuke of the Pardoner as a symptom of how the Pardoner's performance calls into question the orthodox faith in sublimation, or the correspondence of a material object with what Jacques Lacan terms the ineffable Thing *(das Ding)*. The Pardoner's cynical participation with spiritual corruption further raises the question of what queer ideology critique should look like in the age of cynical reason. Looking to other tales including The Miller's Tale and The Summoner's Tale, I suggest that Chaucer finds an answer in *kynicism:* a bawdy, bodily strategy for deflating and debunking ideology that derives from the Greek "antiphilosopher" Diogenes.

I have claimed that this book is promiscuous, but my rather idiosyncratic choice of primary texts certainly warrants some further commentary. Excepting both *The Canterbury Tales* and *Hamlet,* I am concerned here with what one reader of an early draft of this book aptly called the "B-texts" of the early modern English canon — that is, with texts long derided as waste products of writers who could "do better."[38] I focus on these B-texts for the way their scatological investments — especially their investments in playing dirty with various civil discourses — have sullied their perceived artistry. Some of these investments are more explicit, more subject to critical disgust, than others; but I argue that attention to these investments can help us work through the presumptive aesthetic and structural problems these texts present. To these ends, the first four chapters analyze the purification of language, social spaces, the body, and the body politic in Renaissance texts and their scholarship, and each chapter reflects on the ways Renaissance scholars have purified the canon by purging it of these "bad" texts.

I also have reasons for ending with a chapter on *The Canterbury Tales*. First, the promiscuity of this book's engagements draws much of its energy not only from Lacan's notion of signifying play and queer critiques of teleology and chronology, but also from Chaucer's unfinished, tentatively arranged collection of tales from a variety of different genres. Like my chapters (if such a comparison is not too outrageous), these tales speak to one another in sometimes direct, sometimes subtle, sometimes extended, and sometimes fleeting ways. A synonym for promiscuity, play is itself a key term in studies of *The Canterbury Tales,* and while it is sometimes wrapped up there in themes of antagonism and mastery, I use it here to claim for my own project a Chaucerian sense of open-ended variation with respect to the issues I explore. Hence this book has no conclusion, no last word: its end is no real end.

By shifting in the last chapter back from the Renaissance to the Middle Ages, I also want this book to go some way toward traversing the territorializing fantasy of many Renaissance scholars that the Renaissance still (and despite the vigorous critiques of medievalists) maintains a privileged relationship to modernity — to the present, the prescient, and the new.[39] I have chosen to traverse this fantasy using the bridge of "early modernity" — a choice that risks affirming the notion of the modern divide even as I put several different versions of this divide into play over the course of this book. I should thus specify that I use the phrase "early modern" precisely because of its imprecision. Recognizing the modern divide's susceptibility to translation (to historical movement), I recognize it as a useful if highly provisional concept for relating past and present. I should further specify that while my construction of a Chaucerian bridge between the Middle Ages and modernity risks affirming Chaucer's status as the most modern of medieval writers, my goal in chapter 5 is to exploit this status for a queer political purpose by focusing on the possibilities, not simply the limitations, of a narrative of modernization.

The presentist dimensions of this book activate still other senses of *play:* the dramatic and especially the Shakespearean. As currently practiced in Renaissance studies, presentism concerns itself largely with the relevance of Shakespeare's plays in the contemporary moment. Ewan Fernie describes presentism as "a strategy of interpreting texts in relation to current affairs which challenges the dominant fashion of reading Shakespeare historically."[40] In *Shakespeare in the Present,* Terence Hawkes likewise focuses on how the performance of a Shakespeare play brings the play into the present and activates the "here-and-now immediacy that binds performer to audience."[41] I myself touch only once on an adaptation of a Shakespeare play: in chapter 4, I look briefly at Don Roos's film *Happy Endings* as a translation of *All's Well That Ends Well*. Yet while I would happily describe many of this book's analytical moves as presentist, I am more interested in playing with, in the sense of loosening, presentism's fixation of Shakespeare. Certainly, Shakespeare is more present than any other writer in the chapters that follow, just as he is more present than any other Renaissance writer (or perhaps any other writer period) in contemporary Anglo-American culture. That being the case, Shakespeare's works (or even more narrowly, his plays) should nevertheless not become presentism's proper objects of study, lest presentism calcify into a methodology that, despite its claim to novelty, simply reiterates one of the otherwise very old truths about Shakespeare: that he always seems to be our contemporary. Combining chapters on Shakespeare with chapters on his contemporaries and one on Chaucer will hopefully go some way toward expanding presentism's critical purview.[42]

The final sense of play at work in this book derives from the historiographic stylings of Michel Foucault. In a 1977 conversation with a group of psychoanalysts, Foucault describes his strategy for writing the history of sexuality as a "game" he will require six volumes to play.[43] At stake in this game is nothing less than the historicity of sexuality, Foucault's wager being that he can historicize sexuality in much the same way he historicized criminality in *Discipline and Punish*. Foucault's most hostile interlocutor is Jacques-Alain Miller, whose concerns about the erasure of a Freudian "break" in this history prompt Foucault to explain that "the whole business of breaks and non-breaks is at once a point of departure and a very relative thing."[44] Miller does not grant Foucault's point, and when Foucault remarks on Tertullian's pivotal connection of sex with the truth of the self, Miller objects:

MILLER: Here you are looking for an origin again, and now it's all Tertullian's fault . . .

FOUCAULT: I was only joking there.

MILLER: Obviously, you're going to say that things are much more complicated, there are heterogeneous levels, movements from above to below and below to above . . . ! But *seriously,* this search for the point where it all may have begun, all this malady of speech, do you . . . ?

FOUCAULT: I say it in a fictive matter, as a joke, to make a fable.

MILLER: But if one wasn't joking, what would one say?[45]

Foucault's answer approximates the argument for heterogeneity that Miller anticipates, and here the conversation steers away from Foucault's "joke." In introducing a book that approaches history psychoanalytically, I would nonetheless like to suggest that to "forget Foucault" (to play with Jean Baudrillard's imperative, also first issued in 1977) would be to forget this playfulness, to forget that Foucault was himself making a wager and playing a game with potentially serious consequences.[46] My final wager is somewhat similar to his: that in the theory and history of anal eroticism, breaks and origins (or foundations) are at once points of departure and very relative things. I likewise realize that whether this wager pays off depends in no small part on my reader's willingness to play along.

I

The Wandering Anus

Ben Jonson, John Harington, and Humanist Homopoetics

Language is a slut.

— Dominique Laporte, *History of Shit*

IN 1616, FOLLOWING THE FOLIO PUBLICATION OF HIS COLLECTED works, Ben Jonson produced *The Devil Is an Ass,* his last play before his decade-long hiatus from the popular stage. *The Devil Is an Ass* ranks among Jonson's least critically valued comedies, if for no other reason than in following on the heels of such works as *Volpone, Epicene, The Alchemist,* and *Bartholomew Fair,* the play seems self-derivative — the work of a tired playwright reproducing scenes from his earlier masterpieces. Of course, Jonson was always something of a repetitive playwright. As David Riggs remarks, "Any critic of Jonson knows that between 1598 and 1614 he relies on a limited repertory of character types and structural devices. The two gallants, the confidence man, the shaming of the cuckold, and the quarrel that escalates out of control recur again and again."[1] *The Devil Is an Ass* is no exception to this rule, but it is not unremarkable for that reason. "Indeed," Riggs writes, "the whole question of what it means for a playwright like Jonson to repeat himself is sufficiently complicated to warrant our attention for a moment."[2]

For Riggs, *The Devil Is an Ass* caps Jonson's achievements in the genre of comedy in two respects. First, the play "is a parable about the obsolescence of evil in the world of Jonsonian comedy."[3] Jonson's previous comedies turn on obfuscated distinctions between moral categories, as characters mistake vices for virtues and vice versa. When, in the opening scene of *The Devil Is an Ass,* the demon Pug asks Satan for permission to work mischief in London, Satan testifies to Jonson's comic success when he claims that Londoners "have their Vices, there, most like to Vertues; / You cannot know 'em, apart, by any difference" (1.1.121–22).[4] As a comedy in excess of this success, *The Devil Is an Ass* caps Jonson's achievements in a second respect by giving him the opportunity to recant his long-held position that human folly is a proper object of comic mockery. Of the gallant Manly's punning conclusion, "It is not manly to take joy, or pride / In humane errours" (5.8.169–70), Riggs writes that Jonson "tacitly abandons the claim that the comedies published in the 1616 *Works* constitute a timeless model of what 'other plays should bee.'"[5] Only by repeating himself can Jonson produce a "sentimental comedy" out of "his own cynical farces about human life."[6] *The Devil Is an Ass* offers repetition with a difference, self-derivation for the purpose of self-differentiation and artistic evolution.

Beginning a book on comic anal eroticism with a discussion of Ben Jonson might be as predictable as beginning a book on early modern literature and psychoanalysis with a discussion of *Hamlet*. I nonetheless begin again with Ben Jonson because I want to advance a series of interrelated arguments, both textually specific and more broadly theoretical, that likewise repeat with a difference some basic claims about repression and the civilizing process. At the heart of this chapter is an analysis of the humanist conjunction of femininity and excrementality, as well as this conjunction's figuration and disfiguration of sexual difference, in Jonson's poem "On the Famous Voyage" and Sir John Harington's *The Metamorphosis of Ajax*. This analysis follows a shorter discussion of Foucault's and Lacan's critiques of the repressive hypothesis, a discussion that leads into a recuperation of Freud's claim for the constitutive relationship between repression and comedy. By way of introducing to all these arguments, Jonson's repetition in *The Devil Is an Ass* is additionally interesting for what it suggests about Jonson's own antitheatrical imagination of the source of comedy's production. Many of the motifs of the morality play that appear in *The Devil Is an Ass* Jonson had already used in *Bartholomew Fair*. In particular, the Hell Mouth takes to the stage in the earlier play as the criminal headquarters of Ursula's booth — the "very wombe and bedde of enormitie! grosse, as [Ursula] her selfe" (2.2.106–7), according to Adam Overdo. Through this grotesquely feminine booth, follies are born onto the stage where they become the object of comic sport.[7] In *The Devil Is an Ass,* Jonson more distinctly figures the Hell Mouth as the anal foundation of playing when Pug emerges from the "Hole" (1.2.34) of "Divells arse" (1.2.35) to meet Fittzdotrel — a Londoner who wants to be seen in his expensive new cloak at a performance of *The Devil Is an Ass.* This self-referential gimmick through which Jonson makes his play the backdrop for Fittzdottrel's vain self-expression is particularly symptomatic in light of Jonson's own tendency toward dramatic repetition. It suggests Jonson's recognition that to mock vices, the writer of comedy first must "produce" them, giving them a space to play through a process evocative of anal birth. Indeed, I will go farther: because he realizes this production as a constitutive component of comic theater, Jonson abandons the stage after 1616 out of frustration with the ineluctable filthiness of his own creation.

This suggestion is highly speculative, of course, and it does not account for Jonson's later return to both the stage and comedy. Strategically, however, I intend it to recall Edmund Wilson's well-known diagnosis of Jonson as an anal erotic.[8] Although it has been more than half a century since Wilson played analyst to the "morose" Jonson and contrasted Jonson as a writer of limited creativity to Shakespeare as a man for all seasons, many critics still agree that Wilson accurately pinpointed something fundamental about Jonson's character. Jonson certainly exemplifies many of the traits that Freud associates with the anally retentive personality, especially an obsession with order and learning, or a "hoarding" of knowledge.[9] Jonson is also frequently given to troping aggression as an evacuation of the bowels and money as feces. In a 1979 essay, E. Pearlman argued that if "the retentive character is defined by stinginess," Wilson's diagnosis accounts neither for Jonson's virtuoso proficiency in multiple genres, nor for a play like *Bartholomew Fair,* "which not only celebrates the anus, but is a paean to every orifice, every bodily fluid, every quiddity of man's nature." Many later Jonsonians would follow Pearlman in distancing themselves from Wilson's diagnosis, but Pearlman himself did not quite claim that Wilson was wrong. He argued only that Wilson offers "a partial truth, a psychological synecdoche."[10]

As Bruce Boehrer observes in his own discussion of this critical history — a discussion that opens an incisive Deleuzo-Guattarian analysis of Jonson's alimentary imagination — David Riggs has himself "revived the psychoanalytical approach to Jonson's works, correlating anal motifs with patterns of oedipal aggression."[11] Case in point: Riggs reads the scene in *The Case Is Altered* where Jacques (or *jakes,* slang for *privy*) de Prie hides his money in manure as Jonson's staging of his infantile desire to soil his stepfather with feces. Immediately, however, Riggs makes an important qualification that supposedly renders "inadequate" any conclusion that "Jonson 'was' an anal personality": "Composing a comedy is an adaptive, rather than a neurotic act," and through writing comedies like *The Case Is Altered* Jonson "discovered how to turn manure into a valuable commodity."[12] In other words, Jonson found a way to exercise rather than repress his infantile desire, and to turn a profit while doing so. This difference between the adaptive exercise and neurotic repression of desire apparently makes all the difference when it comes to the task of depathologizing Jonson despite his manifest anality. Furthermore, this difference can be all the more beneficial to a psychoanalytic reading of Jonson and his works if, as Boehrer argues, it has a foundation in Freud. According to Boehrer, "the study of anal eroticism . . . functions primarily [in Freud's work] as a study of character formation and only secondarily as a classification of neurosis."[13] Although he then acknowledges that the distinction between character formation and neurosis is tenuous at best, Boehrer writes that "Jonson's preoccupation with excretory processes should arguably be viewed as culturally paradigmatic rather than individually neurotic."[14] I would like to argue here for the very categorical confusion that Boehrer aims to circumvent.

To admit the tenuousness of the distinction between character formation and neurosis is to admit that Jonson is neurotic — *not* in the sense that his preoccupation with excretory processes differentiates him from his peers, but in the sense that this preoccupation is "culturally paradigmatic." As Norman O. Brown demonstrates in his influential account of Western civilization's "excremental vision," the opposition of individual neurosis to culturally paradigmatic or normal character formation elides Freud's argument in *Civilization and Its Discontents* that normal society is itself neurotic, fundamentally uneasy *(unbehagen),* because it is founded on the repression of desire.[15] For Boehrer, Freud's argument in *Civilization and Its Discontents* regarding anal eroticism "is vaguely reminiscent of a

Monty Python comedy routine; there is no anal eroticism in the well-adjusted character, Freud insists, and by none he means that there is a certain amount."[16] Yet perceptive as this joke is, it need not be understood as exposing a self-refuting contradiction in Freud's thought. Rather, the joke illuminates how well-adjusted, normal character is created only through the work of repression that relocates "improper" desires in the unconscious. These desires do not simply cease to exist: through translation they appear in ciphered form as symptoms within the psychopathology of everyday life. Freud can therefore speak at once of the anal eroticism that subtends the civilized values of "parsimony, a sense of order and cleanliness," while also identifying the "intensified" expression of the same values in an anal character.[17] The distinction is quantitative rather than qualitative; or as Brown writes, the "difference between 'neurotic' and 'healthy' is only that the 'healthy' have a socially usual form of neurosis."[18]

If Jonson's notorious obsessions with order and decorum evince Freud's theory of anal retentiveness, Jonson's anal explosive celebration of the excremental in a play like *Bartholomew Fair* is no less conditioned by the civilizing demand to repress the pleasures of anal purgation. For this celebration to even register as a celebration requires that a sense of its impropriety register against the various voices of social propriety, including Zeal-of-the-land Busy, Adam Overdo, and Humphrey Wasp, that the play also mocks. The vicissitudes of Jonsonian comedy are such that it articulates the demand to repress while simultaneously flaunting that demand, often elevating its own moralizing author above its mockery of fools, criminals, and authority figures alike. But in *The Devil Is an Ass,* Jonson completes his descent into the mire — grounding himself, as it were, in the excremental economy of the theater with no further pretense of transcending it save abandoning the theater entirely. Temporarily exhausting what he has to contribute to the genre of theatrical comedy, *The Devil Is an Ass* figures the theater as the source of an anal production that it is now impotent to retain: when, at the end of the play, Iniquity bears Pug back to hell, they retreat from what Riggs calls a "fundamentally corrupt" society that Jonson's comic morality plays first produce but can no longer master.[19] As a farewell to the stage from a playwright whose own antitheatricality forces him to recognize that he breeds what he abhors, *The Devil Is an Ass* demonstrates that what is repressed also repeatedly represents itself in comic play.

Foundational Desire

My revival of the admittedly archaic claim that civilization is itself neurotic presumes a theory of repression that may well raise my reader's suspicion, given Foucault's critique of the repressive hypothesis in the first volume of *The History of Sexuality.* Before continuing with my discussion of Jonson, it therefore seems necessary to cast my analytical net a bit wider and ask in what sense we as literary critics, comic theorists, and historians of sexuality might still speak of repression as a culturally foundational act. As Joan Copjec has argued in *Read My Desire: Lacan against the Historicists,* Foucault's critique underwrites the New Historicist equation of sexuality with discourse. Copjec claims that New Historicism "refuses to believe in repression and proudly professes to be *illiterate in desire.*"[20] While I certainly agree that the psychoanalytic perspective on desire differs from Foucault's (though Foucault himself never actually denies that repression takes place), I have yet to come across any critic who makes such a blustering declaration of disbelief and illiteracy. More often, when historians (New or otherwise) undertake what Bruce Smith calls the task of "search[ing] out the other ideologies that formerly gave sexual behavior a vocabulary, a syntax, and a logic," the ways in which expressions of desire suggest psychoanalytic (and thus anachronistic) notions of repression simply provide the ground for explorations of historical difference.[21] The psychoanalytic method that I am describing as (a)historical should not be understood as inimical to the task that Smith describes. Analyzing both the historical and ahistorical dimensions of sexuality, (a)historicism rejects the disciplinary notion that these are incompatible inquiries.[22]

I therefore begin my attempt to rescue repression from the repressive hypothesis with a point on which Foucault actually purports to agree with psychoanalysis:

> In point of fact, the assertion that sex is not "repressed" is not altogether new. Psychoanalysts have been saying the same thing for some

time. They have challenged the simple little machinery that comes to mind when one speaks of repression; the idea of a rebellious energy that must be throttled has appeared to them inadequate for deciphering the manner in which power and desire are joined to one another; they consider them to be linked in a more complex and primary way than through the interplay of a primitive, natural, and living energy welling up from below, and a higher order seeking to stand in its way; thus one should not think that desire is repressed, for the simple reason that the law is what constitutes both desire and the lack on which it is predicated.[23]

In arguing against those who maintain that the history of sexuality can be written as a history of sexual repression, and that sexual freedom amounts to a liberation of repressed desires, Foucault claims that psychoanalysts have beat him to the punch. Psychoanalysis already opposes the simplistic position that desire is a force independent of the law and "welling up from below" — the assumption of desire as a concealed, independent psychic energy subtending the repressive surface of the ego and the social order.

To be sure, as is often the case in volume 1 of *The History of Sexuality,* it is hard to determine whom exactly Foucault intends to reference as psychoanalysts. Inasmuch as he clearly opposes the liberationist "perversion" of psychoanalysis by Wilhelm Reich, Foucault seems to be aligning himself with Lacan.[24] He would indeed be right to cite Lacan's rejection of the hypothesis that desire can be freed from the law and exercised independently of the force of interdiction. Slavoj Žižek stresses that Lacan develops the concept of the *sinthome* precisely in order to move psychoanalysts beyond the idea that symptoms will dissolve once patients realize their cause: "the symptom is not only a ciphered message, it is at the same time a way for the subject to organize his enjoyment — that is why, even after completed interpretation, the subject is not prepared to renounce his symptom."[25] For Lacan, analysis cannot liberate desire from the law *qua* the demand of the Other. At best, it works through — or, as Laplanche would say, detranslates — the patient's ciphered message to make the patient recognize the fantasy that organizes his or her enjoyment.

Foucault's affinity with Lacan on the critique of sexual liberation nonetheless risks obscuring the latter's distinct understanding of the relationship between desire and the law. When Foucault claims that "one should not think that desire is repressed, for the simple reason that the law is what constitutes desire and the lack on which it is predicated," he harmonizes what Lacan, like Freud before him, more pointedly formulates an antagonism. As Copjec argues,

> [W]hile Foucault conceives desire not only as an *effect,* but also . . . as a *realization* of the law, *psychoanalysis teaches us that the conflation of effect and realization is an error.* To say that the law is only positive, that it does not forbid desire but rather incites it, causes it to flourish by requiring us to contemplate it, confess it, watch for its various manifestations, is to end up saying simply that the law causes us to *have* a desire. . . . Psychoanalysis denies the preposterous proposition that society is founded on desire. . . . Surely, it argues, it is the *repression* of this desire that founds society. The law does not construct a subject who simply and unequivocably has a desire, but one who *rejects* its desire, who wants not to desire it.[26]

The problem with Foucault's formulation of the relationship between desire and the law pivots, in short, around the verb "constitutes" *(constituer).*[27] Although the law affects desire, shaping its experience, it does not follow that the law brings desire into being. Psychoanalysis posits to the contrary that certain desires precede the laws that forbid them. Psychoanalysis also splits the subject from desire, such that "desire itself is conceived as something — precisely — unrealized," and thus as unsatisfied by anything other than its own perpetuation.[28] The differences between these conceptions of the law's relation to desire are considerable. Copjec follows Freud in arguing that an entirely positive concept of the law carried to its logical conclusion renders prohibition superfluous and the experience of conscience inexplicable. But Copjec also risks overstating the difference between these conceptions when she denounces the "preposterous position that society is founded on desire." After all, Copjec herself formulates repression as an expression of one desire against another — as the rejection of desire by a subject who "wants not to desire it." In other words, to repress is *to desire not to desire* in order to be for the Other. So long as we realize that the law does not realize this desire either — for if it did, there would be no such thing as a symptom — we can stake a psychoanalytic claim that the desire to repress is the desire that founds the subject's place in the social order. To wit, to speak of repression as "foundational desire" is perhaps the truly "preposterous" sense in which we can say that society is founded on desire.

Freud suggests in *Jokes and Their Relation to the Unconscious* that the analysis of comedy — especially hostile, antagonistic, or otherwise "tendentious" comedy — provides fertile ground for exploring society's foundation in repression:

> The repressive activity of civilization brings it about that the primary possibilities of enjoyment, which have now, however, been repudiated by the censorship in us, are lost to us. But to the human psyche all renunciation is exceedingly difficult, and so we find that tendentious jokes provide a means of undoing the renunciation and retrieving what was lost.[29]

The subject never represses a desire to the point where it ceases to exist, where it and its object cannot be detected in ciphered form. As the means by which the subject enters into civilized, mature social discourse, repression instead effects the translation of desires that have no proper place in this discourse into ciphered forms such as jokes that, to varying degrees and in varying personalities, color civilized life. Activating the anal connotations of my "preposterous" position about "foundational desire," the two tendentiously comic texts to which I am about to turn my attention — Jonson's poem "On the Famous Voyage" and Sir John Harington's *The Metamorphosis of Ajax* — illustrate how desires subject to repression appear out of place in humanist history and discourse as dually feminine and excremental symptoms that threaten sexual difference. Jean Laplanche's definition of repression as a failure of translation usefully prefaces this illustration: "Translation is always at the same time a failure of translation — that is, repression, the constitution of the unconscious from what translation deposits as waste."[30] In humanist discourse, a law of chronology coded as masculine governs the translation of desires, shaping and ordering events and affects, causes and effects, in narrative form. Simultaneously, adherence to this law creates a personal and collective unconscious as a feminine reservoir of the ahistorical — of what is purged from the organization of time that historical narrative affords.

Although the confluence of the feminine and the excremental is clearly evident in plays like *Bartholomew Fair,* my specific argument about humanism entails a shift from what has so far been a discussion of dramatic comedy to another mode for the play of the signifier: humanist wit. Analyzing the return of the repressed feminine in "On the Famous Voyage" and *The Metamorphosis of Ajax* also leads to an engagement with the status of psychoanalysis as a humanist discipline — a discourse and practice of male homosocial relations. According to Alan Stewart, the "achievement of humanism lies precisely in the social relations that it facilitates, maintains, and transforms. . . . They are essentially relations *between men.*"[31] Maintaining that psychoanalysis can claim a similar "achievement," the readings that I am about to offer are summarily guided by two concerns: first, how within humanist discourse, and through humanist displays of wit, language becomes something dirty and feminine against masculine attempts to purify it; and second, how psychoanalysis subsequently reproduces this most misogynistic of humanist rhetorics.

Latrina Lingua

In *Timber: or Discoveries,* Jonson's observations "made upon men and matter: as they have flow'd out of his daily Readings; or had their refluxe to his peculiar Notion of the Times," Jonson describes "comely" composition as the offspring of a meditated "ranking [of] both matter, and words":

> For all that wee invent doth please us in the conception, or birth; else we would never set it downe. But the safest is to returne to our Judgement, and handle over againe those things, the easinesse of which might make them justly suspected.[32]

In this argument for a balanced rhetorical relationship between *res* (matter) and *verba* (word), Jonson employs the commonplace trope of composition as childbearing. At the same time, Jonson's "or" also more strangely aligns "birth" with "conception," simultaneously troping compositional fecundity as ejaculation (anachronistically, the cum in "comely").[33] This alignment is particularly suggestive given Jonson's attempts throughout *Timbers* to distinguish masculine from feminine composition. In his discussion of the "true artificer," Jonson includes among the artificer's admirable qualities learning, wisdom, subtlety, an ability to inspire, and an ability to jest; these qualities "shew the composition Manly," for "hee hath avoyded faint, obscure, obscene, sordid, humble, improper, or effeminate Phrase."[34] A few pages earlier, Jonson appeals to a masculine community of readers and writers defined against "Womens-Poets." These are not female poets per se, but poets whose writing is stylistically feminine:

> Others there are, that have no composition at all: but a kind of tuneing, and riming fall, in what they write. It runs and slides, and onely makes a sound. Womens-Poets they are call'd: as you have womens-Taylors. . . . You may sound these wits, and find the depth of them, with your middle finger. They are Creame-bowle, or but puddle deep.[35]

This last assertion is arguably obscene; I will leave it to my reader's own imagination. Suffice it only to say that Jonson opposes a shallow, unharmonious, feminine poetics to the deeper, more decorous poetics of male homosociality.

By describing masculine composition as "comely," Jonson also situates what I will call his *homopoetics* within a discourse of sanitation that French psychoanalyst Dominique Laporte has linked to the development of Renaissance waste management policies. Laporte opens his 1978 *History of Shit* by juxtaposing two edicts issued in France in 1539 by the Ordinance of Villers-Cotterêts. The first edict established French as the official language in all matters pertaining to government. The second required the installation of cesspools within residential buildings and ordered citizens to chase their household waste down the public drainage stream with a bucket of water.[36] Seven years earlier, the English Parliament passed a similar statute regulating waste disposal, though Parliament failed to provide funds for the management commission until 1622. There is actually little evidence to suggest the strong enforcement of the French statutes either.[37] Still, for Laporte, who defines humanism "by its penchant for waste, that is, human waste," these ordinances conjoin a desire for clean streets and proper speech into a single discourse: a humanist discourse of civilizing purification.[38] "If language is beautiful," Laporte writes, "it must be because a master bathes it — a master who cleans shit holes, sweeps offal, and expurgates city and speech to confer upon them order and beauty."[39] Jonson's true artificer is one such master, one who knows "what word is proper: which hath ornament: which height: what is beautifully translated."[40] He is one who practices his skill on the streets of England's filthiest city.

Although Jonson's animus toward the Puritans is well known, the fact that his homopoetics form within this humanist discourse suggests that we might still call them puritanical. After all, Jonsonian comedy takes to the streets and wrestles with the familiar paradox of purification: that it actually produces waste. As Laporte writes, waste is the "inevitable outcome" of a systematic cultivation of "cleanliness, order, and beauty."[41] *The Devil Is an Ass* acknowledges this paradox while reflecting on the excremental origins of the comedies that Jonson has previously written. The poem "On the Famous Voyage" likewise acknowledges this paradox at the end of Jonson's collection of neoclassical *Epigrams*. A mock epic, the poem opens with a challenge to its classical precedents:

> No more let Greece her bolder fables tell
> Of Hercules, or Theseus going to hell,
> Orpheus, Ulysses: or the Latine Muse,
> With tales of Troyes just knight, our faiths abuse:
> We have a Shelton, and a Heyden got
> Had power to act, what they to faine had not. (1–6)

Jonson's account of Shelton and Heyden's voyage up Fleet Ditch in London has been ranked "among the filthiest, the most deliberately and insistently disgusting poems in the [English] language."[42] And rightly so. The foul waters of Fleet Ditch carried all sorts of waste — human, animal, and culinary — to the Thames and outside the city. Bringing its heroes into confrontation with all this waste, "On the Famous Voyage" maps out London from the flows of its sewage.

Critics have been interested in this neoclassical satire for its excremental vision of city space and its relation to the rest of the poems in Jonson's collection.[43] As I share these interests, I would like to add that the poem reckons simultaneously with questions of sexual and historical difference through its heroes' confrontation with a metamorphic monster named Mud. Shelton and Heyden immediately encounter Mud on setting out in Fleet Ditch's foul waters:

In the first jawes appear'd that ugly monster,
Ycleped Mud, which, when their oares did once stirre,
Belch'd forth an ayre, as hot, as at the muster
Of all your night-tubs, when the carts doe cluster,
Who shall discharge first his merd-urinous load:
Thorough her wombe they make their famous road,
Betweene two walls; where, on one side, to scar men,
Were seene your ugly Centaures, yee call Car-men,
Gorgonian scolds, and Harpyes: on the other
Hung stench, diseases, and old filth, their mother,
With famine, wants, and sorrowes many a dosen,
The least of which was to the plague a cosen.
But they unfrighted passe, though many a privie
Spake to 'hem louder, than the oxe in Livie;
And many a sinke pour'd out her rage anenst 'hem. (61–75)

A *vagina dentata* with fecal breath, Mud easily beats out Ursula for the dubious honor of being the most grotesque product of Jonson's excremental imagination. Here are all the markers of the grotesque female body: consumptive, flatulent, incontinent, and diseased. The word "sinke" (75) also fuses the vagina, womb, and anus into the source of an amorphously liquid "rage."[44] In Freudian terms, the poem would seem to guard against the threat of sexual indifference by deflecting excrementality onto this devouring, dually engrossing and purgatorial, female body. We might therefore conclude that the poem engages the male desire to return to the maternal body while simultaneously predicating male heroism on successful passage *through* this same body ("Thorough her wombe they make their famous road"). Yet this misogynistic deflection of excrementality ultimately disfigures sexual difference in the very process of figuring it. By braving the excremental assault and passing through Mud's womb, Shelton and Heyden are both born *and shit* out of her body, as upon their exit they immediately encounter an enormous dung barge. Perhaps for reason of the same disfiguration, the poem ultimately climaxes not with a successful escape from Fleet Ditch but with a return "backe, without protraction" (192) to the spot from which they began, Bridewell Dock. What the poem celebrates as Heyden and Shelton's "liquid deed" (193) is not, in the end, a passage through Fleet Ditch and its excremental horrors but an endless and repetitive passage appropriately memorialized by the raising of a "Pyramide" (194), which most likely means a dung heap.

"On the Famous Voyage" scatologically (dis)figures historical difference by way of this (dis)figuration of sexual difference. What Boehrer terms the poem's "congeries of figures and situations from Greco-Roman myth" ironically testify to the superiority of a classical civilization that, while giving birth to Jonson's modern London, has simultaneously been transformed into waste.[45] Fleet Ditch channels the detritus of antiquity through the modern cityscape, encoding Christian modernity's repressive transformation of its own past into excrement. Mud grotesquely embodies this conjunction of the classical and the modern: an (a)historical monster, Mud is a mother to centaurs, Gorgonian scolds, and harpies who has materialized in London's Fleet Ditch. Yet her presence also signals the conspicuous absence of the very underground sewer system that would keep her buried — the Roman *cloaca maxima,* which Laporte identifies as the object of desire in humanist fantasies about civilized waste management, and which likewise encodes both maternal and excremental passage.[46] This detranslation of the poem's excremental vision accords with Laporte's observation that humanism's return to the past to locate the materials for the construction of modern civilization undermines the forward-looking narrative of the civilizing process. "Where its anal constituent is concerned," Laporte writes, "civilization does not follow a rhythm of linear progress," and the circuitous "rebirth" of civilization that defines the Renaissance is to humanists not simply a new historical beginning.[47] Rather, modern civilization becomes in the humanist vision of time an achievement lost — quite literally, in the case of "On the Famous Voyage" — to the sewer of the past. Humanism produces the classical past as that which has been purged from the present and as that which must be recovered for the sake of progress predicated on the concealing management of waste.

In this light, Sir John Harington's long-neglected *New Discourse of a Stale Subject, Called the Metamorphosis of Ajax* (1596) stands out as a humanist treatise par excellence, a manifesto for a prototypical flush-toilet that scripts at great length a history of waste management and heaps praise upon the Roman sewer system as the supreme instrument of urban purification. Boehrer more than once appeals to Harington's *Metamorphosis* as evidence of the heterogeneous attitudes toward feces in Renaissance England. The reading that I am about to offer situates *The Metamorphosis* in the homopoetic discourse of Renaissance humanism, focusing on Harington's failed effort to purify both the space of the privy and the bodies that inhabit it — aristocratic and female bodies in particular. I will argue that the text itself becomes the scatological symptom of this failure, for *The Metamorphosis* is never so much an advertisement for Harington's flush-toilet, which did not catch on and brought Harington only ridicule, as it is a repetitive, neurotic apology for talking about something that it otherwise thoroughly delights him to talk about.

By most accounts, *The Metamorphosis* is a highly unbalanced text. While the flush-toilet takes only a few pages to describe, Harington occupies himself throughout most of his book with citing biblical and classical precedents for his discussion of waste and waste management. Only in the third of the book's three sections does he get around to actually describing the device and its benefits. Elizabeth Story Donno notes in the introduction to her 1962 edition of the text that the excessiveness of Harington's citations and the widely disproportionate relationship of his rhetoric to his subject matter mark *The Metamorphosis* as a mock encomium, the humanist exercise of praising "a trivial or unworthy subject," which it surely is.[48] Yet to read *The Metamorphosis* as merely a mock encomium reinforces the triviality of Harington's subject matter at the expense of what Harington simultaneously perceives as its genuine social importance. Harington explicitly situates himself within the tradition of his humanist predecessors Erasmus and Rabelais (63–64), but just as *The Praise of Folly* and *Gargantua and Pantagruel* are not without their serious purpose, the praise of civilized waste management in *The Metamorphosis of Ajax* stems from Harington's quite serious attempts at linguistic and social reform. Without likewise taking this reformative agenda seriously, we cannot fully appreciate his paranoia regarding the potential assaults made upon his work (both the flush-toilet and the text) by what *The Merchant of Venice*'s Portia would call "lewd interpreter[s]" (3.4.81).

Harington tries to preempt these assaults as he opens his book:

I know that the wiser sort of men wil consider, and I wish that the ignorant sort would learne; how it is not the basenesse, or homlinessse, either of words, or matters, that make them foule & obscenous, but their base minds, filthy conceits, or lewd intents that handle them. (83)

Gilles Deleuze and Félix Guattari would agree: "[O]nly the mind is capable of shitting."[49] But whereas these antihumanists argue for the democratizing consequences of this thesis, Harington defends what Gail Kern Paster terms "reformation semantics," wherein "the social index of a given signifier flows directly from the recognized social legitimacy of its user."[50] Harington "rationalizes" excretion as a universal bodily function only "to claim a high excretory privilege for the aristocratic body."[51] At the same time, Harington repeatedly reveals that the "greatest resistance to a rational agenda of excretory reform comes not from the lowness of matter, but from the limitless circulation of meaning around it, by the very linguistic excesses his own text delights in."[52] The text's titular pun succinctly illustrates Paster's point: by describing the metamorphosis of *a jakes,* Harington founds his text in the same metamorphic potential of signification upon which he tries to foreclose.

In the first prefatory letter of *The Metamorphosis,* Philostilpnos ("Lover of Cleanliness") urges his cousin Misacmos ("Hater of Filth") to publicize his invention for the benefit of all mankind and to do so frankly, without concern for "saving reverence": "[I]f it be so sweet and so cleanely as I heare, it is a wrong to it to use save reverence, for one told me, it is as sweet as my parlor, and I would thinke discortesie, one should say, save-reverence my parlor" (56). Philostilpnos adds that if Misacmos/Harington, already familiar in Elizabethan literary circles for his translation of *Orlando Furioso,* should "tell a homelie tale of this in prose as cleanlie, as you have told in verse a baudie tale or two in Orlando mannerlie, it maie passe among the sowrest censurers verie currantlie" (57–58). Misacmos promises that he will indeed produce clean prose; he vows to "keepe me within the boundes of modestie, and use no wordes, but such as grave presidents in Divinitie, Law, Phisicke, or good Civilitie, will sufficiently warrant me" (63). Yet his failure to bind his own language is nowhere more evident than when he strikes out against his anticipated censurers. For all their apparent civility, these censurers prove quite gifted at perverting Harington's civil discourse:

> And if I should fortunate to effect so good a reformation, in the pal-
> lace of Richmond, or Greenwich . . . I doubt not but some pleasant wit-
> ted Courtier of either sex, would grace me so much at least; as to say,
> that I were worthy for my rare invention, to be made one of the Privie
> (and after a good long parenthesis come out with) chamber, or if they
> be learned and have read *Castalios Courtier* they will say, I am a proper
> scholer, and well seene in *latrina lingua.* (61–62)

Imagining his success at the highest level of Elizabethan society — reforming the privies of his godmother Queen Elizabeth — Harington betrays
the vulnerability of reformation semantics to wit. As the ventriloquized
courtier derisively elides *latina* with *latrina,* and lets the word *privy* hang
in the air before adding *chamber,* Harington brings the humanist valorization of wit as a mark of civility into conflict with wit's effectuation of the
signifier's metamorphosis.

A display of erudition through the manipulation of signifiers, wit
ultimately works against reformation semantics insofar as it sullies language and belies Harington's displacement of the baseness of words and
matter onto other base minds. More precisely, his wit deterritorializes,
as Deleuze and Guattari would say, the bounded terrain of purified language and social space that Harington simultaneously works to create.
Harington is well aware that in so promoting his flush-toilet he risks
sullying his own text: as Misacmos, he jests that if he fails to make his
discourse "mannerly enough, the worst punishment it can have is but
to employ it in the house it shall treat off" (65). Later, Harington takes
another preemptive strike at those who would find *The Metamorphosis*
"noysome and unsavory" (82):

> in citing examples . . . I have bene the more copious, because of this
> captious time, so readie to back-bite every mans worke, and I would
> forewarne men not to bite here, lest they bite an unsavorie morsell. (110)

Much like Jonson, Harington homologizes reading with ingestion and
digestion, composition with defecation.[53] Having divided *The Metamorphosis* into sections to allow for "breathing places" (81), he here compares
the first section to the "coursest meate," which, in its digestive metamorphosis, "make[s] a man winke, drinke, and stinke" (111). As Harington attempts to aristocratically harness the power of signification and

confine the smell of feces behind closed doors, the text itself becomes the excremental product of its own championed reformation of the privy and language — a metamorphosis that seems born out in its long historical neglect.

The late renewal of critical interest in *The Metamorphosis* has much to do with the text's appeal to materialist criticism.[54] As one of the B-texts of the early modern English canon, *The Metamorphosis* renders the material world of late-Elizabethan England in its *b*asest form, founding (pun intended, as usual) discourses of history, rhetoric, and self-fashioning in the process. In a remarkable passage at the beginning of the second section, the section "proving the matter not to be contemptible," Harington weaves all three discourses together by elaborately likening the history of privies to the history of metaphors:

> as Tully saith of Metaphors, that they were like our apparell; first devised to hide nakednesse, then applied for comelinesse, and lastly abused for pride: so I may say of these homely places, that first they were provided for bare necessitie, for indeed till Romulus time I find little mention of them; then they came to be matters of some more cost, as shall appeare in examples following; & I thinke I might also lay pride to their charge: for I have seene them in cases of fugerd sattin, and velvet (which is flat against the statute of apparell) but for sweetnesse or cleanlinesse, I never knew yet any of them guiltie of it. . . . Now, as scholers do daily seeke out new phrases, and metaphors; & Tailores do oft invent new vardingales, and breeches: so I see no reason, but Magistrates may as well now as heretofore, devise new orders for cleanlinesse, & wholesomnesse. (112–13)

As Harington translates the history of metaphors into the history of privies, he translates humanist concerns about self-display and linguistic decorum into concerns about waste management. The scholars' invention of new phrases and metaphors is here no different from the tailors' fashioning of new apparel, and both are no different from the installation of flush-toilets in privies: each is instrumental in the fashioning of the eloquent and clean self. This equation may be one reason that, as Paster observes, *The Metamorphosis* has largely been "unintelligible to humanist critique."[55] Humanism's advocacy of personal decorum and the display of wit at one and the same time negates *and* necessitates Harrington's efforts — efforts ostensibly aimed at the concealment of shit, and thus unavailable to detranslation within the most familiar humanist code for scatological revelry, the Rabelaisian carnivalesque.[56] Bruce Boehrer describes the other early modern B-text that I have discussed here, "On the Famous Voyage," as "the external limit of Jonsonian classicism, both negating and necessitating all that has gone before it" by virtue of the fact that it "sits like pile of untreated garbage" at the end of "Jonson's meticulous epideictic and satirical discriminations."[57] Similarly, I am suggesting that *The Metamorphosis* marks the external limit of Renaissance humanism in two related ways: first, it provides scholars of humanism with no way around humanism's often disappeared foundation in waste management; and second, in all its scatological playfulness, it stages the irresolvable conflict within humanism between the purification of language and the celebration of language's witty manipulation.

To consider further the gendered dynamics of this scatological playfulness, we should pause on Harington's remarks regarding the comparative pleasures of sex and defecation. At first, Harington's civilized subject seems to differ from the Freudian subject who experiences defecation as a secret and shameful pleasure:

> I say this surpassing pleasure [sex], that is so much in request, and counted such a principall solace, I have heard confessed before a most honourable person, by a man of middle age, strong constitution, and well practised in this occupation, to have bred no more delectation to him (after the first heate of his youth was past) then to go to a good easie close stoole, when he hath had a lust thereto (for that was his verie phrase). (84)

Reversing the Freudian trajectory from excretory to genital pleasure, this anecdote relies on the humoral equation of sex and defecation as modes of purgation. Yet Harington's appeal to an "honourable," middle-aged man in *defense* of excretory pleasures indicates that not only may Harington be more of a Freudian subject than he initially seems, but that he is uneasily situated within a culture that is recalibrating the relationship between the excretory and the sexual, and doing so along the lines of both gender and age.[58] Harington defends defecation as a mature, masculine pleasure, such that genital sex becomes a youthful, effeminate

pleasure by contrast. Though culturally commonplace, this effeminiz-
ing of genital sexual pleasure is then made explicit — and in a way that
dissolves the very distinction between scatology and sexuality that Harington simultaneously works to set up — in the immediately subsequent
anecdote about an angel and a hermit's city stroll. On the approach of a
dung farmer, the hermit crosses to the other side of the street while "the
Angell [keeps] on his way, seeming no whit offended with the savour"
(85). Only on encountering a courtesan does the Angel pinch his nose
and hasten away, thereafter explaining to the hermit that "this fine courtesan laden with sinne, was a more stinking savour afore God & his holy
Angels, then that beastly cart, laden with excrements" (85). Harington
writes that he "will not spend time to allegorize this storie" beyond urging his readers to purify the "sinkes" of their homes as they purify their
souls (85). But this anecdote does far more work than Harington's mea-
ger gloss would allow. Namely, it works despite its ostensible differentiation of shit's stench from the courtesan's sin to both scatologically sully
and effeminize what Harington calls "the sweet sinne of letcherie" (84).
Throughout *The Metamorphosis,* Harington expends considerable repressive energy over this stench of the feminine.

   Julian Yates rightly observes that Harington's privy differs from contemporary bathrooms insofar as Lacan's laws of urinary segregation gov-
ern the latter: "[D]efecation, not urination, is the defining aspect of the
privy."[59] Harington even opens *The Metamorphosis* by explicitly acknowledging that, in the privy, "*Lords and Ladies do the same*" (83, original italics).
Irrespective of the privy's gender-democratizing capacity, however, Harington repeatedly stresses the need to protect women from the shame
attendant upon the olfactory and visual exposure of their feces. As
Paster demonstrates at more length than I will here, Harington obsesses
over the stench caused by the collection of women's feces in a close stool,
which "wold have made a man (at his next entrance into the chamber)
have sayd, so, good speed ye" (113), and the stench that wells up from the
cesspit, circulates through the houses, and "prease[s] to the faire Ladies
chambers" (160). Of Harington's repeated recourse to images of defecating women and women's feces, Paster aptly notes, "The contents of a
Lord's close-stool would have the same olfactory effects, but not the
same textual ones: gender difference, although threatened by the close-

stool, . . . creates a sense of social urgency about reforming the privy by simultaneously protecting and exposing great women at stool."[60] Troping women as texts, Harington at another point equates women with privies through his equation of privies with metaphors: "deformed" privies, he tells us, are "of the feminine gender" (220). By cordoning off the pleasure of defecation as mature and masculine, and the sight and smell of feces as feminine, Harington strings himself a thin rhetorical tightrope to walk in urging the installation of flush-toilets. For the flush-toilet would not help repress the desire to defecate, but the desire to expose women at stool — a desire Harington desires not to desire, and which he exercises even as he protests the shamefulness of such sights and smells.

Harington and Jonson have this in common: in their anxious exposure of grotesque women, both betray the failure of a repressive homopoetic reformation of language and sanitation. Another anecdote from *The Metamorphosis,* this one about a woman who soils her linens, perhaps best illustrates how this exposure betrays homopoetic failure. Despite Harington's allowance that he may be censured by "some pleasant witted Courtier of *either* sex" — a notably un-Jonsonian allowance that women can be witty — this anecdote also indicates how the female body figures in *The Metamorphosis* as an object of homopoetic contestation:

> Which mishap a faire Lady once having, a serving man of the disposition of Mydas Barber, that could not keepe counsell had spyed it, & wrate in the grossest termes it could be exprest, upon a wall, what he had seene; but a certaine pleasant conceited Gentleman, corrected the barbarisme, adding ryme to the reason in this sort.
> *My Lady hath polluted her linneall vesture:*
> *With the superfluitie, of her corporall digesture.* (65)

Harington offers this anecdote simply to illustrate the inevitability of defecation and the consequences of delaying one's response to the call of nature. Yet much like the anecdote about the angel and the hermit, it suggests more than Harington admits. In this contest between the servant and the gentleman, the base mind belongs to the servant who crassly exposes his mistress's "mishap," while the gentleman's "correction" of the barbarism through rhyme reclaims aristocratic privilege over semantics through the exercise of wit. This correction certainly does not abrogate the exposure, however. It arguably *enhances* the exposure through its witty translation.[61] The filthiness of the rhyme in any case immediately prompts Harington to back off the implications of the anecdote:

> But soft, I feare I give you to great a tast of my slovenly eloquence, in this sluttish argument. (65)

By its nature, Harington confesses, his own "slovenly" wit has carried his argument into the realm of feminine promiscuity, the realm of the courtesan and the slut.

Paster argues that such anecdotes "reveal how gender works to maximize exposure and differentiate excrement, and reciprocally, how the exposure and the differentiation of excrement work to maximize gender."[62] We are now in a position to further realize that this exposure and differentiation of excrement both correlate with the establishment of homopoetic discourse as a masculine instrument of control over a promiscuous, feminine rhetorical mode. Harington's sudden concern with his "sluttish argument" suggests that this process of exposure and differentiation operates first along the lines of gender, and second along the lines of status. It moreover illustrates how, regardless of his promise to keep his discourse within the bounds of modesty and civility, Harington's own wit proves corrosive to the homopoetic decorum he advocates. As his neurotic *sinthome,* which persists even after the recognition of its consequences for his own discourse, Harington's wit organizes and *engenders* his own ongoing enjoyment and presentation of his subject matter.

Before turning in the next chapter to a play that places a contest over linguistic propriety at the center of its comic crafting of a body politic, I would like to end with the suggestion that Harington's *Metamorphosis* does not simply demonstrate how the civilizing process engenders neuroses, but that it does so in such a way as to more uniquely warrant a place within a genealogy of hysteria. In several ways, the psychoanalytic approach to hysteria mirrors Harington's approach to defecation — chiefly in that, despite its claim that men and women are both susceptible to hysteria, psychoanalysis rarely focuses on male hysterics. In practice and in theory, psychoanalysis has so overlooked the existence of male hysterics that, as Juliet Mitchell complains, it has shifted from "looking at the symptoms of hysteria to trying to replace them with an understanding of femininity in general."[63] This shift is partially attributable to the fact that psychoanalysis has inherited hysteria's medical history as the condition of the wandering womb. But the blindness of psychoanalysis toward male hysterics might also be partially attributable to hysteria's homosocial birth within psychoanalysis — to the way hysteria originally facilitated relations between men collaborating over the treatment of a female body.

I take my cue here from Wayne Koestenbaum's account of the homoerotics of collaboration in the case of Anna O. (Bertha Pappenheim) from Freud and Josef Breuer's seminal *Studies in Hysteria.* "By collaborating with Breuer," Koestenbaum argues, "Freud sought to fuse male bonding and scientific labor, and to appropriate the power of female reproduction, a force embodied in Anna O.'s hysterical pregnancy."[64] Curing Anna O. entails Freud and Breuer's homosocial translation of her maternal body into their theoretical and textual progeny, the product of their joint "labor." Freud's subsequent exchanges with Wilhelm Fliess — letters wherein the two men discuss the labor of theoretical production, Fliess's theory of male menstruation, and the etymological derivation of reproductive from excremental terms — only further foregrounds "the anus as a primary center of metamorphic energy in [Freud's] first approaches to psychoanalysis."[65] The ways in which these collaborations situate psychoanalysis in the tradition of humanist disciplines would seem in retrospect to develop Harington's and Jonson's homopoetic fantasies. As the anus wanders between male analysts and female patient, translating and retranslating the "o" of Anna's fictional name, might the case of Anna O. come into focus as the psychoanalytic reiteration of humanist discourses on scatology? To put the same question more broadly, might humanist concerns about scatology afford access to the very foundations of psychoanalysis?

2

Shakespeare's Ass

The Merry Wives of Windsor and the Butt of the Joke

THE PREVIOUS CHAPTER TRACED THE RETURN OF THE FEMI-
nine repressed in Ben Jonson's poem "On the Famous Voyage"
and Sir John Harington's *Metamorphosis of Ajax.* In the process,
it touched on a trope of great familiarity to early modernists: that of
the female body as a text over which men vie for rights of authorship.
This chapter extends my discussion of this trope by focusing on two
women in Shakespeare's corpus who redeploy the trope in authoring — or
translating — a fat male body. Jean Laplanche's description of psychoanalysis as a method of detranslation has a particular resonance in this
context, considering translation's function as a trope of textual and linguistic movement within numerous cultural discourses, including educa-
tion *(translatio studii)* and colonization *(translatio imperii).* In *Literary Fat
Ladies* and *Shakespeare from the Margins,* Patricia Parker has richly explored
the Shakespearean life of both tropes central to this chapter: that of
female and fat bodies as texts, and that of translation as the eroticized
movement of women and female desire by men who figure themselves
as authors.[1] Parker's work, together with other studies on early modern
translation, suggests that desire is well understood in the period as a
text — one to be mastered and its movement controlled. My own study
of *The Merry Wives of Windsor,* a play to which Parker devotes a chapter in
Shakespeare from the Margins, leads me to further suggest that the exercise

of authorial control over desire is at the same time an exercise of control over waste.

This chapter also analyzes the comic ass as the "butt" of a joke, exploring the possibility that the ass is one of the alimentary metaphors that helps shape understandings of social status and mobility in the early modern period.[2] This possibility hinges in part on whether Renaissance English allows a pun between *ass* and *arse*. The *OED* says no: it points to an 1860 text as the pun's first recorded instance, and it provides no etymological connection between the words.[3] Nor does the pun appear in Gordon Williams's authoritative *Dictionary of Sexual Language and Imagery in Shakespearean and Stuart Literature*.[4] A number of critics of early English literature, and of drama in particular, sense a pun nonetheless and have suggested various chains of signification that bring it into being. In her reading of *A Midsummer Night's Dream*, for example, Gail Kern Paster argues for a "somatic troping on Bottom's name" by tracing the logic of purgation that structures the ass-headed Bottom's love affair with Titania.[5] Likewise, in an older essay on Shakespeare's use of the ass motif in *A Midsummer Night's Dream* and *The Comedy of Errors*, Deborah Baker Wyrick hears the pun as a consequence of Renaissance pronunciation; for her, the pun is purely homonymic.[6] Undoubtedly the most emphatic assertion of the pun's presence in Shakespeare belongs to Frankie Rubenstein, who boldly proclaims in her *Dictionary of Shakespeare's Sexual Puns and Their Significance*, "Shakespeare never used 'arse'; like his contemporaries, he used 'ass' to pun on the ass that gets beaten with a stick and the arse that gets thumped sexually, the ass that bears a burden and the arse that bears or carries in intercourse."[7] Annabel Patterson agrees with Rubenstein's assessment, and she reads the translated Bottom as "a political allegory of status inversion and corporal punishment."[8] Finally, Mario DiGangi argues that the pun can be heard outside Shakespearean contexts in the homoerotic relation of masters to asses in seventeenth-century city comedies.[9]

DiGangi aside, this minor critical consensus that Renaissance English locution did allow for a pun between *ass* and *arse* draws exclusively upon Shakespearean evidence, and chiefly upon *A Midsummer Night's Dream* at that. I would maintain that the pun is also audible in Jonson's *The Devil Is an Ass*, which unlike *Midsummer* voids the term of its animalistic referent in translating the iconographic traditions of demonic anality. At the risk of further restricting the pun to Shakespearean contexts, however, this chapter argues that the pun reverberates within larger networks of word-play that contribute to Falstaff's translation into an ass at the end of *The Merry Wives of Windsor.* Mine is not an argument for the pun's factual presence in the play. The pun's presence is (a)historical, enabled at one and the same time by the play of signifiers in the play-text and the con-temporary ear with which I hear this play. When Falstaff admits that he has been "made an ass" (5.5.115) in Windsor Forest, I hear him identifying as the butt of the communal joke — the anal object of humiliation whose etymological roots lie in the use of *butt* (from Old French) to refer to a hunter's mark or target.[10] I also hear him identifying as the butt of Wind-sor's body politic — a body politic that gets into shape, so to speak, by purging gender, national, and class excesses. I hear both identifications despite the fact that the word *butt* is nowhere to be found in *Merry Wives,* for Falstaff, costumed as Herne the Hunter, identifies as a *target* of ridi-cule using a word wrapped up in the play's pervasive scatological humor.

Falstaff's "way of waste"

In *Comedy: The Mastery of Discourse,* Susan Purdie contends that comedy turns on the "ab-use" of language. Comedy is essentially a contest over language, and as we have seen in the last chapter, jokers manipulate sig-nification so as to demonstrate their mastery over linguistic systems. Purdie also claims that jokes work by displacing "semantic excess" onto "butts." At the expense of butts, and in relation to joke tellers and audi-ences, jokes reinforce the rules of language.[11] Purdie summarily offers a structuralist analysis of the comic butt that is useful, as we will see, for detranslating Falstaff's identification as an ass. Yet in this assessment, the butt's anatomy and etymology go unaddressed, as if the word *butt* simply constituted an unremarkable, ahistorical correlation between a shameful body part and a humiliated other. Among the many comedies that feature asses as butts of jokes, *The Merry Wives of Windsor* stages the convoluted construction of this neglected correlation. The play fore-grounds the labor-intensive processes of shaping and partitioning the body — both the individual body and the body politic — as a contest over linguistic propriety. Fittingly, the play has as its comic villain a knight whose grotesque body by definition exceeds normative boundaries. Like the play's scatological wordplay, Falstaff's body is excessive, and both bespeak a social order in the making through processes of consumption and purgation.[12]

Merry Wives is full of puns, a word that is itself an anachronistic narrowing of what Renaissance rhetoricians call *clenches:* witty wordplay that includes and exceeds the conjunction of inconsonant signifieds under a single signifier.[13] Tracing the chain of signifiers that becomes audible in light of Falstaff's identification as an ass requires working through much of this wordplay to link the pun on *ass* back to another pun between *waste* and *waist* that Falstaff employs when he tells Pistol and Nim of his plan to woo Mistress Ford. This pun blurs the line between consumption and purgation — between what Falstaff has consumed, what he has turned into refuse, and where such refuse is located:

> FALSTAFF: My honest lads, I will tell you what I am about.
>
> PISTOL: Two yards and more.
>
> FALSTAFF: No quips now, Pistol. Indeed, I am in the waist two yards about. But I am now about no waste; I am about thrift. Briefly, I do mean to make love to Ford's wife. I spy entertainment in her. She discourses, she carves, she gives the leer of invitation. I can construe the action of her familiar style; and the hardest voice of her behaviour, to be Englished rightly, is "I am Sir John Falstaff's." (1.3.33–41)

In Falstaff's construal, *waste* (as in "I am now about no waste") refers first and foremost to his financial expenditures. Having wasted all of his money on sack, women, and residency at the Garter Inn, Falstaff devises his wife-wooing plan as a perverse method of thrift through thievery: he will gain access to Ford's coffers through the seduction of Ford's wife. The pun links both sexual and financial profligacy (wastefulness) to Falstaff's fat (waist-full) body, though Falstaff seeks to distance the connection. To seduce Mistress Ford, he needs his large waist not to signify "waste" — a body in financial, sexual, and gluttonous excess — but "thrift." Rebounding from Pistol's quibble on "about," Falstaff figures himself as the master of a thrifty bodily economy. Yet in claiming such mastery, Falstaff will find that he actually has quite a limited domain. Just as his waste-full waist, which is still "two yards about," bodies forth his conspicuous consumerism, the play repeatedly shows that Falstaff cannot dictate the terms of what Michael Moon and Eve Sedgwick have called "*the representational contract* between one's body and one's world."[14]

Of course, Falstaff takes pride in his girth. Throughout both parts of *Henry IV* and *Merry Wives* he speaks of his weight as something he must protect, something valuable. In *1 Henry IV,* he worries that he wastes away after his humiliation at Gad's Hill: "Bardolph, am I not fallen away vilely since this last action? Do I not bate? Do I not dwindle?" (3.3.1–2). In *Merry Wives,* he expresses similar concern after he has been twice tricked by Mistress Page and Mistress Ford: "If it should come to the ear of the court how I have been transformed, and how my transformation hath been washed and cudgelled, they would melt me out of my fat, drop by drop, and liquor fishermen's boots with me" (4.5.77–81). For Falstaff, his fatness equates with self-possession: he controls himself and his body insofar as he remains large. And the comic effect of this equation arises from its inversion of the more familiar association between girth and a *lack* of control. Falstaff insists that he controls the significance of his own fat body, which corresponds not, as those around him see it, with uncontrolled excess — with the riot of sexual and consumerist pleasures that other members of Windsor's community disavow — but with "thrift" and conservation. For the rest of Windsor, Falstaff's large waist signifies what Mistress Page calls his "wantonness of spirit" (4.3.182) and his "way of waste" (4.3.184). One purpose of duping Falstaff is to enforce this semiotic correspondence between *waist* and *waste* that his assertion of their distinction would challenge.

This enforcement is thus itself a translation, an inscription of Falstaff as a waste-/waist-full thief who seeks to translate (purvey or steal) wives and their *wills* — both their sexual propriety and the property to which they are entitled through their husbands. Pistol succinctly encapsulates Falstaff's translative intentions in his reply to the knight's claim to have interpreted Mistress Ford's "familiar style": "He hath studied her well, and translated her will: out of honesty, into English" (1.3.42–43). The revenge jests arise within this same translative context. Reacting to the identical love letters Falstaff sends them — "He will print them, out of doubt," Mistress Page says, "for he cares not what he puts into the press when he would put us two" (2.1.67–69) — the wives agree to engage "in any villainy against him that may not sully the chariness of our honesty" (2.1.86–87). Though Falstaff locates a sort of phallic authority in his waist that measures "two yards about," his waist marks for the wives the ultimate impotency, or wasted energy, of his attempts at seduction; his waist is nothing but a heavy press from whose weight they must escape without losing their chastity. The wives additionally activate the very flaccidity Falstaff's name suggests as they seek to preserve their wills by translating or conveying the knight into the comic position of the butt for which his fat body particularly suits him. As Purdie writes, "Butts are precisely degraded from the power to construct and define *us,* within *their* language making."[15]

The buck-basket trick figures as the first such attempt at translation in its play upon Falstaff's fat body:

> MISTRESS PAGE: Look, here is a basket. If he be of any reasonable stature, he may creep in here; and throw foul linen upon him as if it were going to bucking. Or — it is whiting time — send him by your two men to Datchet Mead.
>
> MISTRESS FORD: He's too big to go in there. What shall I do?
>
> FALSTAFF *[coming forward]:* Let me see't, let me see't, O let me see't! I'll in, I'll in. Follow your friend's counsel; I'll in. (3.3.106–12)

Falstaff squeezes in with the dirty laundry, only to be carried to the banks of the Thames and dumped out, as he later describes, "like a barrow of butcher's offal" (3.5.4–6). The jest works in this way to enforce the degrading relationship between Falstaff's waist and waste, yet unable to construe *this* action, Falstaff is undeterred. I will have more to say about Falstaff's stupidity later. Suffice it now to suggest that it is precisely because Falstaff is so stupid that the jests can continue, ultimately transforming him into the butt of Windsor's body politic. Thus the second trick, while similarly an inside joke between the wives, has with respect to this suggestion an important difference from the first: the assault upon the wives' wills is no longer so private, having been publicized by Pistol and Nim and having roused the jealousy of Francis Ford. Now duping Falstaff becomes more than an act of private revenge and more than an act of rebuffing his sexual advances. It becomes what Mistress Page calls a "double excellency" (3.3.148) — a chance to trick Ford in front of his male friends and school him on spousal trust. Ford and Falstaff become conjoined — or *brooked,* as it were, given Ford's disguise as Master Brooke — as men to be instructed in sexual decorum by the wives; and their common position is reinforced rhetorically: Ford's jealousy, like Falstaff's body, is "gross" (3.3.158), and Falstaff, nearly drowned in the Thames, declares his "belly full of ford" (3.5.32). If the second trick draws particular attention to Falstaff's butt, as I am about to argue, both Falstaff and Ford are, in another sense, its like targets: both are the butts of a jest whose disciplining efficacy extends to multiple male bodies in the wives' assertion of mastery over their domestic arena.[16]

This second trick consists of dressing Falstaff as a woman to hide him from the raging Ford:

> MISTRESS PAGE: . . . There is no woman's gown big enough for him; otherwise, he might put on a hat, a muffler, and a kerchief, and so escape.
>
> FALSTAFF: Good hearts, devise something. Any extremity rather than a mischief.
>
> MISTRESS FORD: My maid's aunt, the fat woman of Brentford, has a gown above.
>
> MISTRESS PAGE: On my word, it will serve him; she's as big as he is. . . .
> (4.2.56–64)

This "fat woman of Brentford," whom Mistress Page also calls "Mother Prat" (4.2.158), may have been recognizable to an Elizabethan audience as Gillian of Brentford, a comic figure about whom little is now known. Particularly germane for my purposes, however, is Thomas Nashe's remark that she "bequeathed a score of farts among her friends" in her will.[17] The name *Prat* may also have been heard as slang for *buttocks,* an appropriate name for the woman of Brentford given her bequest.[18] Allowing these evocations, Falstaff's fatness now evokes a will-full (desirous) but debased and textualized anality that, much like the epithet "fat ass," would restrict obesity to a single body part. Moreover, as Falstaff's body becomes a dumping ground of significations (a sort of semiotic cesspit), we can begin to see how he is being drafted into the service of healing rifts within the Windsor community. Literally pratted or beaten from the

Fords' home — "I'll prat her" (4.2.160), Ford rages of a woman he calls a "witch, a quean, an old cozening quean" (4.2.149) — Falstaff's fat ass becomes the repository for Ford's anxieties about feminine agency.[19]

As the butt of this jest, Falstaff/Mother Prat is not simply masculine *or* feminine, but a figure whose own somatic and semantic excessiveness — whose "extremity" — retains the most socially disruptive characteristics of both sexes: the masculine proclivity for controlling and translating women's "wills" and the presumptive female proclivity for secretive, adulterous plotting.[20] Because Anne successfully schemes to elope with Fenton, the play proves the security of the latter translation especially elusive. But here, nonetheless, Ford expels his anger and is able to ask his wife's "pardon" (4.4.5), and the wives can let their husbands in on their secret that they have been plotting against the knight rather than plotting to sleep with him. As the symptom for what is rotten in Windsor's domestic body politic, Falstaff and the gender troubles he retains are momentarily purged.

An Ass by Any Other Name

Falstaff's identification as an ass in Windsor Forest arises out of what Rosemary Kegl has referred to as the "network of insults" that constitutes the Windsor citizens' "shifting and uneven relationships to one another."[21] The term *cuckold* also passes through this network, and its passage is instructive to map because both it and *ass* come to rest on the shamed knight. Alone after having learned from Falstaff that Mistress Ford has summoned the knight to her house, Ford cries, "I shall not only receive this villainous wrong, but stand under the adoption of abominable terms, and by him that does me this wrong. . . . But 'cuckold,' 'wittol'! 'Cuckold' — the devil himself hath not such a name" (2.2.258–60, 262–64). Ford protests the adoption but recognizes that exposing his wife's infidelity would only publicize the "fact" that he has been cuckolded. Later, Ford resigns himself to the term, determined to work within it rather than against it: "Though what I am I cannot avoid, yet to be what I would not shall not make me tame. If I have horns to make one mad, let the proverb go with me: I'll be horn-mad" (3.5.128–30). Falstaff's shaming in Windsor Forest nonetheless gives Ford the opportunity to displace the assault, even if the actual crisis of adultery has passed. As Kegl observes, "By costuming Falstaff with a buck's head and orchestrating his ritual humiliation, they [the wives] allow Ford to repudiate his earlier jealousy and to turn Falstaff's slanderous speech upon the knight's own head."[22] And Ford relishes the turning: "Now, sir, who's a cuckold now? Master Brooke, Falstaff's a knave, a cuckoldy knave. Here are his horns, Master Brooke" (5.5.106–8). Strictly speaking, Falstaff (like Ford) is not a cuckold. Yet Falstaff's horned disguise as Herne the Hunter makes the knight available for the accusation and gives Ford the opportunity to repudiate the "abominable term." *Cuckold* comes to rest on Falstaff whether it fits him or not.

Ass circulates similarly throughout *Merry Wives,* and it connects with the term *cuckold* so as to suggest an underwriting opposition. In the play's first scene, Slender tries to discover who picked his pocket. After accusing Nim, who threatens to fight him, he accuses Bardolph: "By this hat, then, he in the red face had it. For though I cannot remember what I did when you made me drunk, yet I am not altogether an ass" (1.1.141–43). For Slender, whose name parodies the equation between thinness and self-possession, to be an ass is not only to admit the humiliating loss of control over one's person and property but also to lack suspicion about the theft of one's property. Ford uses the same term to characterize the incredulous Page: "Page is an ass, a secure ass. He will trust his wife, he will not be jealous" (2.2.264–65). That both wives are actually faithful to their husbands, that Page is right not to be jealous, is irrelevant: asses refuse to accept that they are cuckolds. In both Slender's and Ford's constructions of the term, an ass is a man insufficiently vigilant of his property — a man foolish enough to believe that no one has tricked him out of it.

When Falstaff admits that he has been made an ass, he identifies himself as just such a man foolish enough to believe he was not being tricked out of property to which he had (illegitimately) laid claim. To connect his admission to Slender's and Ford's statements in this way is only to establish the most audible path along which the term *ass* moves, however. The Oxford editors, and the Norton editors following them, realize the potential of punning Anne Page's first name with *âne,* French for *ass* (as in the animal), when they emend the folio's use of "fools head" to "ass head" in Mistress Quickly's double-tongued assurance to Caius:

CAIUS: By Gar, if I have not Anne Page, I shall turn your head out of my door...

MISTRESS QUICKLY: You shall have Anne —
> *Exeunt Doctor* [CAIUS *and* RUGBY]
— ass-head of your own. (1.4.108–11)

As Stanley Wells and Gary Taylor explain, "The double function of An[ne] as a name and an article is completely spoiled by the following noun beginning with a consonant." Besides, "an ass-head of your own" and a "fool's head of your own" are "parallel proverbial phrases, so substitution would be particularly easy."[23] The purity of these lines can apparently only be maintained through a translation that also echoes the "translated" (3.1.105) Bottom's retort to an astonished Snout in *A Midsummer Night's Dream:* "What do you see? You see an ass-head of your own, do you?" (3.1.103–4). The translation of *fool* to *ass* situates Anne within the network of asinine insults that I am mapping. Moreover, when heard as a scatological pun, Anne's name also helps enable French puns on the names of two other characters: Caius, or *cas (buttocks),* and Hugh Evans, whose first name is synonymous with *colour,* perhaps punning on *culier* (meaning that which pertains to the arse) when he declares himself "full of cholers" (3.1.8).[24] I do not presume that these puns, like the wordplay surrounding Falstaff's disguise as Mother Prat, would have been audible to every member of Shakespeare's audience. Nor am I making any sort of claim for Shakespeare's intentions. My detranslation of these puns rather capitalizes on the play's recognized preoccupation with the possibilities of multilingual wordplay.[25] When Caius challenges Evans (who is actually acting on Slender's behalf) for the right to pursue Anne — setting up the sodomitical joke that ends the play as Slender and Caius find themselves nearly married to boys — the Host of the Garter Inn brings the doctor and the parson together in Frogmore, a wasteland or a dung-depot. Caius and Evans reconcile with each other and agree to take revenge on the Host for making them "laughing-stocks" (3.1.73). But at least Caius does not leave his scatological associations on Frogmore's moist field. After Ford's first failure to expose his wife as an adulteress, Page invites everyone bird hunting the next morning. Ford agrees, as does Evans, and Caius follows: "If there be one or two, I shall make-a the turd" (3.3.200).

Importantly, those persons who are not scatologically sullied are all married. Ford nearly slanders himself when his anger swells and he declares himself "gross" like Falstaff, but by and large the Fords and the Pages are clean. Preserving the purity of these married couples depends, it seems, on the scatological denigration of other possible sexual unions — be it between Caius and Anne, which might be read as a kind of adulteration of English stock, or between Falstaff and the wives. Falstaff is immediately denigrated when he announces that he has written a love-letter to Mistress Ford:

> FALSTAFF: I have writ me here a letter to her — and here another to Page's wife, who even now gave me good eyes too, examined my parts with most judicious oeillades; sometimes the beam of her view gilded my foot, sometimes my portly belly.
>
> PISTOL: Then did the sun on dunghill shine. (1.3.49–54)

Pistol's equation of Falstaff's belly with a dunghill thwarts Falstaff's attempt to divorce *waist* and *waste,* while it also sullies the knight's assertion of Mistress Ford's attraction. Such a quick quip further anticipates the often critically maligned ease with which Falstaff plays into the hands of his detractors. A. C. Bradley encapsulated generations of critical sentiment with his complaint that Falstaff is "baffled, duped, treated like dirty linen, beaten, burnt, pricked, mocked, insulted, and worst of all, repentant and didactic." Bradley then concluded with the simple judgment, "It is horrible" — the ambiguous pronoun presumably referring to Falstaff, his treatment, and the play as a whole.[26]

I suspect that most contemporary critics of *Merry Wives* tacitly agree with Bradley that the play is neither a satisfying comedy in its own right nor a play that does justice to Falstaff. Without working through these aesthetic shortcomings, most recent work on the play has simply turned toward its domestic, gender, class, and national politics. Walter Cohen's introduction to the play exemplifies this critical turn. In his final paragraph, Cohen surmises not that the play is bad but that "the hierarchies and conflicts that separate man from woman, parent from child, sexual normality from sexual deviancy, town from crown, Englishman from foreigner, upper class from middle class, and middle class from lower are resolved — or, more accurately, evaded — through the good-natured, universal inclusiveness of the conclusion."[27] Cohen recognizes that this evasion requires Falstaff's public shaming, but he also betrays a slight Bradlarian misgiving about the necessity of the public shaming when he notes that it proceeds despite his sense that the Fords and Pages "are confident that he [Falstaff] no longer poses a threat."[28] At the end of 4.2, Mistress Page does assert that pratting Falstaff has put an end to his assault upon their wills: "The spirit of wantonness is sure scared out of him. If the devil have him not in fee-simple, with fine and recovery, he will never, I think, in the way of waste attempt us again" (4.2.183–85). Mistress Ford's subsequent assertion that "there would be no end to the jest should he not be publicly shamed" (4.2.193–94) thus indeed seems unjustified, and the perpetuation of the jest excessively vindictive. I submit, however, that engaging such questions of necessity requires engaging *Merry Wives* as a play about symptomatic excess. Falstaff's public shaming is excessive, but as Jerry Aline Flieger observes (following Freud), jokes often produce a "vague sense of excess, an unfinished feeling."[29] Just as this unfinished feeling leads someone who hears a joke to tell the same joke to someone else, it drives the "public sport" (4.4.13) of Falstaff's shaming.

Luring Falstaff into the woods and ambushing him also crucially allows the citizens of Windsor to ally themselves against a knight whose fat body can figure other types of excessive difference beyond gender. These differences include, especially, differences in nationality. Richard Helgerson has situated *Merry Wives* within the historical context of England's attempt to legitimate English as a sovereign language, one derived from but not equal to Latin, and one capable of imperial translation into foreign lands.[30] The play's "language lessons," as Helgerson calls them, focus attention on embattled concepts of national identity and language — on questions about how the English language is supposed to sound sovereignty throughout the world when it is simultaneously derived from a colonizing Roman power and so easily debased by foreign accents and bawdy misconstructions. The foreign degradation of Falstaff's English body temporarily neutralizes these nationalist concerns:

> FALSTAFF: Have I laid my brain in the sun and dried it, that it wants matter to prevent so gross o'er reaching as this? Am I ridden with a Welsh goat too? Shall I have a coxcomb of frieze? 'Tis time I were choked with a piece of toasted cheese.

EVANS: Seese is not good to give putter; your belly is all putter.

FALSTAFF: 'Seese' and 'putter'? Have I lived to stand at the taunt of one
that makes fritters of English? This is enough to be the decay of lust
and late walking through the realm. (5.5.130–37)

The cultural superiority awarded by Englishness, like the superiority
awarded by masculinity, here fails Falstaff. The Windsor citizens inscribe
upon his consuming body the markers of abject Welsh identity: the goats,
frieze, and toasted cheese. Furthermore, Evans's identity as a Welshman
has simultaneously been emptied of these negative associations through
his participation in a jest that, in Mistress Quickly's encouragement of
the "fairies," more or less replicates Elizabeth I's ceremonial blessing of
the aristocratic fraternity the Order of the Garter (see 5.5.52–70).[31] Only
now that Falstaff is shamefully exposed — that his position as an ass is, as
it were, uncovered — does Evans regain his accent, which he lost while
playing the part of the satyr (see 5.5.46–51, 74–77). This accent has heretofore marked Evans's national difference, but now his difference is not
so different because the mockery that it invites has been displaced onto
the fat knight. Falstaff's sense that he has been "ridden," costumed, and
force-fed only affirms that he no longer maintains control over his body
and its significations. He has been dispossessed of his own flesh, and he
can be melted, deflated, stuffed, swollen, and choked.

It is more than curious, though, that the only translated national difference here is Welsh. Caius, the French doctor fluent in a language that
governs much of the play's scatological wordplay, has eloped with his boy
in green. That Caius returns at the very end of the play and threatens to
"raise all of Windsor" (5.5.190) suggests that, although Falstaff now wears
the ass-head Quickly promised Caius, the humiliation of the knight has
not entirely purged the threat of the foreign from Windsor's English
body politic. Likewise, Falstaff's punishment for attempted thievery in
Windsor Forest may be read as proxy punishment for the Germans who
steal the Host's horses in 4.5, but this punishment only provides the necessary cover for Anne and Fenton to steal away. As an ass whose humiliation momentarily deflects attention away from the theft of another ass
(Anne), Falstaff serves as a repository for the purgation of *some* foreign
and gendered attributes that will not be assimilated into patriarchal

English culture. But the purge is clearly not complete, the body politic not freed from the threat of the foreign. Furthermore, the mechanisms of this purge — its workings through the discourse of the fat, anal body — remain crucial to engaging with the play's tenuous resolution of another hierarchical conflict. In the next section, I turn specifically to the class politics of the play in order to investigate the particular ways in which Falstaff's translation provides a foundation for the formation of Windsor's middle-class community.

(Cl)ass

Few critical paradigms have resurrected interest in *Merry Wives* as much as class — a term that would seem to emerge, as distinct from status, within early modern city comedies. As Rosemary Kegl reminds us, "the middle class" is not a "*thing* to be defined but, instead, a *process* of constructing alliances among groups" that are positioned "within very different structures of oppression."[32] Nowhere is this process more evident than in the play's final scene, where the "middle class" emerges in and around the distinction between "true aristocracy" and "aristocratic imposture" afforded by Falstaff's translation into an ass and Fenton's marriage to Anne.[33] Because Fenton and Falstaff, true aristocrat and aristocratic impostor respectively, gain a place within the Windsor body politic, there is, in the end, no absolute distinction to be made between the retained and the purged in Windsor's middle class. Nor, really, is there any end to the process of translation, as the end of the jest is repeatedly deflected.

This second point first: Mistress Ford is wrong to assume that the jest will end with Falstaff's public shaming. After Falstaff's humiliation, Page initiates what Walter Cohen terms an "antiscapegoating outcome" by inviting Falstaff to "eat a posset tonight at my house" (5.5.158–59).[34] Once home, however, Page plans to continue jesting, this time at his wife's expense. As he tells Falstaff, "I will desire thee to laugh at my wife that now laughs at thee" (5.5.159–60). This new jest turns on Anne's marriage: Page believes his daughter has married Slender, while Mistress Page believes she has married Caius. Perpetuating the public sport in excess of Falstaff's shaming would potentially displace the "abominable term" of *ass* onto the Page whose parental propriety is denied. Thus, when Anne returns instead with Fenton, potentially humiliating both Pages, Falstaff revels in the deflection of their original aim: "I am glad, though you have ta'en special stand to strike at me, that your arrow hath glanced" (5.5.211–12). Only the arrow does not in turn strike either Page. Refusing to be similarly shamed — and taking it upon himself to speak for his wife — Page embraces his daughter's marriage to Fenton in a move that enables the formulaic comic dénouement while also signaling a significant adjustment of class boundaries.

Page has heretofore disapproved of Fenton on the grounds that he is a gentleman "of no having" (3.2.60–61) and "of too high a region" (3.2.62). From Page's perspective, Fenton and Falstaff, no matter their differences in character, are part of the same social constituency: both belong to that faction of the aristocracy supplying the stock figures of city comedies, men dispossessed of the wealth that ostensibly elevates them into the upper strata of society.[35] One presumes that Page would feel differently if Fenton were wealthy. Nevertheless, his prejudice helps shape Windsor's body politic, distinguishing its citizens (foreign nationals or not) from its aristocratic outsiders, Fenton and Falstaff, both of whom share a further acquaintance in the Host of the Garter Inn. As its name implies, the Garter Inn is a restrictive residence for transients; it fashions the body politic in such a way as to staunch middle-class excess. Page's ultimate acceptance of Anne and Fenton's marriage on the grounds that "[w]hat cannot be eschewed must be embraced" (5.5.214) thus signals nothing if not a relaxation of his prejudice. He correctly claims that the marriage cannot simply be eschewed, but he still posits something of a false alternative in claiming that it *must* be embraced. He could seek revenge on Fenton, Anne, or Mistress Quickly, and such a turn would certainly be in keeping with the play's compounding plots of revenge and cozening. Acceptance of the marriage suggests, by contrast, that the final trick on Falstaff has opened Windsor's body politic to include this compromised version of the aristocracy — this aristocracy in title but "of no having."

The performance of the Garter Ceremony is instrumental in this expansion. Early in the play, Mistress Quickly recalls a time when "the court lay at Windsor" (2.2.59), marking court culture as both constitutive of Windsor's continuing significance as an English town and a vestige of its past. Quickly and her fellow citizens are not aristocrats, but the town's historical relation to the court serves as the backdrop against which they can undergo their own translative experiences, becoming the guardians of a social, domestic, and courtly order by asserting their assumed moral authority over the debauched knight. This translation also occasions a pivotal inversion: Mistress Quickly, formerly the go-between for Anne and her three suitors, and hardly a paragon of chastity, assumes the role of the Fairy Queen and takes out her hatred of "sluts and sluttery" (5.5.43) on Falstaff's body. The otherwise differentiated Windsor citizens, while performing the roles of ideological guardians, cohere atop the dregs or waste of the aristocracy, as signified by the burned and pinched Falstaff. This bottoming-out of the aristocracy quells anxieties about mixing the highborn with the lowborn by first defining lowness as "sluttery" and then displacing it onto Falstaff's fat body. Windsor's body politic can thus expand to incorporate those members of the aristocracy whose class-status is compromised by their lack of property. But just as it thereby absorbs Fenton, Windsor must also absorb Falstaff, whose retentive body serves as the site and orifice of the purge, the butt of the body politic.

As a performance that reshapes Windsor's body politic through purgation, relaxing the pressure on this body's middle, the performance of the Garter Ceremony does not merely hearken back to an aristocratic culture or nostalgically resurrect the spirit of an old regime. At one and the same time, it looks backward toward an older aristocratic ideal and forward toward a unification and valorization of an otherwise polymorphous polity under the banner of English, patriarchal virtue. Through the translation of the ceremony by people who are markedly not aristocrats, the very notions of aristocracy, the middle class, and class itself are being tailored to fit the gendered and nationalist realities of life in Windsor. The repeated punning on *deer* and *dear* in the final scene attests to this fitting. Formerly the deer/dear of Mistresses Page and Ford ("Art thou there," Mistress Ford calls on arriving in Windsor Forest, "my deer, my male deer?" [5.5.15–16]), Falstaff redeploys the pun after he learns of Anne and Fenton's elopement: "When night-dogs run, all sorts of deer are chased" (5.5.215). Fenton's "thievery" of Anne has heretofore been the stuff of Falstaff's villainy (the play of course opens with Justice Shallow accusing Falstaff of poaching his deer), yet Fenton is now protected from parental and patriarchal retribution because Falstaff retains the thieving associations that have displaced onto him. Consequent to this retention, Falstaff's significance in this final scene becomes even more excessive than when he is outfitted as Mother Prat. Costumed as the horned Herne the Hunter, he is a scapegoat, taking on the "sins" of others, as well as the hunter and the hunted, a stag and a deer, a cuckold, a butt that everyone has "ta'en special stand to strike," the arse of the body politic, and an ass who bears the burden of bringing Windsor together. In Windsor Forest's Ovidian landscape, he is four-part animal — goat, stag, ass, and ox — and he evokes classical figures including Actaeon, Jove, Midas, and Lucius (from Apuleius's *The Golden Ass*).[36] In short, he signifies excessively, but only through the production of this excessive signification, and at his expense, does Windsor's body politic take shape.

Because every body needs an ass, Falstaff cannot simply be cast out from the community. His scatological degradation has produced the foundation of Windsor's body politic. The Ovidian end of the play nevertheless highlights how this body politic is also fundamentally metamorphic. Caius's phallic threat that he will "raise all Windsor" (5.5.190) promises to change the shape of this body. So too, the Pages' attempts to outmaneuver each other in marrying Anne off to different suitors suggest the domestic foundations of this body politic may be tenuous. Through the consumption of otherwise inconsonant signifiers, Falstaff momentarily becomes the ass, the repository for what is ostensibly in excess of bourgeois English patriarchy. Yet he will not be in this position for long.

But(t)

In *The Four Fundamental Concepts of Psychoanalysis,* Lacan distinguishes the four elements of the partial drive using language that we are now in a position to describe as Shakespearean. To illustrate the relationship between these four elements, Lacan draws a parabola designating the *aim* (1), which leaves from one side of the circular *rim* (2), circles its *object* (3), and returns again to the other side of the rim in achieving its *goal* (4). Lacan uses the diagram to illustrate the drive's "return to its circuit," and in light of Falstaff's temporary position as the ass, Lacan's claim that English is more helpful than French in distinguishing the *aim* from the *goal* is especially significant:

[L]et us concentrate on this term *but,* and on the two meanings it may present. In order to differentiate them, I have chosen to notate them here in a language in which they are particularly expressive, English. When you entrust someone with a mission, the *aim* is not what he brings back, but the itinerary he must take. The *aim* is the way taken. The French word *but* may be translated by another word in English, *goal.* In archery, the *goal* is not the *but* either, it is not the bird you shoot, it is having scored a hit and thereby attained your *but.*[37]

The French word *but* translates as *aim* (1) and *goal* (4), and is thereby distinct from the object (3): "It is not the bird you shoot." But the bird, in this case, is not actually the object either. The object is "simply the presence of a hollow, a void, which can be occupied, Freud tells us, by any object, and whose agency we know only in the form of the lost object, the *petit a.*"[38] Like Falstaff, against whom Windsor takes aim, the bird's tenure as the object is only temporary. The drive returns to its circuit — and the jest continues — around a void that *Merry Wives* metaphorizes as an anus.

In this chapter, I have argued that the wives' revenge jests reinscribe the degrading relationship between *waste* and *waist* back onto Falstaff's fat body, translating the knight into the butt of Windsor's body politic. I have further argued that the play emphasizes the fragility of this "scapegoating" translation and the other social positions that take shape through it. Lacan's Shakespearean elaboration of the elements of the partial drive now underscores the illimitability of scapegoating as itself an eroticized process of translation: the ass is not only a site of social production but one of perpetual metamorphosis in its irreducible metaphoricity. I will return to the subject of translative scapegoating in chapter 4 apropos of Freud's account of the goal of the obscene joke: in that chapter, the object of the drive, of the jest, metaphorizes as both the anus and the vagina, as one and the same orifice. First, however, I turn to another Shakespeare comedy, *All's Well That Ends Well,* which also plays with the translative dimensions of scatological debasement in its anal inscription of Paroles (whose name means *words*). When Paroles returns to the French court "muddied in Fortune's mood, and smell[ing] somewhat strong of her strong displeasure" (5.2.3–5), Lavatch, the clown, insists on the scent of Paroles's metaphor: "Indeed, sir, if your metaphor stink I will stop my nose, or against any man's metaphor" (5.2.11–12). Paroles's humiliation by his fellow soldiers is arguably necessary to bringing about the comic resolution that reconstitutes Bertram as an honorable nobleman and husband. But I submit that the scent of Paroles's metaphor is the scent of his own excessive inscription as the play's ass. Like Falstaff, Paroles cannot ultimately retain the anal signifier that has been written onto him. I will argue that the wandering anal signifier forces a reassessment of the play's comic teleology — its drive toward a happy ending.

3

Happy Endings
Healing Sick Desires in *All's Well That Ends Well*

[G]ive thyself unto my sick desires[.]
— Bertram to Diana, *All's Well That Ends Well*, 4.2.36

FRAMING THEIR MISSION IN MOSAIC TERMS, EXODUS INTER-
national, one of the leading ministries in the contemporary ex-
gay movement, equates sexual reorientation with liberation. As
the author of one Exodus testimonial writes, God "not only saved me,
He liberated me and continues to liberate me. . . . I am not only free of
the bondage of unwanted same-sex attraction, I continue to walk free
of anything that hinders my relationship with Him."[1] Yet Exodus's name
alone does not suggest the ways in which the ministry also intertwines
the discourse of abolition with the discourse of pathology, such that liberation from homosexuality is at one and the same time a cure of some
sickness that has arrested the development of a heterosexual subject. In
the words of the ministry's statement on "Healing," this cure begins with
a "reconciling of ones [sic] identity with Jesus Christ," a reconciliation
that "enables growth towards Godly heterosexuality." Although Exodus
measures this sexual and spiritual conversion by "a growing capacity to
turn away from temptations," the statement ends by identifying a "lifelong and healthy marriage" and a "Godly single life" as "good indicators
of this transformation."[2]

As socially conservative and psychologically pernicious as sexual-
conversion therapy may be, there is also something remarkably queer
about it — or so Tanya Erzen argues in her ethnography of the ex-gay
movement, *Straight to Jesus*. According to Erzen, ex-gays share with queer

theorists an understanding "that a person's sexual orientation, behaviors, and desires can fluctuate."[3] Many ex-gays do not believe, for instance, that their desires will always correspond with the married or single heterosexual identities that they strive to inhabit. "Recovery and relapse are built into the creation of an ex-gay identity," Erzen writes, "and sexual falls are expected. Rather than becoming heterosexual, men and women become part of a new identity group in which it is the norm to submit to temptation and return to ex-gay ministry over and over again."[4] (As Erzen also points out, the ex-gay identity itself "represents their sense of being in flux between identities."[5]) The movement's official literature, including its testimonials, does not always reflect this queer understanding that desire and identity are fluid and often incongruous. It holds out the prospect of "freedom" and promises that transformation is possible. In short, it rarely admits that the teleological "growth towards Godly heterosexuality" is often a lifelong struggle with "illness," an endless journey to a promised land.

Erzen's work raises a provocative and complex set of questions about the relationship between sexual identity and desire in the ex-gay movement. For my purposes in this chapter, the movement's specific correlation of homosexuality with arrested development and sin facilitates an (a)historical inquiry into the relationship between desire and identity in Shakespeare's *All's Well That Ends Well*. As Bruce Smith writes of male homoeroticism in the Renaissance, "The structures of knowledge that impinged on what we would now call 'homosexuality' did not ask a man who had sexual relations with another man to think of himself as fundamentally different from his peers. Just the opposite was true. Prevailing ideas asked him to castigate himself for falling into the general depravity to which *all* mankind is subject."[6] Exodus International maintains a similar position; according to one of their policy statements, "homosexual tendencies [are] one of many disorders that beset fallen humanity."[7] Exodus rejects any claim that homosexuals comprise a fixed percentage of the population and posits instead that a struggle with same-sex desire is simply part of the lapsed human condition. The fact that ex-gays often trace their homosexual desires back to a traumatic but chance instance of childhood molestation helps substantiate this claim: anyone may fall victim to sexual disorders by virtue of what happens in his or her child-hood, but not everyone does.

Insofar as the development of the modern epoch is coterminous with the development of essentializing and minoritizing discourses of sexual identity, the ex-gay movement's perspective on homosexuality seems quite retrograde.[8] While granting the reality of heterosexuality, ex-gay ideol-ogy denies that homosexuality is a sexual orientation, that a person can be a homosexual. At the same time, the movement's use of the discourse of sexual pathology also indicates its debt to what Foucault describes as modern regimes of *scientia sexualis.* The movement correlates homosex-ual "tendencies" with original sin, but it stakes the possibility of healing on the essentialist ground that all human beings are, by default, hetero-sexual. There is no such ground in the Renaissance, for there is no such thing there as heterosexual identity.[9] There are, however, moral norms and social expectations against which sexual relations can be judged devi-ant, and which are hardly absent from contemporary heterosexual ide-ology: first, that reproduction is the purpose of sex, and second, that young men and women will grow up and get married.[10] Taking a cue from those many critics (like Bruce Smith) who locate a nascent understanding of homosexual identity in Renaissance articulations of same-sex desires and erotic practices, I want to (a)historically approach the *evidentiary* limits of heterosexual identity that I locate in this reservation of sex for reproduction and this equation of maturation with marriage.[11] The ex-gay movement both insists on the possibility of sexual conversion and admits desire's original and ongoing susceptibility to perversion. It assumes that desire is malleable, its objects always vulnerable to shift, while it also posits a healthy or pure sexual state against which sick desires signify. In staking out this vexed ideological terrain, the ex-gay move-ment raises the question of what heterosexual identity *looks* like, or what signs — like marriage — serve as visual evidence of everyone's supposedly core sexual identity.

In this chapter, I consider the ex-gay as someone whose represented reorientation at the end of the conversion process comes into con-flict with the "invisible" persistence of perverse desires. These desires upset the teleological conversion narratives offered by the movement as evidence for the possibility of change. These desires also challenge the marital evidence frequently cited in claims for the success of sexual reorientation. Thinking this challenge through *All's Well That Ends Well,* I will argue that the play aligns sexual conversion with the comic fantasy of a happy ending, and in the process raises evidentiary questions that the ex-gay movement seems unwilling or unable to address. Whereas dramatic comedy traditionally aims to reorient desires so as to bring about a happy ending, Shakespeare seems to have grown disillusioned with the possibility of reorientation by the time he wrote his so-called problem comedies. These plays — *Troilus and Cressida, Measure for Measure,* and *All's Well That Ends Well* — all foreground concerns about sexual health, suggesting, in various ways, that the social order is itself sick, and that there can be no happy endings in the midst of such pervasive illness.[12] David Scott Kastan remarks that the latter two plays make "the gratification of desire appear so willfully manipulated and contrived" that their audiences cannot but doubt the optimism of their own conclusions.[13] *All's Well* invites this doubt with its own title. A play about a female doctor who heals "sick desires," *All's Well* also illustrates the conflict between minoritizing understandings of sexual identity and universalizing theories of psychosexual development susceptible to arrest. To perceive this conflict, we must focus on what the play locates off stage. We must focus on the way desire's perverse loyalty to improper objects persists against the staged fiction of sexual reorientation. By attending to the play's strategic occlusions and to the relationship of the invisible with the temporal deformations that derail the conventional teleology of comic narrative, I will argue that Helen does not cure or liberate Bertram from his sick desires.[14] Rather, she finds a way to queerly accommodate them within the institution of marriage.

The Curbèd Time

Let me begin by stating my claim as simply as I can: Bertram is a sodomite.

Simple as this claim may seem, it warrants qualification. Nevertheless, let us consider some evidence. First, Bertram keeps very queer company — namely, Paroles, whom the Countess charges with corrupting her son's "well-derivèd nature / With his inducement" (3.2.88–89). Always dressed to the nines and frequently bragging about spurious martial victories, Paroles wields considerable influence over the young nobleman.

Patricia Parker has argued that Paroles represents a new breed of "counterfeit" (4.3.95) men associated throughout the play with the monetary
language of principle and interest.[15] I would add that such association
also places Paroles squarely within the discourse of sodomy, of unnatural
and usurious creation *ex nihilo*.[16]

Second, Bertram rebels against the ideological injunction to marry
and produce legitimate heirs.[17] When Bertram protests his marriage to
Helen, the king sharply rebukes his disobedience. But Bertram's disobedience registers in this play as more than a dishonorable affront to the
king's authority. Absconding with Paroles to the Florentine wars where
he tries instead to seduce Diana, Bertram also refuses to carry on the family name. This refusal — what Garrett A. Sullivan Jr. describes as a violent
act of self-forgetting, a betrayal of "family memory and identity" —
sounds the threat of termination that sodomites pose to the order of the
family and the state.[18]

I am interested here in homologies between the early modern discourse of sodomy and the ex-gay movement's construction of homosexuality, but it is important to recall that sodomy does not simply equate
with homosexuality or with male homosexual intercourse. Sodomy encom-
passes a wide range of transgressive acts, including adultery, heresy, and
treason — crimes that are all predicated on the creation of illegitimate
alliances. As Jonathan Goldberg memorably defines it,

> [S]odomy is, as a sexual act, anything that threatens alliance — any sexual
> act, that is, that does not promote the aim of married, procreative sex
> (anal intercourse, fellatio, masturbation, bestiality — any of these may
> fall under the label of sodomy in various early modern legal codifications
> and learned discourses), and while sodomy involves therefore acts that
> men might perform with men, women with women (a possibility rarely
> envisioned), men and women with each other, and anyone with a goat,
> a pig, or a horse, these acts — or accusations of their performance —
> *emerge into visibility* only when those who are said to have done them can
> also be called traitors, heretics, or the like, at the very least, disturbers
> of the social order that alliance — marital arrangements — maintained.[19]

Of course, no one in this play explicitly charges Bertram (or Paroles) with
sodomy — a fact not unimportant considering that, in the period, sodomy
is a distinct legal and theological accusation of monstrous criminality, and

that numerous same-sex and otherwise transgressive sexual relationships escape the charge entirely. My claim that Bertram is a sodomite rests on a strategic decision to use "sodomy" to trope dead-end sexualities — or sexualities "oriented" around the disillusion of the social order, and the anus. My claim also rests on circumstantial evidence, which is by definition subject to inference. We might easily read Bertram's rejection of Helen as motivated by the fact that he is a nobleman and she a "poor physician's daughter" (2.3.111), and thus argue that Bertram is a social conservative rather than a sodomite. But considering the numerous elements in the discourse of sodomy that otherwise circulate throughout the play, my argument is rather that Bertram's conservative posture "visibly" signifies as sodomitical in its defiance of the king's command. To make this argument is to frame sodomy's visibility in *All's Well* as itself a matter of inference — a frame constructed by the very play of signifiers for sodomy in the play. Furthermore, it is to suggest that the king's command is itself instrumental in the identification of Bertram as a sodomite. Like the relationship of homosexuality to heterosexuality in ex-gay ideology, the relationship of sodomy to normative sexuality in *All's Well* is one Jonathan Dollimore would describe as paradoxically perverse; in both relationships, perversity is "perceived as at once utterly alien to what it threatens, and yet, mysteriously inherent within it."[20] Bertram and Paroles may be the play's most visible sodomites, but their perversions are endemic to the same social order they threaten.

The king betrays his concern about the sodomitical nature of the French body politic in his nostalgic portrait of Bertram's late father. A brave man who "did look far / Into the service of the time" (1.2.26–27), whose honor was a "Clock to itself [knowing] the true minute when / Exception bid him speak" (1.2.39–40), and who "scattered not [his words] in ears, but grafted them / To grow there and bear" (1.2.54–55), Bertram's father paradoxically (because he is dead) represents everything that sodomy is not: proper reproduction, forward thinking, and productive expenditure. The king paints the French youth, in contrast, as loquacious "goers-backward" (1.2.48) who "may jest / Till their own scorn return to them unnoted / Ere they can hide their levity in honour" (1.2.33–35). Like Paroles, who stands with Bertram in front of the king, these youths are also fickle fashionistas "whose judgments are / Mere fathers of their garments" (1.2.61–62). The king never directly outs the French youth as sodomites, but accusations abound in this memorial speech. Offering far more than kind words to a grieving son, the king eroticizes generational conflict, warning the still obedient Bertram — whom the Countess has charged with succeeding his father "In manners as in shape" (1.1.55) — against the perversions of his fellow youth.

In light of this portrait of the times, Helen's earlier exchange with Paroles on the subject of virginity stands out for its manipulation of common signifiers for sodomy. Paroles admonishes her,

> 'Tis against the rule of nature. To speak on the part of virginity is to accuse your mothers, which is most infallible disobedience. He that hangs himself is a virgin: virginity murders itself, and should be buried in highways, out of all sanctified limit, as a desperate offendress against nature. Virginity breeds mites, much like a cheese; consumes itself to the very paring, and so dies with feeding his own stomach. Besides, virginity is peevish, proud, idle, made of self-love — which is the most inhibited sin in the canon. Keep it not, you cannot choose but lose by't. Out with't! Within t'one year it will make itself two, which is a goodly increase, and the principal itself not much the worse. Away with't. (1.1.127–39)

By casting virginity as a narcissistic and self-devouring crime against nature, then framing its loss in terms of usury ("goodly increase"), Paroles effectively sodomizes virginity — shifting the familiar terms of sodomy's condemnation onto virginity while simultaneously celebrating an erotics of interest. Considering that Paroles is often accounted another poor copy of Falstaff (another, that is, if the Falstaff of *Merry Wives* is also a poor copy of his Henriad self), Paroles's rhetorically dexterous resignification of virginity as sodomitical should recall Falstaff's equally dexterous attempt to redefine the relationship between *waste* and *waist* in *Merry Wives*. Like his dramatic predecessor, Paroles is outwitted by a better female wordsmith:

HELEN: Monsieur Paroles, you were born under a charitable star.

PAROLES: Under Mars, I.

HELEN: I especially think *under* Mars.

PAROLES: Why '*under* Mars'?

HELEN: The wars hath so kept you under that you must needs be born under Mars.

PAROLES: When he was predominant.

HELEN: When he was retrograde, I think rather.

PAROLES: Why think you so?

HELEN: You go so much backward when you fight.

    (1.1.177–86, original emphasis)

Returning his scorn unnoted, Helen translates the fearful and fashionable fop into Mars's catamite ("*under* Mars"), re-inscribing him within the very same sodomitical terrain that Paroles sought to position virginity. It will be Paroles's Falstaff-like fate to rebound from this insult, only later to be "found an ass" (4.3.313) and "muddied in Fortune's mood" (5.2.3–4). But here he is outwitted and stunned, left for once without much to say, if still swollen: "I am so full of businesses I cannot answer thee acutely" (1.1.191).

Helen's jest with Paroles foreshadows her later outwitting of Bertram, whose riddling letters prove him to be as rhetorically dexterous as his friend. Her jest also illustrates the common association of sodomy with backward movement, both temporal and spatial: Paroles was born when Mars was retrograde, moving backward as Paroles does when he retreats from battle. Helen's wit effectively promotes the "straight" ideology of her elders against the preposterous movements of Paroles and the French youth. After the marriage of Bertram and Helen, Paroles additionally opposes women's time, as the time of marital dues and due dates, to the temporality of Bertram's retreat:

> Madam, my lord will go away tonight.
> A very serious business calls on him.
> The great prerogative and rite of love,
> Which as your due time claims, he does acknowledge,
> But puts it off to a compelled restraint:
> Whose want and whose delay is strewed with sweets,
> Which they distil now in *the curbèd time,*
> To make the coming hour o'erflow with joy,
> And pleasure drown the brim. (2.4.36–44, emphasis added)[21]

Paroles excuses Bertram from immediate consummation of the marriage with the vagary of "serious business," but he acknowledges Helen's "due" and paints the future with orgasmic promise. What Paroles does not say is that Bertram aims only to delay forever "the coming hour," to curb time permanently, such that Helen will never receive what is hers.[22]

In her work on contemporary queer subcultures, Judith Halberstam makes a distinction between normative and queer temporality that seems equally relevant for Paroles's distinction between due and curbed time. Normative temporality, within which the developmental stages of psychoanalysis take shape, prescribes a growth "out of childish dependency through marriage and into adult responsibility through reproduction."[23] To resist marriage and/or parenthood — the ostensible happy endings of the process of maturation — is to potentially enter a queer temporality that registers against the norm as a prolongation of adolescence. Endless adolescence does indeed seem the state in which Bertram, described by his mother as a "rash and unbridled boy" (3.2.27) suffering from a "careless lapse / Of youth and ignorance" (2.3.159–60), is trapped by his decision to flee Helen; and much psychoanalytic criticism has accordingly situated him within the Oedipal paradigm of immature rebellion against the (here surrogate) father.[24] At the same time, it is crucial to any assessment of Bertram's maturity to note that the king would have Bertram grow up too quickly by forcing him into marriage. The king has already set war before women when cautioning the two lords Dumaine:

> Those girls of Italy, take heed of them.
> They say our French lack language to deny
> If they demand. Beware of being captives
> Before you serve. (2.1.19–22)

The king has also stayed Bertram from the wars by telling him that he is "'Too young' . . . and 'tis too early'"(2.1.28). Both Helen, in demanding Bertram's hand, and the king, lacking the language to deny her, therefore do their part to throw time and social alliances out of joint. Acting out normativity's perverse dynamic, the sodomite who flees a woman for the wars paradoxically preserves the prescribed sequence of events in the course of male maturation.

Yet Bertram's flight to fight is not for this reason a flight away from the play of sodomitical signifiers. As Paroles depicts them, the wars are themselves queer grounds:

> To th' wars, my boy, to th' wars!
> He wears his honour in a box unseen
> That hugs his kicky-wicky here at home,
> Spending his manly marrow in her arms,
> Which should sustain the bound and high curvet
> Of Mars's fiery steed. To other regions! (2.3.262–67)

Additionally equating marriage with castration — "Why these balls bound, there's noise in it. 'Tis hard: / A young man married is a man that's marred" (2.3.281–82) — Paroles denigrates the marital expenditure of "manly marrow" and valorizes, in turn, martial, equestrian showmanship. Going to war may be instrumental in the making of a Renaissance man, but the line between martial and sodomitical erotics (which Shakespeare traces and transgresses most formidably in *Troilus and Cressida* and *Coriolanus*) is a particularly thin one; and Paroles's call arguably crosses this line by eroticizing war as a phallic performance among other men and horses.[25] A possible quibble on the "box unseen" as the vaginal grave of honor further allows "other regions" to be heard both geographically, from France to Florence, and somatically, from vagina to anus — a conflation Bertram then echoes in his riddling letter to Helen: "'Til I have no wife, I have *nothing* in France" (3.2.72, emphasis added). This detranslation of Bertram's and Paroles's wordplay constitutes the first step in showing how sodomitical desire, in opposition to marital desire, is troped as anal in the play. I will argue that independent of any corresponding orificial rhetoric within the ex-gay movement, but in ways that bring questions about fantasy life to bear on the process of sexual conversion, the anus in *All's Well* becomes the signifying orifice for sodomy as the dead-end erotics of improper alliance and temporal perversion. On the eve of his escape to "other regions," Bertram confirms his induction into this realm of the preposterous:

> I have writ my letters, casketed my treasure,
> Given orders for our horses, and tonight,
> When I should take possession of the bride,
> End ere I do begin. (2.5.22–25)

Bertram exempts himself from the strictures of straight time, the sequence of which now demands the consummation of his marriage, and seeks instead to end his life with Helen before it even begins. The question remains whether Helen can prove herself a better time traveler.

Cuts

In an influential essay on Alfred Hitchcock's *Rope* — a film long understood to focus on two homosexual men, though it offers no direct evidence of their sexual identity — D. A. Miller argues that the truth of the men's homosexuality is sutured to the film's notorious single shot structure. Because cameras only held ten minutes worth of film, Hitchcock had to manage ten cuts, the first four of which involve a blackout as the camera focuses on the rear of a man's suit. "Under cover of these blackouts," Miller argues, "two things get 'hidden.' One is the popularly privileged site of gay male sex, the orifice whose sexual use general opinion considers . . . the least dispensable element in defining the true homosexual. The other is the cut, for whose pure technicity a claim can hardly be sustained at so overwhelmingly hallucinatory a moment."[26] In the darkness of the blackout, both the anus and the film cut seem "to come in place of one another, [to] configure one and the same thing: the anus is a cut, and vice-versa."[27] As that which bespeaks the truth of gay male identity, the anus appears at the moment of its vanishing, reproducing homosexuality as an epistemological problem "of *being able to tell* " that makes itself felt in critical obsession with the film's technical originality.[28]

By and large, critics of *All's Well* have been more attuned than critics of *Rope* to the erotics of occlusion. As David McCandless observes, "the play seems to suppress its own erotic subdrama."[29] Miller's analysis of *Rope* can nonetheless be of some help in approaching the question of what happens in *All's Well* — or more specifically, what enables the comedy to play itself out to its "happy ending." While drama and film are different media, Miller's connection of *Rope*'s celluloid cuts to the film's production of sexual identity suggests why the action offstage, or behind the scenes, in *All's Well* is no less significant to the conversion narrative — and perhaps it is even more significant — than what happens on it.[30] Just as *Rope* generates a desire to see what it does not show, *All's*

Well does the same by shifting offstage, or cutting away from, two "sex scenes": the cure of the king's fistula and the bed trick. These cuts in the dramatic action are not themselves coded as anal, but I suggest that the anus nonetheless does trope the sex of which we are denied sight. This trope does not allow us to specify what exactly happens in each cut scene. Rather, it confounds the distinction between sodomitical and non-sodomitical sex that the play's plot seems intent on forging as it drives in fits and starts toward its happy ending.

Perhaps nothing in the play is more empirically obscure than the location of the king's fistula — that ulcerous canal, or cut, in his own body. Taking their cue from Lafeu's wish that the fistula "were not notorious" (1.1.32), many critics have argued, if not simply assumed, that it is anal.[31] This argument makes a great deal of sense. *Fistulas in ano* were the most common type of fistulas according to Renaissance physicians.[32] The pervasive rhetoric of the preposterous also arguably overdetermines the fistula's rear location. Because Shakespeare's sources — both Boccaccio in *The Decameron* and William Painter in the 1575 *Palace of Pleasures* — clearly locate the fistula on the king's chest, however, the fact that Shakespeare does not seems significant in its own right. Shakespeare would seem to have strategically mystified the location of the fistula, and thus to have rendered it *anally indeterminate.* That is to say, the fistula *seems* anal regardless as to where it resides on the king's body. The method of Helen's Viagran cure — "powerful to arise King Pépin" (2.1.74), Lefeu promises — is likewise indeterminate: at once mysterious and erotic, it takes place off stage, raising the question of what Helen has that, according to her own testimony, supersedes her "father's skill" (1.3.229).[33]

Both indeterminacies are profoundly consequential for a reading of *All's Well* as a sexual conversion narrative, the king's conversion preceding Bertram's. For much like the Karposi's Sarcoma legion that presents as a symptom of AIDS, the fistula symptomatizes a terminal illness of desire that we can say the nostalgic, backward-looking king shares with his youthful subjects as the head of France's sick body politic. In the cut between Helen and the king's scenes, 2.1 and 2.3, we see a short scene in which Lavatch jests with the Countess about "an answer that fits all questions" (2.2.13): this bawdy answer is "like a barber's chair that fits all buttocks" (2.2.14) and "of most monstrous size that must fit all demands"

(2.2.28–29). But the answer itself, "Oh Lord, Sir!" (2.2.36), actually *evades* an answer, the comedy of the scene distracting from but also giving voice to the ambiguity in the hidden spectacle of what Wendy Wall would call "queer physic" (female medical treatment of the male body).[34] Helen's methods are not clear, but if she is a disciple of the late medieval physician John Arderne, she is herself a skilled cutter: Arderne's often highly successful procedure involved inserting a probe into the rectum and cutting the fistula open.[35] ("Oh Lord, Sir!" indeed.) At the very least, she probably has to insert her fingers into his body. The king's phallic salvation depends on the occlusion of such a potentially obscene reversal in the gendered roles of penetrator and penetrated, but the fact that the spectacle is hidden makes it no less perverse. "They say miracles are past," Lefeu wonders at the opening of 2.3, "and we have our philosophers to make modern and familiar things supernatural and causeless" (2.3.1–3). In what Kiernan Ryan has described as Shakespeare's secular miracle play, Helen's sexual healing of the king is itself a preposterous event.[36]

The bed trick likewise takes place off stage, but in its place appears a conversation between the two lords Dumaine as they wait for Bertram. Using language that evokes the construction of homosexuality as the "open secret," the second lord claims to know something that "must dwell darkly with" (4.3.11) the first:

> FIRST LORD DUMAINE: When you have spoken it 'tis dead, and I am the grave of it.
>
> SECOND LORD DUMAINE: He [Bertram] hath perverted a young gentlewoman here in Florence of a most chaste renown, and this night he fleshes his will in the spoil of her honour. He hath given her his monumental ring, and thinks himself made in the unchaste composition.
>
> FIRST LORD DUMAINE: Now God delay our rebellion! As we are ourselves, what things we are.
>
> SECOND LORD DUMAINE: Merely our own traitors. And as in the common course of all treasons we still see them reveal themselves till they attain to their abhorred ends, so he that in this action contrives against his own nobility, in his proper stream o'erflows himself. (4.3.12–25)

Bertram's perversion of the "proper stream" of social alliances, as well as the second lord's transmission of this secret into the "grave" of the first lord's body, here takes on a sodomitical — which is to say, an anally indeterminate — tone. The first lord's exclamatory plea for divine aid implicitly links the salvation of Bertram's "end," or his treason's "abhorred end," to the salvation of the king's end, while more explicitly linking the need for Bertram's salvation to the need for humankind's salvation ("God delay *our* rebellion. . . ."). The lords here signal that Bertram's sodomitical fallenness is paradigmatic, not idiosyncratic, and that it manifests itself in the sin of illicit "heterosexual" sex. As we will see, the bed trick mediates between such sodomitical (perverse) and nonsodomitical (straight, chaste) sexuality. As part of Helen's method of curing Bertram's sick desires, the bed trick turns on the fungibility of the anus and the vagina endemic to the discourse of sodomy, the same fungibility that arguably underwrites the king's fistula as a penetrable orifice. Helen raises the king from his "sickly bed" (2.3.107) only by sealing (if first by cutting open even wider) a hole in his body. In turn, only if the orifices cease to be fungible, only if the procreative female end is secured as the proper end of Bertram's desire, can we likewise say that the young nobleman has been cured.

Equally instrumental in Bertram's sexual healing is the exposure of Paroles for which the two lords wait in anticipation. That Paroles is nothing more than the shell of an honorable man seems plain to everyone but Bertram, who mistakes emptiness for substance and who must witness Paroles's treason in order to see the difference. Or perhaps *hear* the difference, considering that Paroles is repeatedly associated with hollow objects: he is a "vessel" (2.3.198), a "casement" (2.3.205), a "light nut" without a kernel (2.5.40), a "bubble" (3.6.6), a "pasty" (4.3.120), and a "drum" (5.3.253). Jonathan Gil Harris argues that with all these homophonic associations, Paroles sounds the condition of dropsy, a pathological swelling in the belly that was frequently mistaken for pregnancy. Insofar as this swelling "bears no fruit other than itself," I would add that the sounds of dropsy also homophonically slide into the sounds of sodomy.[37] Both dropsical and sodomitical conceptions lack issue, and both are associated throughout the period with backward movement. For Bertram to be set on the straight path that all the youth need to follow, he must witness the dead ends to which he will come under Paroles's corrupting influence. For Bertram to be cured of his sick desires, he must see and hear Paroles — captured by his disguised fellow soldiers while searching for his lost drum, and held prisoner in a "dark and safely locked" (4.1.89–90) place — as an unregenerate hollow vessel.[38]

If this reading is to hold any water (as it were), it is important to note how Paroles betrays Bertram: not only by willingly divulging military information and "betray[ing] us all unto ourselves" (4.1.87), as the Second Lord Dumaine says (the collective equivalent of Bertram's self-betrayal with Diana), but also by planning to expose Bertram to Diana as one who "ne'er pays after-debts" (4.3.214). Paroles admits no motive for the betrayal other than "honest[y] in the behalf of the maid" (4.3.206–7); he claims that he knows "the young Count to be a dangerous and lascivious boy, who is a whale to virginity, and devours up all the fry it finds" (4.3.207–9). But that Paroles has such genuine concern for Diana is highly doubtful. It might be more useful to understand Paroles as a jealous lover, and this exposure of his treachery as part of the plot's attempt to sort out and cure sodomitical desires, aligning Bertram's desire with Helen's and bringing the play to a happy ending. ("Who cannot be crushed with a plot?" Paroles asks [4.3.302].) Reading Paroles as a jealous lover might likewise help explain Bertram's bitter aside: "I could endure anything before but a cat, and now he's a cat to me" (4.3.225–26). *Cat* is common enough slang for *slut,* and such an accusation alone encodes the sexual nature of Paroles's betrayal. Yet as Stanley Wells acknowledges while simultaneously cautioning against "lewd interpretations" of Shakespeare's plays, *cat* might also have been heard as *catamite.* For Wells, this accusation is "not inconsistent with what we know about Paroles, though at the same time it is not supported by anything else in the play" — a hermeneutic impasse, to be sure.[39] When *cat* instead takes its place in the play of sodomitical signifiers, it illustrates Jonathan Gil Harris's claim that the play's series of "homophonic slippages . . . not only enables but also obstructs what playgoers believe themselves to see."[40] *All's Well* seems, in sum, uniquely invested as part of its salvational project in the manipulation and frustration of knowledge derived from the senses. To the extent that comic teleology requires clarifying Bertram's vision — Bertram will later claim to have seen Helen through a glass darkly, his "perspective" framed by "Contempt" (5.3.49) and Helen transformed out of "all proportions /

To a most hideous object" (5.3.52–53) — the play simultaneously muddies the transactions of its own sensory economy. Consequently, it destabilizes the very conversions the plot seeks to effect, leaving open the question of what exactly Bertram sees in Helen at the end.

This Mortal Coil

Lavatch speaks to the anal erotics of the bed trick when he jests with Paroles on the latter's return to court:

> Truly, Fortune's displeasure is but sluttish if it smell so strongly as thou speakest of. I will henceforth eat no fish of Fortune's butt'ring. Prithee allow the wind. (5.2.6–8)

Like other clowns in Shakespeare's plays, Lavatch is "a voice available to say the unsayable," to speak the obscene.[41] In much the same way that he and Lefeu both speak to the anal location of the king's fistula in act 2, here he speaks to the way in which the anus tropes promiscuous or "sluttish" desire. As "Fortune's close-stool" (5.2.14–5), Paroles bears the scent of this trope, which Lavatch attributes to the "fish of Fortune's butt'ring" — not only, that is, to Fortune's buttering, but also to her *butt ring*.

The audibility of Lavatch's pun is no doubt overdetermined, if not entirely enabled, by the anal focus of my own reading. Nevertheless, whether Lavatch is punning is a question of "being able to tell" that I attribute to the play of sodomitical signifiers in *All's Well*. Rings are themselves slippery signifiers, sometimes facilitating a pun on the vagina, and sometimes generating a Latinate pun on the anus. Stephen Orgel hears both puns in Gratiano's final lines in *The Merchant of Venice*:

> But were the day come, I should wish it dark
> Till I were couching with the doctor's clerk.
> Well, while I live I'll fear no other thing
> So sore as keeping safe Nerissa's ring. (5.1.303–6)

For Orgel, Gratiano's implication that "Nerissa and the doctor's clerk are equivalents and alternatives" — that Nerissa's "ring" is at once her vagina (her "no . . . thing") and the clerk's anus (the "other" nothing) — reintroduces the homoerotic desires that Portia's transvestite intercession in Venice worked to redirect toward marital sexuality.[42] I would add that this joke is also one of the many references on the English Renaissance stage to the Italian practice of "gynosodomy." As Celia Daileader uses the term in her essay on English fantasies of this "exotic" practice, gyno-sodomy denotes the male penetration of the female anus.[43] The ring pun broadens this definition of gynosodomy, however, by suggesting the anus can also trope the vagina, and the vagina the anus — that vaginal sex can also signify as anal sex, and vice-versa. The pun summarily wreaks havoc on the image of marital sexuality at the end of *The Merchant of Venice,* raising questions about the orificial propriety of hetero sex and — what often goes unthought within ex-gay literature — the possibilities of homo-erotic fantasy within heterosexual marriage.

With this trope in mind, we might read Bertram's "monumental ring" — given to Diana (or so he thinks) in exchange for both the "ring" (4.2.46) of her chastity and the ring she slips on his finger in return — as something more than a symbol of his ancestral lineage or their engage-ment. What does it mean for Bertram to possess her ring(s), and Diana/ Helen to possess his, if "ring" is possibly an anal signifier?[44] And how does the ring trick facilitate Bertram's sexual healing, or the reorienta-tion of his desire toward productively vaginal ends? We should notice first that the messy effects of *Merchant*'s ring trick recur in *All's Well* with an important difference. In the latter play, Helen's trick depends not on transvestite disguise but on recruiting another woman to help purge Ber-tram of his sick desires. Critics have long recognized Diana's function as Helen's double, though without suggesting (as far as I know) that one effect of this doubling may be written into the strange route of Helen's pilgrimage. Like the mystery of the fistula, the choice of the shrine of St. Jacques for Helen's destination is a curious Shakespearean addition to the tale considering that Florence, as Samuel Johnson notes with no small measure of understatement, "is somewhat out of the road from Rousillon to Compostella."[45] We might make some symbolic sense out of the errant path of this pilgrimage if we not only recognize that Florence is actually in the other direction (so Helen goes backward to get where she's going) but also hear *Jacques* as a pun on *jakes.* This pun suggests that Helen finds in Diana a privy for Bertram's lust — a site for the purgation of his sick desires.[46] According to Helen, Bertram's "sweet use" of this privy defiles even the darkness of the cut in which it happens:

But O, strange men,
That can such sweet use make of what they hate,
When saucy trusting of the cozened thoughts
Defiles the pitchy night; so lust doth play
With what it loathes, for that which is away. (4.4.21–25)

As a curative, the bed trick uses the anal erotic conjunction of sex and purgation, taking advantage of the "pitchy night" to turn purgation toward reproduction. As particularly salvational curatives, the ring trick and the bed trick together also allow Helen to emerge at the play's dénouement as a chaste saint: "'Tis but the shadow of a wife you see, / The name and not the thing" (5.3.303–4). This differentiation between spiritual name and fleshy "nothing" (or "not the thing") itself depends on what the widow suggestively terms the "bottom" of Helen's "purpose" (3.7.29). Helen's purpose has been a substitution of bottom parts — of sodomitical dead ends for spiritually sanctioned, procreative ends.

The concluding revelation of Helen's pregnancy thus resounds against the revelation of what the first lord Dumaine calls the "bottom" (3.6.32) of Paroles's wasted efforts to find his lost drum. Diana's claim that Bertram "knows himself my bed he hath defiled, / And at that time he got his wife with child" (5.3.297–98) also sounds the success of the plot's attempt to differentiate sodomy from legitimate, reproductive sexuality, as well as the satisfaction of the bottomless desire for Bertram that Helen articulates early in the play:

I know I love in vain, strive against hope;
Yet in this captious and intenable sieve
I still pour in the waters of my love
And lack not to lose still. (1.3.185–89)

When Helen's purpose is understood as that of securing a bottom for her desire, and thereby securing her own position as a dutiful wife, we can read her as what Natalie Zemon Davis calls a "woman on top," one whose positional inversion works to preserve the "order and stability in hierarchical society."[47] This inversion registers in Helen's representation of herself as the source of seminal "waters" and of Bertram as the leaky vessel, the "intenable sieve."[48] It registers in her sexual healing of the king — a procedure that I would claim also registers as gynosodomitical. Finally, it registers in Helen's ethics, as she repeatedly seeks to justify her tricks on Bertram by appealing to their ends. "Let us essay our plot," she tells the widow, "which if it speed / Is wicked meaning in a lawful deed / And lawful meaning in a wicked act" (3.7.44–46). And later: "All's well that ends well; still the fine's the crown / Whate'er the course, the end is the renown" (4.4.35–36). For many critics of the play, Helen's ethics of inversion are highly suspect. But in *All's Well* (as in *Measure for Measure* and *Troilus and Cressida*), Shakespeare seems to give quite serious consideration to the question of whether ends do in fact justify means. Moreover, Shakespeare seems to base this consideration in large part on the function of language in marking temporal movement.

As Madhavi Menon remarks in her own study of the metaleptic construction of sexuality in *All's Well,* the title of the play declares the plot's intention to "bridge ends and means, to make sure things end well so that they can always have *been* well."[49] If Helen builds this bridge, Bertram designs it in the letters he writes to Helen and his mother. To his mother he writes, "I have wedded her, not bedded her, and sworn to make the 'not' eternal" (3.2.20–01). And to Helen, an even more "dreadful sentence" (3.2.59):

> When thou canst get the ring upon my finger, which never shall come off, and show me a child begotten of thy body that I am father to, then call me husband; but in such a "then" I write a "never." (3.2.55–58)

The first letter puns on *not* as both a negation and a wedding knot, simultaneously affirming the eternity of a marriage whose rites Bertram claims he will never complete. The second letter prescribes the preposterous condition that Helen become pregnant with Bertram's child before he will sleep with her, and the equally impossible condition that she remove from his finger an immovable ring. For Menon, Bertram's letters "allow for an exploration of possibility precisely by marking the possible as impossible."[50] The riddling nature of these letters (the "when . . . then" clause conditioned by the "never," and the ambiguity of *not* in confirming the eternal existence of the nonexistent-because-incomplete bond) "ensure that the text embarks on a rhetorical *tour de force* during which it attempts to reconcile Helen's happiness with Bertram's, and vice-versa."[51] I will suggest that we should be particularly skeptical about the satisfaction of

Bertram's desire, but I would first like to add that nothing is so impossible within this rhetorical tour de force as Bertram's *straight* salvation. The riddling letters require Helen's entrance into the queer temporality from which she seeks to rescue her husband.

As a material signifier of the wedding (k)not and what Menon calls "a physical marker of metalepsis," the ring Helen places on Bertram's finger during the bed trick also simultaneously figures straight and queer temporalities.[52] Diana suggests as much when she states the condition of giving the ring of her chastity to Bertram:

> And on your finger in the night I'll put
> Another ring that, what in time proceeds,
> May token to the future our past deeds. (4.2.62–64)

Having just pledged himself to Diana in marriage, Bertram most likely hears that this ring will "token" this bond to the future. But if so, Diana's words are also a perfect example of what Henri Bergson calls the comic scenario of "the reciprocal interference of series." In this scenario, the same utterance or event "is capable of being interpreted in two entirely different meanings at the same time."[53] Knowing that Helen will substitute for her in bed, Diana means something quite different than what Bertram hears. For Diana, the ring that Helen will place on his finger will identify Bertram to posterity as Helen's husband — *as what he has already become.* The ring thus tokens a curvature of time such that time's movement into the future is at the same time a movement into the past, securing Bertram's return to Helen to honor his original vows. The ring indexes this paradoxically perverse dynamic whereby a circular curvature of time and sexuality works to set both straight.

In vanishing to be replaced by Helen's, Diana's phantasmatic rings — both the ring of her chastity and the ring she promises to put on Bertram's finger — mediate between sodomitical and chaste sexualities. The rings facilitate Helen's substitution of bottom parts. Yet the bed trick is only the first of two occasions in which Diana and "her" rings must perform this mediating function. The second takes place in front of the king and prepares the way for Helen's apparent resurrection. Helen's otherwise strange act of dragging Diana to court and having Bertram condemn her as a whore publicly stages the mediation that the bed trick worked to accomplish beneath the cover of darkness. Now we learn, however, that the ring Bertram wears (Diana's, or so he thinks) was actually a gift to Helen from the king. This origin has tainted Helen's ring with the anal erotics of the king's fistula, a terminal erotics of the flesh; and Helen needs to publicly shuffle off this mortal coil if she is to end as the chaste saint she wants to be rather than as someone haunted by the specter of sodomy. Only by publicly staging the displacement of sodomitical erotics from her own to Diana's body can Helen emerge at the play's end as the sanctified woman who has reoriented her husband's desires by accomplishing the impossible.

All's Well's own happy ending hinges on this staged production of Helen's resurrection and Bertram's reorientation. When Bertram returns to the French court, a patch of velvet on his left cheek, he repents his rejection of Helen and offense to the king. If read as a testimonial of conversion, however, what renders the possibly syphilitic Bertram's apology suspect is nothing so much as Bertram's belief that Helen is now dead. Helen's subsequent conversion of Bertram through her own reappearance might thus be more convincing, but it too depends on the fact that Bertram has all along been ignorant of Helen's physic — that, as Diana reveals, Bertram exercised his sick desires not knowing that he was actually fathering a legitimate heir. Helen's conversion therapy works with, rather than against, Bertram's sodomitical "tendencies," and Helen's self-sanctification does not escape the consequences of Bertram's ignorance. When we consider that Bertram thought he was having sex with Diana in the "pitchy night," Helen's Marian staging of immaculate conception readily detranslates into sodomitical conception.[54] Through Diana, Helen has attempted to displace her own base humanity, resurrecting herself as "the shadow of a wife . . . / The name and not the thing." Yet Bertram's cry of "Both, both. O, pardon!" (5.3.305) can be heard as a denial of this displacement in rejoining name and thing, vagina and anus, spirit and flesh. Bertram's cry heralds Helen's success in outwitting him, but simultaneously re-inscribes Helen as a being of flesh and blood, a woman capable of sin, and of sodomy.

All's Well's resistance to its own titular pronouncement therefore registers in this endless play of sodomitical signifiers that disrupts even this sight of Bertram and Helen's reunion. The king's final lines — "All yet seems well; and if it end so meet, / The bitter past, more welcome is the sweet" (5.3.329–30) — foregrounds the tenuousness of the play's resolution by stressing *seeming* over *being,* the *all seems* over the *all is.* David Scott Kastan remarks, "Helen's desire for Bertram, the King's for wholeness, and even our own for comic satisfaction can only be fulfilled by assuming that 'the shows of things' exist primarily for our own pleasure and purpose."[55] Important for my purposes, too, Kastan's insight into the way "our" desire for a happy ending compensates for the otherwise palpable lack of one resonates with Tanya Erzen's conclusions regarding the ends of conversion therapy:

> While the Christian Right speaks with assurance that men and women can become heterosexual, using testimonies as proof of healing, men and women in ex-gay ministries know that walking in a dark room [one man's apt metaphor for his faith in God] means that hope for sexual and religious transformation is at best a leap of faith. Rather than concrete evidence that change happens, ex-gays retain the belief that change is possible. It is that possibility which keeps them stumbling forward despite sexual falls, statistics, and public scandals.[56]

Within the ex-gay movement, faith underwrites the possibility of conversion, the "truth" of reorientation, and the repression of homoerotic desires. Yet *All's Well* skeptically probes the limits of such faith, exploring the tensions between efforts at sexual healing and the queer fluctuation of desire on which a pathologizing narrative of redemptive sexuality depends in the first place. If the play's happy heterosexual ending is predicated on Helen's pregnancy, on legitimate reproduction, then the play simultaneously admits that her pregnancy is not itself predicated on Bertram's conversion, or on the partitioning of vaginal/reproductive and anal/sodomitical ends, but only on the end-determined supersession of these means. Neither marriage nor reproduction is therefore a "good indicator" of conversion, for this claim rests on the dubious evidentiary standard that both generic and institutional forms can contain desire and render it fully legible. In the end, *All's Well*'s preoccupation with the limits of this standard, with the fungibility of orifices and the misperception of the senses, suggests quite the opposite: that such forms may at best have a false bottom, that converted desire may actually remain within a looped circuit from which there is no exodus.

4

Happy Endings II

The Unfortunate Traveller, the "Frenzy of the Visible," and the Comedy of Anti-Semitism

The sexual material which forms the content of smut
includes more than what is peculiar to each sex; it also
includes what is *common* to both sexes and to which
the feeling of shame extends — that is to say, what is
excremental in the most comprehensive sense. This is,
however, the sense covered by sexuality in childhood, an
age at which there is, as it were, a cloaca within which
what is sexual and what is excremental are barely or not
at all distinguished. Throughout the whole range of the
psychology of the neuroses, what is sexual includes what
is excremental, and is understood in the old, infantile
sense.

— Sigmund Freud,
Jokes and Their Relation to the Unconscious

THE PRIMAL SCENE OF THE OBSCENE JOKE FROM FREUD'S *JOKES and Their Relation to the Unconscious* is perhaps so familiar that it needs no more than a brief recitation.[1] Born out of a man's frustration with a woman's resistance to his sexual advances, the obscene joke provides an outlet for aggression that would otherwise be directed toward the coital satisfaction of the libido. Enlisting a third man, the teller exposes the woman through the joke, which disguises (albeit sometimes quite thinly) his aggression and sanctions his otherwise unacceptable speech. ("The smut becomes a joke and is only tolerated when it has the character of the joke."[2]) My epigraph suggests that there may be more to this familiar scene than meets the eye, however.[3] Although he situates obscenity, or smut, within the terrain of anal eroticism, Freud does not return to the conflation of the sexual and the excremental in his account of the joke's primal scene that immediately follows. Rendered at once integral to and absent from the primal scene, anal eroticism appears only to vanish immediately out of sight of the scene's misogynistic heterosexuality.

For Freud, a joke is obscene not merely because it violates community standards of sexual propriety, but because it makes sex, both the genitals and the acts, visible to the mind's eye. The libido comprises desires to both touch and see, and through the avenue of sight the obscene joke affords the same pleasure as smut, "the intentional bringing into prominence of sexual facts and relations by speech."[4] This dependency of sight on speech suggests, in Joan Copjec's words, that "[s]emiotics, not optics, is the science that enlightens for us the structure of the visible domain. Because it alone is capable of lending things sense, the signifier alone makes vision possible. There is and can be no brute vision, no vision totally independent of language."[5] Any psychoanalytic account of the anal erotics of obscene joking must accordingly recognize that a conflation of the sexual and the excremental, the vaginal and the anal, within the joke's visual field is predicated upon the primary (Freud's "infantile") conflation of signifiers.

In the previous chapter, I argued that the fiction of orificial difference that constitutes *All's Well*'s happy ending is simultaneously enabled and undermined by the strategic cuts made in the play's visual field. Here I would like to shift focus to consider the similar effects on narrative resolution of what Linda Williams has famously analyzed as hard-core pornography's "frenzy of the visible." *Frenzy* bespeaks a dual tantalization and frustration of desire — specifically, in Williams's account of twentieth-century cinematic hard core, the desire to see *real* female enjoyment:

> Hard core desires assurance that it is witnessing not the voluntary performance of feminine pleasure, but its involuntary confession. The woman's ability to fake the orgasm that the man can never fake (at least according to certain standards of evidence) seems to be at the root of all the genre's attempts to solicit what it can never be sure of: the out-of-control confession of pleasure, a hard-core "frenzy of the visible."[6]

For Williams, the production of this hard-core frenzy of the visible depends on twentieth-century developments in the technology of photography that allow for an ever-more spectacular realization of the female body, its orifices and its pleasures. Following Copjec, however, I hope to demonstrate that this frenzy, and pornography itself, is first and foremost an effect of the signifier's structuring of the visual field. Frenzies of the visible can therefore appear even within the visually unprepossessing medium of early modern print.[7]

Both Freud, in his account of the obscene joke, and Williams, in her account of hard-core pornography, maintain that the frenzy of the visible draws its energies from male frustration with female resistance — be it resistance to the signification of authentic pleasure (Williams) or to sex itself (Freud). Williams theorizes this resistance in terms of the inscrutability of the female body to the male gaze, and I would suggest that these terms also operate in Freud's brief suggestion about smut's conflation of the vagina and the anus.[8] Both accounts of visual frenzy are thus germane to an assessment of the strange ending to John Donne's "Elegie XVIII (Love's Progress)." This blazon of the female body, troped as a commercial voyage south, climaxes in a cryptic confrontation with two "purses":

> Rich Nature hath in women wisely made
> Two purses, and their mouths aversely laid:
> They then, which to the lower tribute owe,
> That way which that Exchequer looks, must go:
> He which doth not, his error is as great,
> As who by Clyster gave the Stomack meat. (91–96)[9]

Whereas the obfuscation of sex in *All's Well* underwrites the fantasy of the comedy's happy ending, the success of the erotic prescription at the end of this poem hinges entirely upon making sex visible. The problem is that the word *aversely* muddies the spectacle. The word is most often glossed as "at an angle," but as Jonathan Sawday argues in *The Body Emblazoned,* "backwards" may be a more appropriate translation, at least one more in line with period uses of the term. In Sawday's reading, the "lower purse" is not the vagina but the anus, and the speaker instructs his presumably male reader on the proper technique of anal sex as entrance from behind, the direction of the Exchequer's look. "[U]nable to resist the joke," however, the speaker then reverses himself in the last two lines by equating anal sex with the "error," or misdirection, of trying to feed the stomach through the anus.[10]

I am not as sure as Sawday about how to read these aversely laid purses, but his reading of the poem's orificial confusion illustrates nothing if not how even after the meticulous metaphorization of female body parts proper to a blazon, the speaker fails to clearly distinguish between anatomical ends at the end of the poem. Such philological confusion in a poem predicated on the tight correlation of language and sight also calls to mind Kaja Silverman's important corrective to film theory's traditional understanding of the gaze as masculine and the object of the gaze as feminine. Distinguishing between the look and the gaze, Silverman argues that "the male look both transfers its own lack to the female subject, and attempts to pass itself off as the gaze."[11] Through the persistent ambiguity of the orifices Donne's speaker tries to describe, the poem correlates his inability to inhabit this identifying space of the gaze with his inability to master the signifier. Consequently, even if the last couplet is best understood as a joke, as Sawday suggests, the joke is rather difficult to "get," the signifier's hold on orificial difference impossible to sustain.

Silverman's argument about the male cinematic gaze also helps facilitate a presentist connection between Donne's elegy and the promotional images to Don Roos's 2005 film *Happy Endings,* a comedy that intertwines the stories and sex lives of ten different individuals living in present-day Los Angeles.[12] The most ubiquitous of these images, the one that now appears on the DVD cover, displays the naked back of a woman (Figure 1). The list of actors' names guides the spectator's eyes down the curvature of her shadowed spine to her buttocks, the upper part of which is covered in a white towel and overwritten with the film's title. I say that this back belongs to a woman because of the width of the hips relative to the narrow waist, and because this image is the companion of another featuring a body with a wider waist and hairier buttocks. But I simultaneously want to claim that the sex of this body is ultimately indeterminate, held in suspension by the absence of more definitive signifiers to be found on the body's front side. In comparison to Donne's

FIGURE 1. Female body, from *Happy Endings,* 2005. Photo provided through the courtesy of Lions Gate Films.

poem, this image does not warn against the error of improper entrance. It rather offers a teasing invitation to the viewer — an invitation that conflates the body's ends and entrances and blurs the distinction between anal sex and *coitus a tergo*. Put another way, through the placement of the towel and the play of shadows, the image manages to be anal erotic but not obscene. It erotically withholds, in Roland Barthes's sense of the word *erotic,* the spectacle of the fundament, blocking sight of what lies below the clothing of the signifier.[13] We might say that the joke here is on obscenity itself — that the towel is to this image what metaphors are to Donne and shot structures and acting are to hard-core pornography: they are the garments that enwrap the female body as an object of desire, that confound the libidinal aim to see what is *really* there and what is *really* happening.

FIGURE 2. Male body, from *Happy Endings,* 2005. Photo provided through the courtesy of Lions Gate Films.

One of the film's taglines, "All's well that ends swell," which accompanies the promotional images featuring the more recognizably male body (Figure 2), invites yet another presentist connection, this time to Shakespeare's problem play, and even further to Jonathan Gil Harris's reading of it:

> This might be a play in which All's Well That Ends Well, as is suggested by the providential movement from crisis to resolution embodied in Helen's seemingly successful conception and the promise of a next generation. But it is also a play in which All Swell That End Swell, with its intimation of a movement that is recursive or pleonastic, embodied in a sick swelling that bears no fruit other than itself. For if the trajectory of All's Well That Ends Well is exocentric, directed toward a future that transcends and redeems current dilemmas, the movement of All

Swell That End Swell is relentlessly endocentric, where the "end" is both syntactically and chronologically impossible to differentiate from the "beginning."[14]

Roos's film begins near its end, with one of its main characters, Mamie, being hit by a car as she runs down the street. "She's not dead," a title card tells us. "Nobody dies in this movie, not on-screen. It's a comedy, sort of." In the next sequence, which takes place twenty years earlier, we see Mamie, age seventeen, seduce her new stepbrother, get pregnant, and give the baby up for adoption. We later learn that Mamie (an abortion counselor with a masseuse boyfriend who delivers "happy endings") just met her son before the car hit her. She has been blackmailed by an unscrupulous young filmmaker who promises to introduce her to her son so long as she allows him to film the reunion for his film school application. Another storyline focuses on Mamie's stepbrother Charley, and his obsessive efforts to prove that his partner Gil fathered the child of a lesbian couple. (Gil donated his sperm, though the couple insists that he isn't the father.) The trajectory of both plots from conception to crisis, as well as the film's endocentric frame, strains what Lee Edelman calls the heteronormative fantasy of "reproductive futurism" that so frequently structures the happy endings of romantic comedies.[15] In Roos's meditation on personal candor and sexual healing, a happy ending is neither transcendent nor redemptive, but tongue-in-cheek — not pregnant with meaning, but swollen with the pathological dishonesty that infects almost every character in the film.

The third storyline is the most direct adaptation of Shakespeare's play about an upwardly mobile and dishonest woman. A young nightclub singer named Jude — whom we first meet as she croons Billy Joel's "Honesty" — becomes sexually involved with a closeted young gay man named Otis, the son of a wealthy and naive widower named Frank. Jude suspects that Otis is gay, and when she and Otis sleep together for the first time, she turns herself onto her stomach in order to afford him a "better" (her word) way in. After she and Otis break up, Jude seduces a smitten Frank; yet her motives for doing so are monetary, and she blackmails Otis to keep silent lest she out him to his father. When Frank and Jude become engaged, Otis steps out of the closet and immediately outs Jude, who then reveals that she is pregnant (either Otis or Frank is father). Neither man believes her, however, and she aborts the child. The thematic conjunction of pathological and pregnant swelling, dishonesty and honesty, gives the lie to Shakespeare's happy ending: in this comedy, sort of, there is no simple "happily ever after," no honest romance predicated on reproduction. Both Otis and Frank do move on to new relationships — Frank with Mamie and Otis with Alvin, a member of his band — but here too the film plays with the conventional equation of a happy ending with permanent coupling. Frank and Mamie marry, and may well be happy, but Otis and Alvin's relationship comes to an end after six years, and a title card tells us that twenty years into the future Otis is "happier than anyone else here." No one sees Jude again, including the author of the film's many title cards. "Whenever I try to see what happens to her," he or she writes, "this is all I can get, the last ending": Jude's performance of another Billy Joel song, "Just the Way You Are." The complement to the first Joel song's plea for candor, "Just the Way You Are" sounds a longing for honesty and stasis that the film's dually progressive and recursive temporality, pregnant and pleonastic, has left unsatisfied.

In the spirit of Roos's play with happy endings, this chapter turns to yet another meditation on anal erotic obscenity, dishonesty, romance, and the limits of "cinematic" vision: Thomas Nashe's fictional narrative of an English trickster who begins his European travels in the English war with France and ends them in Italy, where he is apprehended by Jews and nearly put to death on an anatomy table. Like *Happy Endings, The Unfortunate Traveller* is a comedy, sort of — one known for its frenzy of violence that more than one critic has argued resists critical interpretation.[16] I will argue that psychoanalysis can situate the violent spectacles for which *The Unfortunate Traveller* is well known within an erotic economy that, conflating the sexual and the excremental, pivots around the gruesome scene of Heraclide's rape. I will also argue that a text so concerned with the stakes and limits of comic enjoyment invites the revision of Freud's primal scene of the obscene joke into a spectacle of sodomy. This revision raises important questions about the ethics of comedy that pertain most immediately to the anti-Semitism of *The Unfortunate Traveller.* While the Jews ostensibly come to bear responsibility for the narrative's comic, horrific, and pornographic violence, I want to suggest, apropos of Nashe's own philosophical skepticism, a way of refusing this scapegoating. This refusal is predicated on the (a)historical aspects of *The Unfortunate Traveller* and the provisional nature of happy endings.

The Eye of Honesty

In an essay entitled "The Heroine as Courtesan: Dishonesty, Romance, and the Sense of an Ending in *The Unfortunate Traveller*," Steven R. Mentz provocatively argues that Thomas Nashe's generically heterogeneous text can be usefully understood as what Frank Kermode terms an "end-determined fiction."[17] Whereas other critics have long derided *The Unfortunate Traveller* as generically incoherent, especially when read in light of the modern novel, Mentz follows the recent critical trend of framing its presumptive incoherence as a deliberate and experimental engagement with a broad range of genres, including trickster tales, coney-catching pamphlets, travelogues, picaresque novels, urban journalism, and revenge tragedy.[18] For Mentz, specifically, the marriage of Jack Wilton and Diamante upon their final return to the English camp in France (historically, the Field of the Cloth of Gold in 1520, a brief happy ending to England's ongoing war with France) retroactively scripts *The Unfortunate Traveller* as a romance. Although the term is admittedly "broad and imprecise," Mentz argues that Nashe's hybrid of comedy and tragedy follows the romance pattern of wandering, suffering, courtship, and marriage.[19] At the same time, Nashe evinces a skeptical attitude toward romance through the character of Diamante, a heroine who is no conventional paragon of chastity.[20] Diamante is a Venetian woman whose husband imprisons her on false suspicion of infidelity, but whom Wilton successfully seduces during his own stint in the same prison. We never see Diamante accept money in exchange for sex (we actually see Wilton accept money from her), but Wilton repeatedly refers to her as his "courtesan" — another broad and imprecise term that connotes sexual dishonesty and signals Nashe's strategic manipulation of romance conventions to bring about a happy ending.

Even when framed as a skeptical romance, *The Unfortunate Traveller* remains a bewildering narrative, one resistant to summary in its episodic construction. I nonetheless agree with Mentz that it deserves to be read backwards. Such a preposterous approach does not make *The Unfortunate*

Traveller any less bewildering. Quite the opposite, it may work to enhance readers' alienation from what Margaret Ferguson aptly terms Nashe's "looking-glass world" — a world wherein the identities of both characters and readers are endlessly mirrored, deflected and reflected, by others.[21] Nashe invites a preposterous reading not only by manipulating the sexual conventions of romance, a genre that Mentz contends "defines itself retrospectively," but also through his titular character's appeal to divine justice, one manifestation of the hand of providence that traditionally brings romance to its happy ending.[22] I therefore follow Mentz's lead in beginning at the end, though not the one where Wilton and Diamante live happily ever after, if indeed that is what happens. (Wilton's words on introducing Diamante, "it doth me good when I remember her" [306], may imply otherwise.[23]) Rather, I begin with the end of one of the narrative's two Jews, Zadoch. His and Cutwolfe's executions, along with Juliana's "accidental" suicide, constitute the narrative's hyperviolent climax.

Hardly the "short work" Wilton promises, the scene of Zadoch's execution is worth quoting in full:

> To the execution place he was brought, where first and foremost he was stripped; then on a sharp iron stake fastened in the ground he had his fundament pitched, which stake ran up along into the body like a spit. Under his armholes two of like sort. A great bonfire they made round about him, wherewith his flesh roasted, not burned; and ever as with the heat his skin blistered, the fire was drawn aside and they basted him with a mixture of aqua fortis, alum water and mercury sublimatum, which smarted to the very soul of him, and searched him to the marrow. Then did they scourge his back parts so blistered and blasted with burning whips of red-hot wire. His head they nointed over with pitch and tar and so inflamed it. To his privy members they tied streaming fireworks. The skin from the crest of his shoulder, as also from his elbows, his huckle bones, his knees, his ankles, they plucked and gnawed off with sparkling pincers. His breast and belly with seal-skins they grated over, which as fast as they grated and rawed, one stood over and laved with smith's cindery water and aqua vitae. His nails they half raised up, and then underpropped them with sharp pricks, like a tailor's shop window half-open on a holiday. Every one of his fingers they rent up to the wrist; his toes they brake off by the roots, and let them still hang by a little skin. In conclusion, they had a small oil fire, such as

men blow light bubbles of glass with, and beginning at his feet, they let him lingeringly burn up limb by limb, till his heart was consumed, and then he died. (359)

In graphic detail not lacking in poetic flare (his fingernails "underpropped . . . like a tailor's shop window half-open on a holiday"), this hard-core "spectacle of the scaffold" realizes the anatomizing end to which Wilton nearly came at the hands of the Jewish doctor Zacharie.[24] Yet to call this spectacle hard core is obviously not to claim that it solicits the sight of authentic female pleasure. It is rather to claim that this detailed evisceration of Zadoch's Jewish body is no less frenzied than hard-core pornography's "evisceration" of the female body, or no less an object of spectatorial titillation.[25]

Another appeal to film theory helps develop this claim. As critics of horror films frequently note, the boundary between pornography and horror, especially slasher films, is quite thin: both genres visually fetishize the body's interior.[26] In *The Unfortunate Taveller,* both modes of representation come together in the anatomy theater — that "theater of desire," in Jonathan Sawday's phrase, which offers spectators a dually morbid and erotic display of the opened corpse.[27] Wilton evokes this duality when describing Zacharie's inspection of his body:

> The purblind Doctor put on his spectacles and looked upon me; and when he had thoroughly viewed my face, he caused me to be stripped naked, to feel and grope whether each limb were sound and my skin not infected. Then he pierced my arm to see how my blood ran. . . . Not a drop of sweat trickled down my breast and my sides, but I dreamt it was a smooth-edged razor tenderly slicing down my breast and sides. (349)

The erotics of feeling, groping, piercing, stripping, and slicing are even more fully activated when — in what Foucault would describe as "an almost theatrical reproduction of the crime in the execution of the guilty man" — the Jewish anatomizer (Zacharie) becomes the anatomized Jew (Zadoch).[28]

Wilton is not present at this execution, having at this point become Juliana's prisoner, yet he elaborately fantasizes Zadoch's execution in such a way as to suggest that, although Zacharie has fled Rome, the remaining Jew is being punished for the crimes of his fellow Jews. Flayed, dismembered, and burned, Zadoch is erected onto a stake driven into his anus, and in a parody of the crucifixion two more stakes are driven under his arms. Such a spectacle of punishing criminal anality testifies to Zadoch's role as the "excremental Jew" that Jonathan Gil Harris, in another work, has identified as a fantasy of early modern anti-Semitism — the poisonous, vengeful, and mimicking creature who "gains entry to the body politic through apertures that are subtly coded as its anus."[29] Glancing briefly at *The Unfortunate Traveller,* Harris suggests that "lurking in Nashe's description" of Zadoch's execution is "a phobic fantasy which conflates Jewish infiltration of the Christian body politic with the crime of sodomy."[30] Especially significant to the spectacularization of this fantasy, I would add, is Wilton's attribution of victory over the Jew(s) to two women, Juliana and Diamante: "Triumph women, this was the end of the whipping Jew, contrived by women, in revenge of two women, herself and her maid" (359). Here, as in Frank Whigham's reading of *All's Well That Ends Well* and *The Merchant of Venice,* "the opponent of anal evil is a woman."[31] Only Nashe has doubled the opposition, dividing the role of heroine between Juliana and Diamante, two dishonest women who complement a dishonest hero in Nashe's dishonest manipulation of romance conventions. The ostensible difference between these two heroines amounts, I will argue, to a Jewish difference that necessitates Juliana's death after their "triumph."

As instrumental to the purification of Bertram's desire as Helen proves — which is perhaps to say not instrumental at all — Juliana and Diamante prove to the purification of Wilton's desires. This process of purification begins with Wilton's fall into Zadoch's cellar, which Wilton describes as a fall into "purgatory" (339). Having just been saved from hanging on the charge of Heraclide's murder, Wilton falls into a confrontation with one of his own original sins: he finds Diamante kissing Zadoch's apprentice, betraying Wilton just as Wilton seduced her into betraying her husband. From there, events bring Wilton twice more near death: first, as a specimen on Zacharie's anatomy table, in preparation for which he is administered a "plumporridge of purgations" (349); and second, as a sex-slave to Juliana, whom Wilton believes has plans to use him until he is "consumed and worn to the bones," then poison him and toss him "into a privy" (357). Juliana is clearly no friend of the Jews:

she orchestrates their banishment and Zadoch's execution. Yet Juliana's murderous crimes are no less "Jewish" for that reason, as the comic scenario of her demise suggests: driven into a frenzy by Diamante and Wilton's escape, Juliana orders her maid to bring her a glass of *spiritus vini,* but the maid mistakenly retrieves the poison Juliana intends to administer later to Wilton. If Zadoch's gruesome dismemberment constitutes "justice" for the crime of offering Wilton up for the yearly anatomy, Juliana's self-poisoning is equally just retribution for what we can describe as her sodomitical efforts to waste Wilton through sex and then (like the Jew of English Christian phobic fantasy) poison him. Such poetic justice indeed suggests that in what Wilton calls the purgatorial "Sodom of Italy" (370), Judaism and sodomy are one and the same thing. Both lay waste to Christian bodies.

Not unlike Carol Clover's Final Girl, the lone survivor of the slasher film who triumphs over the killer, Diamante ultimately rescues Jack from purgatory.[32] She alone defeats the anal enemies, including Juliana, not because she is honest (like the virginal Final Girl) but because she is dishonest — because she embodies what might be called the *repressed supplement* to the formulaic chaste romantic heroine. The erotic transgressions with which a romantic heroine like Shakespeare's Helen or Portia flirts while "technically" protecting her own chastity, Diamante — whose original fault, according to Wilton, lies in "being too melancholy chaste" (306) — learns to undertake without a moral qualm. Diamante needs only to be taught, as Wilton surmises: "Many are honest because they know not how to be dishonest" (306). For Mentz, this statement is the philosophical key to Nashe's skeptical play with the conventions of romance, specifically to the disjunction of the genre's providential plot from the virtue of its characters. According to Mentz, "Nashe's innovation makes these two aspects of the genre totally independent of each other. Jack and Diamante's actions have no impact on their final reward."[33] Yet here I part company with Mentz, for I would argue that this disjunction marks a particularly "obscene" demonstration of the providential plot's *fundamental dependency* on dishonest behavior. Nashe's creation of a comparatively brazen dishonest heroine differentiates his skeptical romance from Shakespeare's own arguably more subtle experimentations with the genre, but in essence Diamante can marry Wilton for the same reason that Helen can reorient Bertram: because her dishonesty underwrites the operations of providence that bring the romance to its expected end.[34]

Furthermore, Diamante survives Nashe's blood-bath romance only because Juliana — first Diamante's ally against the Jews and then her enemy in the contest over Wilton — dies for her sins. Like Diana in *All's Well,* Juliana helps purge the hero of his own sick desires through her wasting of his body, while her sins function as a foil for the virtue of the romantic heroine. The above discussion of Zadoch's execution suggests that similar instances of scapegoating help bring an end to *The Unfortunate Traveller* — instances that as an aggregate perhaps readily recall René Girard's thesis about scapegoats bearing the burden of collective violence. I will argue later that Wilton himself, for whose sins others ultimately pay, refuses the offer of final collective redemption, the end of scapegoating, that Girard locates in the Christian Passion.[35] Suffice it now to say that as a series of deaths, some quite grisly, move Wilton through purgatory, *The Unfortunate Traveller* gradually assumes the form of a hard-core divine comedy — a dark comedy of sin and salvation in which Judaism becomes synonymous with punishing cruelty, and Jews function as scapegoats for the sins of Christians.

Wilton enters purgatory immediately upon witnessing the rape of Heraclide, *The Unfortunate Traveller*'s only chaste female character. In plague-ravaged Rome, Heraclide has buried fourteen of her children in the past five days. Now she falls victim to the first of two "sworn brothers in sensuality" (340), Esdras and Bartol, who pillage the homes of rich men, raping wives and maidens. While Nashe never outs Esdras as a Jew, Michael Keefer quite persuasively contends that he is one. Esdras shares his name with the Old Testament prophet Ezra and with Moses ibn Esdras of Granada, the Hebrew poet of late twelfth-century Spain. Moreover, "Moses ibn Esdras of Granada was himself an unfortunate traveller . . . [who] spent the last four decades of his life wandering among the 'barbarians' of Christian Castile."[36] Esdras not only doubles the Jews who will help purge Wilton of his sins but also Wilton himself: all are wandering agents of violence. Little wonder then that Wilton's symptomatic tale nearly reaches its end as he recounts the "sad spectacle" of Heraclide's rape:

On the hard boards he [Esdras] threw her, and used his knee as an iron ram to beat ope the two-leaved gate of her chastity. Her husband's dead body he made a pillow to his abomination. Conjecture the rest, my words stick fast in the mire and are clean tired; would I had never undertook this tragical tale. Whatsoever is born, is born to have an end. Thus ends my tale: his whorish lust was glutted, his beastly desire satisfied. (336)

To understand why Wilton cannot complete his otherwise verbose and pornographic account, it helps to consider the stakes of the highly rhetorical exchange between Heraclide and Esdras that precedes this moment of descriptive impotency. Heraclide alternatively pleads for Christian mercy and threatens Esdras with death, damnation, and plague-infected breath: "A hundred's infection is mixed with my breath. Lo, now I breathe upon thee, a hundred deaths come upon thee" (334). Yet Esdras retorts that he has already suffered "plagues" (including "diseases, imprisonment, poverty, banishment" [335]) worse than she can name, having repeatedly escaped death despite living a life of incessant crime. Lorna Hutson describes this exchange as one in which Heraclide's "[c]hameleon-like persuasive oratory, alleging whatever it hopes will authorize its own desires, vies with an equally deceitful providential discourse, which inevitably falls back on locating moral power within itself."[37] Esdras later dies when Cutwolfe shoots him in the mouth, appropriately enough; but here, following Wilton's ventriloquism of Esdras's deceitful and violent providentialism, Wilton reveals how his own rhetorical abilities are similarly predicated on the production of waste, or the wasting of bodies. This exposure of the foundation of rhetorical production — rendered as the "mire" in which his words "stick fast" and are paradoxically "clean tired" — brings Wilton's description of the rape, and the tale itself, to a screeching halt.

At this point Heraclide's rape begins to take on the characteristics of a primal scene. I am chiefly interested in the primal scene of the obscene joke, but equally relevant here is the primal scene of Freud's Wolfman (Sergei Pankejeff), who at eighteen months, and ignorant of sexual difference, witnesses his parents having sex from behind. Confronted with the threat of castration at the age of four, and consequently beset with doubts about his "cloaca theory," the Wolfman responds by clinging to the familiar: "He decided in favour of the bowel and against the vagina" as the penetrable female orifice.[38] Among the results of this decision are chronic constipation and various episodes of incontinence related to thoughts of financial expenditure; both symptoms of pathological swelling and purgation originate in the Wolfman's infantile spectatorship of *coitus a tergo* and his resulting failure to negotiate sexual difference. What we gain by situating the Wolfman's primal scene alongside the scene of Heraclide's rape is a way to account for the latter's similar indistinction between vaginal sex and sodomy. As Julian Yates observes, "the anus tropes the belly" throughout the Roman episodes of *The Unfortunate Traveller*; Heraclide's rape is only the most obscene, primal reduction of the belly to "a conduit through which matter flows."[39] In this sense at least, Heraclide is anally raped.

Consider that when Heraclide pleads with Esdras, "If thou ever camst of a woman, or hopest to be saved by the seed of a woman, pity a woman," Esdras denies her maternal capacity. He boasts that he turns women into whores:

> My own mother gave I a box of the ear to, and brake her neck down a pair of stairs, because she would not go in to a gentleman when I bad her. My sister I sold to an old leno, to make his best of her. Any kinswoman that I have, knew I she were not a whore, myself would make her one. Thou art a whore: though shalt be a whore, in spite of religion or precise ceremonies. (335)

"Heraclide metaphorically directs Esdras's attention to her womb," Yates writes, but Esdras "sees only her stomach, the process of consumption and defecation."[40] He sees not generational fecundity, but a body to be wasted in sex and prostitution. Diamante's pregnancy, mentioned only once after she and Wilton are released from prison and never brought to fruition, similarly fails to signify except as an index of Wilton's financial "enlargement" (312). Through the efforts of none other than Renaissance Italy's most famous pornographer, Pietro Aretino, Diamante is freed into the company of Nashe's early modern Wolfman with a sizable amount of her husband's money — money Wilton immediately spends in order to pose as Henry Howard, Earl of Surrey.[41] Like Heraclide's body, which produced children who became plague victims, and to which Esdras himself lays waste, Diamante's pregnant body becomes one more symptom in this endocentric narrative's repetition of pathological swelling and wasteful expenditure.

As Yates further notes, Heraclide's rape restages the scene of penetration that lies at the very beginning of *The Unfortunate Traveller,* where Wilton states that he "followed the Court or the camp, or the camp and the court, when Turwin lost her maidenhead and opened her gates to more than Jane Trosse did" (254).[42] Wilton founds his narrative in this act of martial rape, so *The Unfortunate Traveller* both comes back to its beginning and nearly reaches its end as Wilton witnesses a hard-core spectacle of the reproductive female body's transformation into an excremental body, a sodomitical receptacle for "whorish lust." Of course, no one forces him to watch: he beholds this sad spectacle, including Heraclide's suicide, "thorough a cranny of [his] upper chamber unsealed" (339). Critics have accordingly remarked on the suggestion of Wilton's voyeuristic complicity with the rape itself.[43] But crucial to my own analysis of Wilton's voyeurism is the related point that Wilton's representation of the rape is actually a *re* -presentation. Lost between the unrecoverable primal scene of Heraclide's rape and its "graphic," written copy is Wilton's own enjoyment of a spectacle from which he originally did not turn away, the same enjoyment evident in the jesting nonchalance of his description of the rape of Tournai and Térouanne.[44] The horror that Wilton expresses regarding Heraclide's rape is precisely the *retrospective* assumption of guilt in a scene of primordial enjoyment.

Wilton's regret for his own tale thus swells as Heraclide's rape comes to occupy the overdetermined end of every episode that came before: "would I had never undertook this tragical tale. Whatsoever is born is born to have an end. Thus ends my tale. . . ." Yet the tale does not end here. As far as reconstructed primal scenes go, this one drives a demand for accountability, a demand that someone pay for these crimes against the reproductive female body. This payment begins immediately. Heraclide stabs herself, but falling down, she knocks her head against the body of her husband, who awakens "as out of a dream" to find his wife "defiled and massacred" (339), and subsequently charges Wilton with the crime.[45] The juxtaposition of rape and suicide with the farcical comedy of the husband's resurrection further suggests that the joke is now turning on Wilton the trickster, who was no mere spectator to the crime. Through his double, Esdras, Wilton has witnessed what has all along been his own crime on the level of the signifier: a breaching of the excremental and the erotic.

Heraclide's rape exemplifies the signifying violence — the orificial collapse — that attends the primal scene of the obscene joke. It foregrounds the anal eroticism latent in Freud's account, exposing what is "common to both sexes" by conflating the anus and the vagina, and thereby reflecting the male gaze as a look that, as Kaja Silverman says, has attempted to displace its own lack, its own penetrability, onto a female body. In Freud's account of the obscene joke's primal scene, based on the economy of libidinal energies, the joke affords the same pleasure as vaginal intercourse: the joke "make[s] possible the satisfaction of an instinct (whether lustful or hostile) in the face of an obstacle that stands in its way."[46] But reading this primal scene through *The Unfortunate Traveller* suggests that such "satisfaction" is predicated only on the repetition of the very attempt to render into sense something that perpetually resists translation. Some distinct female "thing" is always sliding out of sight. Heraclide's rape is therefore only one end among *The Unfortunate Traveller*'s many endings, while at one and the same time it begins the most unfortunate but also seemingly providential episodes of the trickster's journey. In these episodes, jesting becomes brutal "Jewish" anatomization.

Matthew Biberman's argument that early modern Jews frequently figure "hypermasculine" behavior — including "misogyny, contemptuousness, resourcefulness, cynicism, egotism, and avarice" — becomes especially important here, for in these latter episodes of Nashe's wandering tale, Judaism serves to discipline Christian masculinity, demarcating its proper behavioral boundaries.[47] The Jews enact the sadism that lies at the heart of jesting, transforming Wilton from a victimizing man to a "feminine," penetrable victim. Assessing this transformation therefore requires reading Wilton as more than the sadistic double agent of Heraclide's rape. His double agency is equally masochistic. Having been locked in his upper chamber after Bartol punningly pursues him with a "rapier" (332), Wilton also becomes a passive victim, doubling Heraclide just as he doubles Esdras. To allow such multiple identifications is to enter into yet another dimension of this scene's complex geometry of anal erotic spectatorship. Here the sadomasochistic desire to do harm and be harmed forms the parameters of what Slavoj Žižek calls the "fundamental fantasy" — a fantasy realized through the shameful process of "actively assuming passivity":

> [I]f I am raped, I have nothing to be ashamed of; but if I enjoy being raped, then I deserved to feel ashamed. Actively assuming passivity thus means, in Lacanian terms, finding jouissance in the passive situation in which one is caught. And since the coordinates of jouissance are ultimately those of the fundamental fantasy, which is the fantasy of (finding jouissance in) being put in the passive position . . . [s]hame emerges only when such a passive position in social reality touches upon the (disavowed intimate) fantasy.[48]

This claim risks discounting the ways in which rape victims can feel ashamed for violations they do not enjoy. When Heraclide blames herself for her beauty — "If any guilt be mine, this is my fault, that I did not deform my face, ere it should so impiously allure" (338) — we may hear not a confession of her own desire to be raped but an assumption of culpability following from her subscription to a patriarchal ideology that holds women responsible for misogynistic violence. Whatever Heraclide's desire, however, Wilton's reconstruction of the scene and his subsequent transformation into a victim of Jewish violence nevertheless does suggest that Heraclide's rape touches upon *his* fundamental fantasy.

Like many contemporary cinematic scenes of hard-core sex and violence, Heraclide's rape facilitates its viewers' identification with victimizer and victim, penetrator and penetrated. Along with Heraclide, Wilton loses his "eye of honesty" in a horrific event that was somehow bound to happen:

> [W]hy should not I [Heraclide] hold myself damned (if predestination's opinions be true) that am predestinate to this horrible abuse? The hog dieth presently if he loseth an eye; with the hog I have wallowed in the mire, I have lost my eye of honesty, it is clean plucked out with a strong hand of unchastity. (337–38)

Yet if Heraclide speaks for herself and Wilton here, I suggest that she also speaks for us, the readers, whose "eye of honesty" is likewise at stake.

Wilton's earlier invitation to "conjecture the rest" suddenly aborts the frenzied account of the rape, but it also assumes the reader's sadomasochistic, voyeuristic desire for the scene to continue. I should also stress that this geometry of spectatorial identification undercuts the simple correlation of female with masochistic enjoyment. Like the slasher film, *The Unfortunate Traveller* correlates masochistic enjoyment with female embodiment while also bending gender codes in such a way that women ultimately triumph in their own sadistic turn. As Carol Clover argues of the slasher film, the heroine's triumph helps define a teenage male viewer's sense of proper masculinity. We might say something similar of the way Diamante's ultimate triumph works to define proper male Christianity by (quite literally) carving out Jewish and sodomitical difference.

So far I have argued that Heraclide's rape, as the primal scene of *The Unfortunate Traveller,* comes to mean only after-the-fact, in its reconstruction, and read in hindsight of the narrative as a whole. In what Jean Laplanche would call its "afterwardsness," it retroactively focuses the narrative's creation of doubles.[49] Moving back to the beginning of *The Unfortunate Traveller* in the next section of this chapter, I would like to argue that this doubling breaches the boundary between horror and comedy in partial keeping with Freud's observations about the uncanny *(Unheimliche)*. (As Freud notes, "The prefix *'un '* is the token of repression."[50]) The presence of uncanny doubles only proliferates as Wilton moves farther away from his English home *(Heim)* — a home that was itself always a home away from home, the English camp in France. Heraclide's rape would certainly seem exemplary of Freud's argument for the primal uncanniness of the female genitals. Yet in Wilton's anatomy theater of the self, uncanny doubles arise within an anal erotic economy occluded by too exclusive a genital focus.

The Even-Balanced Eye of the Almighty

Let us turn for a moment to another primal scene. In *Totem and Taboo,* Freud tells the story of a primitive band of brothers who murder their cruel father and erect in his place a law of mutual prohibition. This civilizing, phallic law assures their own equality under the law and their equal entitlement to women. The guilty brothers then resurrect their father as the ghostly guarantor of this law, but no longer is he someone who selfishly enjoys without restriction. Now he promises "protection, care, and indulgence."[51] The law becomes synonymous with his name, the Name of the Father, but only on the condition that he remain pre-Symbolic, constitutively excluded from the order of civilization that preserves the fantasy of his benevolence. If he does appear in the Symbolic, he does so as a pre-phallic double of himself that Žižek terms the *anal father:*

> [T]he reverse of the Name of the Father . . . the obscene little man . . . is the clearest embodiment of the phenomenon of the "uncanny" *(Unheimliche)*. He is the subject's double who accompanies him like a shadow and gives body to a certain surplus, to what is "in the subject more than himself"; this surplus represents what the subject must renounce, sacrifice even, the part of himself that the subject must murder in order to live as a "normal" member of the community.[52]

When Lacan theorizes the appearance of this "obscene little man," he does so apropos of Martin Luther's God and this God's "eternal hatred of men, not simply of their failures and the works of their free will, but a hatred that existed even before the world was created." Hardly the memorialized figure of "sweetness and light," Luther's God is the anal father, the very figure of the evil each person must renounce in order to live in civilized society.[53] *The Unfortunate Traveller*'s Cutwolfe voices a similarly Lutheran belief about God when he boasts about killing Esdras:

> Revenge is the glory of arms and the highest performance of valour; revenge is whatsoever we call law or justice. The farther we wade in revenge, the nearer come we to the throne of the Almighty. To His sceptre it is properly ascribed; His sceptre He lends unto man when He lets one man scourge another. (369)

Once again *The Unfortunate Traveller* returns to its beginning, as Cutwolfe echoes Wilton's early claim that he was "ordained God's scourge" (271) to punish the avaricious and fastidious (read: anal) clerks of the English camp. Yet from the unbearable conclusion that Luther transforms into the foundation of his theology, Wilton retreats in horror. Cutwolfe is put to death, and Wilton, "[m]ortifiedly abjected and daunted . . . with this truculent tragedy" (370), flees with Diamante to the safety of the English camp in France. Cutwolfe's death on the rack brings an end to Wilton's stay in the purgatorial Sodom of Italy, and, finally, to *The Unfortunate*

Traveller, but his death also, and just as importantly, works to purge God of his anal double.

Critics have long framed the presence of doubles in *The Unfortunate Traveller* in terms of Nashe's political, economic, and/or aesthetic meditation on counterfeiting. Margaret Ferguson argues that "Nashe presents the artist as a 'maker' who plays an inherently dangerous game when he creates fictions or 'counterfeits' that subvert established forms of authority."[54] For Joan Pong Linton, Wilton's "irresponsible" counterfeiting of sovereign authority works to challenge both coney-catching pamphlets' and citizen-romances' cultivation of a "responsible disposition" to domestic government.[55] In keeping with such observations, I suggest that counterfeiting — which Ferguson observes is "a process that may be infinitely extendable" — might also be understood as part of *The Unfortunate Traveller*'s dangerous theological game. The players in this game are the figures of sovereign authority — namely, God and king — as well as their obscene, anal doubles. And this game begins when Wilton, as "an appendix or page" to King Henry's court, anoints himself "sole King of the Cans and Black-jacks, Prince of the Pigmies, County Palatine of Clean Straw and Provant, and, to conclude, Lord High Regent of Rashers of the Coals and Red-herring Cobs" (254). In the English camp in France, Wilton reigns not merely as holiday mischief-maker, or rival to Henry's sober paternal authority, but as the anal father who embodies what is in Henry but more than him — an obscene enjoyment of the excremental realized through jesting.

Wilton's claim to command a superior allegiance proves critical to the visual economy of *The Unfortunate Traveller*: "The prince could but command men spend their blood in his service; I could make them spend all the money they had for my pleasure" (255). Repeatedly predicated on the deterritorialization of matter — ultimately *materia,* Heraclide's maternal body — in the orgasmic climax of jesting, the narrative's frenzy of the visible collapses different forms of social currency, including sovereignty and rhetoric, into methods of commanding and controlling flows of excremental expenditure. Wilton first spends his rhetorical skills to trick the camp's cider merchant, a slumming "old servitor" and "cavalier" (256) who is unashamed "to have his great velvet breeches larded with the droppings of his dainty liquor" (256).[56] To punish the merchant for his transgressions against status, Wilton tells him that he (Wilton) was "privily informed" by "privy informers" (258) of the king's suspicion that the merchant is a French spy. *Priv(il)y* means *secret(ly),* but Wilton activates the word's excremental referent (as well as the general fungibility of the humoral body's orifices and fluids) when he feigns distress with the king's suspicion and claims to be so upset that he "wept all my urine upward . . . so immoderately and lavishly that I thought verily my palate had been turned to Pissing Conduit in London" (258). As his urine becomes his tears, Wilton manipulates both the excremental and privileged connotations of privacy. He fabricates the scene in which he was "privily informed" of the king's suspicions, as well as the king's belief that the merchant is a "miser and a snudge" (260), but the merchant believes him because he claims the private honor of the page to "attend where the King and his lords and many chief leaders sat in council" (258). Persuaded by Wilton's offer to help "pluck" him "out of the mire," the merchant takes Wilton's advice and opens his taps, free of charge, allowing the soldiers to "burst their bellies with cider and bathe in it" (260). The result is a Rabelaisian scene of excremental expenditure in which the soldiers fill their helmets, scuppets, and boots with free cider, while the merchant sues the king for mercy. Wilton is then "pitifully whipped for his holiday lie," though he notes that "they [presumably including the king] made themselves merry with it many a winter's evening after" (261).

Heraclide's rape later works to shame Wilton for commanding just such excremental expenditures, but at this initial point in the text Wilton's "holiday lie" needs also to be understood as a carnivalesque fusion of sustenance and waste, a paradigmatic exploitation of excrement's ambivalent semiotics. In his essay "Filthy Rites," Stephen Greenblatt briefly traces the demise of this ambivalence — this doubling — through the historical evolution of another appendix to the monarch, the Groom of the Stool:

> During the regime of Rabelais's contemporary, Henry VIII, the working head of the Privy Chamber was a high-ranking and influential gentleman called the Groom of the Stool, whose status originated in his duty to attend on the king when he made use of the royal close-stool. This attendance signaled the groom's publicly acknowledged intimacy

with the king, an intimacy that conferred power not only by virtue of the king's evident confidence, but by virtue as well of a charisma that extended even to the barest functions of the king's body. By the later seventeenth century, that charisma had drastically waned, and royal bodily service had begun to seem an embarrassment.[57]

As feces loses its carnivalesque association with renewal and rebirth throughout the sixteenth and seventeenth centuries, the Groom of the Stool becomes less intimate with the king's body, and he moves his station from the close-stool to the dressing room. Yet in observing this semiotic and professional shift, Greenblatt cautions against any simple equation of popular culture in Henry's England with the Rabelaisian carnivalesque: "Indeed," he argues, "some of Rabelais's power derives from the evanescence of the festival tradition, or more accurately, from the sense of a literary, social, and religious world hardening in its commitment to order, discipline, and decorum."[58] This hardening makes Henry's Groom of the Stool, while not a carnival figure, already something of an anachronism, the stage having been set for the reformation of his position. Likewise, it makes Rabelais's work no mere exercise in the carnivalesque, but the response of a Renaissance sophisticate to "the carnivalesque threatened in its very existence."[59] Published in 1594 but set in the reign of the "only true subject of the chronicles" (254), *The Unfortunate Traveller* registers a later and far less consistently revelatory response to this same threat. *The Unfortunate Traveller* celebrates the carnivalesque tricks of its hero, his manipulation of the semiotic ambivalence of excrement and privacy, only to then shame him through Heraclide's rape for the same.

The Unfortunate Traveller's refusal to move straight forward, its unsettling recursiveness and its multiple endings, are part and parcel of its further attempt to capture Europe's recent history within a single, textual movement: the travels of its titular *page* who wanders back and forth throughout the sixteenth century. *The Unfortunate Traveller* opens at the siege of Tournai and Térouanne in 1513, but from there Wilton proceeds to the Battle of Marignano in 1515; to John Leiden's 1534 Anabaptist uprising in Münster; to Rotterdam, where he and the Earl of Surrey meet with Erasmus and Thomas More sometime before the publication of *The Praise of Folly* in 1509; and back to Germany, where Wilton witnesses Luther and Carolostadius dispute John Eckius in 1519 (in Leipzig, though Wilton places them in Wittenberg). The Italy of *The Unfortunate Traveller* is more difficult to date, though Zacharie's escape to the Duke of Burbon could take place no later than 1527 given that Burbon was killed that year in his attack on Rome. Finally, Wilton's own flight from Rome returns him to the Field of the Cloth of Gold in France in 1520.[60] Wilton's "gloss upon the text" of Cutwolfe's execution — "Chaste Heraclide, thy blood is laid up in heaven's treasury. Not one drop of it was lost, but lent out to usury" (363) — suggests that the narrative's conjunction of disparate events might well be understood as the condensation of time into an (a)historical demonstration of divine providence.[61] For indeed this gloss strains the facts in much the same way that Wilton's account of his travels strains historical credulity. Cutwolfe is executed for murdering Esdras, not for raping Heraclide. Cutwolfe is thus guilty of the rape only in the sense that his crime doubles Esdras's crime. I suggest that this gloss in turn strains the providential theology underwriting *The Unfortunate Traveller*'s hybridization of romance and revenge tragedy, allowing us to read Wilton's quick retreat in horror from Cutwolfe's execution as a retreat from the obscene conjunction of providence with vengeance. Through Cutwolfe's execution, God's benevolence, justice, and guardianship are not so much affirmed as exploded in a Jewish (usurious) frenzy of anal enjoyment.

Wilton's gloss on Cutwolfe's execution continues:

> Water poured forth sinks down quietly into the earth, but blood spilt on the ground sprinkles up to the firmament. Murder is wide-mouthed and will not let God rest till he grant revenge. Not only the blood of the slaughtered innocent, but the soul, ascendeth to His throne, and there cries out and exclaims for justice and recompense. Guiltless souls that live every hour subject to violence, and with your despairing fears do much impair God's providence, fasten your eyes on this spectacle that will add to your faith. Refer all your oppressions, afflictions and injuries to *the even-balanced eye of the Almighty;* He it is that when your patience sleepeth will be most exceeding mindful of you. (363, emphasis added)

After Wilton finishes, Cutwolfe delivers the speech in which he declares himself a divine avenger, and the executioner sets to work on the faith-enhancing spectacle. The executioner stretches Cutwolfe out on the wheel, fractures his bones with a hammer, solders his wounds with hot lead, pulls out his tongue, thrusts "[v]enemous stinging worms" (369) into his ears, crushes the cankers in his mouth, "lingeringly" (369) splinters each limb, and then leaves him to die while his flesh is eaten away by birds. According to Wilton, this spectacle evinces God's justice, but Cutwolfe's speech also transforms this spectacle into a Lutheran revelation of God as the anal father. Indicative of this transformation is Wilton's own immediate shift in message. Cutwolfe dead, Wilton declares the text of the future inscrutable: "Unsearchable is the book of our destinies: One murder begetteth another; was never yet bloodshed barren from the beginning of the world to this day" (369–70). Cutwolfe's execution first spectacularized the guidance of God's providential hand, but now Wilton sees nothing but the inevitability of bloodshed itself, the endless perpetuation of violence, now divorced from divine purpose.[62] The result of this translation is not just an end to the narrative but another narrative impasse as Wilton gives up trying to read his book.

In the dedicatory letter to his patron Lord Henry Wriothesley, Nashe writes, "How well or ill I have done in it, I am ignorant (the eye that sees round about itself sees not into itself)" (251). By the end of *The Unfortunate Traveller*, this statement reflects the limits of Wilton's own skills as a reader of his life's series of unfortunate events. The text invites us as readers to critique Wilton's shortsightedness, just as Nashe invites Wriothesley's judgment of a text that Nashe claims he does not have the proper perspective to provide. We may therefore recognize, for instance, that throughout *The Unfortunate Traveller*, and long before he witnesses Heraclide's rape, Wilton confronts his own doubles but fails to recognize them as such. Wilton fails to see himself reflected in the clerks of the camp. Likewise, he does not see himself reflected in Jack of Leiden, the leader of the Anabaptist uprising in Münster. (Leiden assumes a divine commission for the rebellion, but Wilton, who also doubles Nashe here as the scourge of Martin Marprelate, fiercely denounces him as a seditionist.) Wilton further fails to recognize in either the plague of sweating sickness that sweeps suddenly across England or the massacre of the French and Swiss soldiers at the Battle of Marignano the recurrence of the liquefying effects of his own jests. Nor does he see in the summer banquet house — the Golden Age, technological marvel that Wilton visits in Rome — a spectacle of perfectly managed material flows that functions as a counterpoint for all his narrative's other deterritorializing spectacles.[63] Such observations belong to critics who claim an insight into the narrative distinct from Wilton's own. But we as critics should also recognize through the limitations of Wilton's vision that we too are barred the position of the gaze. We too lack the "even-balanced eye of the Almighty" that sees all. Moreover, our vision and Wilton's are often compact — both blinded to an aspect of the self with which we are nonetheless brought into confrontation during the scene of Heraclide's rape.

Keeping an eye on the way this confrontation may shift one's perspective on the Freudian theory about obscene joking — translating heterosexual into sodomitical aggression, different bodies into the same — I suggest we return to the homophobic anti-Semitism of *The Unfortunate Traveller*'s ending. The perception of this ending as Nashe's sincere attribution of anatomizing violence to a wandering excremental Judaism would be, I think, short-sighted, for among other reasons it would overlook the consequence of another moment in the rape scene when Nashe reveals the reader and Wilton's vision to be compact. I propose instead to take Nashe's own cue and see the ending skeptically, just as I and most everyone see the ending of *All's Well That Ends Well*. A skeptical reading has the power to recast the ending's homophobic anti-Semitism as profoundly comic — as the absurd scapegoating of the Jews who embody the motivating desires of the page. To be clear, a skeptical reading does not change the fact that this scapegoating is itself anti-Semitic, as well as homophobic. It does, however, condition this prejudice as the consequence of repression — as a displacement of enjoyment onto a "monstrous" other. Perhaps, in the end, laughter at such displacement constitutes the only proper, ethical response to Nashe's skeptical romance.

Ethical Laughter

My use of the word *ethical* should not be taken to imply that laughter somehow "humanizes" the excremental Jew, or, in Emmanuel Levinas's terms, puts a face on the Other. Freud's antipathy toward Christ's commandment to love one's neighbor is well known and well explained by Slavoj Žižek in his own objection to Levinas:

Is there not, in the very heart of the Judeo-Freudian inhuman neighbor, a monstrous dimension which is already minimally "gentrified," domesticated, once it is conceived in the Levinasian sense? What if the Levinasian face is yet another defense against this monstrous dimension of subjectivity? . . . In short, the temptation to be resisted here is the ethical "gentrification" of the neighbor, the reduction of the radically ambiguous monstrosity of the Neighbor-Thing into an Other as the abyssal point from which the call of ethical responsibility emanates.[64]

From this point of view, "humanization" is itself unethical, a denial of the Real, radical inhumanity within the human itself. The ethics of psychoanalysis therefore begins with recognizing the Other's inhumanity as one's own — as the excremental, monstrous dimension of subjectivity. Laughter, in turn, need not constitute a defense against this monstrosity — an attempt to neutralize it, rendering it harmless or otherwise distant from the self. This laughter does not sound one's superiority, as Thomas Hobbes understood laughter.[65] Nor does it betray, in Henri Bergson's words, "an absence of feeling."[66] Rather, this laughter results from the recognition of the Other as one's self. It sounds what Joan Copjec describes as "the discharge of an excess of energy called up by our expectation of the new and made superfluous by the recognition of the same."[67]

In this ethical laughter at the homophobic anti-Semitism of *The Unfortunate Traveller* lies the recognition that the act of reading the text has been an obscene exercise in our own anal enjoyment. As a "privy token of his [Wilton's] good will" written out on "waste paper" (253), *The Unfortunate Traveller* affords the reader the opportunity to realize the fundamental fantasy alongside Wilton, to revel in fascination at the violent evisceration of bodies. In Nashe's imagination, this readership is likely Christian, but the enjoyment the text affords is certainly not so restricted. A properly ethical response to this realization among believers and nonbelievers alike hinges on acknowledging and owning this enjoyment. The Christian Wilton acknowledges his enjoyment only to then find a scapegoat for its "sinfulness" in the Jews, while Nashe scholars have long denounced (while continuing to read) *The Unfortunate Traveller* as an exercise in Nashe's "bad taste."[68] Both responses abscond on the significance of Heraclide's blush, which follows her meditation on the predestination of her rape:

> Having passioned thus awhile, she hastily ran and looked herself in her
> glass, to see if her sin were not written on her forehead. With look-
> ing she blushed, though none looked upon her but her own reflected
> image. (338)

As Wilton's and the reader's double, Heraclide here realizes our collective fundamental fantasy, and her blush signals our culpability for her
lost eye of honesty. At the same time, however, the blush also crucially
registers an ethical possibility: as the only ones looking at Heraclide
besides herself, and thus as Heraclide's double, we are being given the
opportunity to cast judgment on ourselves, to recognize our enjoyment
as victimizing, and even to be ashamed of ourselves.

At this moment, the eye that sees round itself can also see into itself,
but what it sees is not a self that can gaze; the enjoying self does not have
an "even-balanced" perspective, one without the base partiality that psychoanalysis dubs "lack." The ethical choice hinges on how, so implicated,
we respond to the self we see. Few recent films have offered a similar
choice more starkly than Mel Gibson's *The Passion of the Christ,* which like
The Unfortunate Traveller recruits the Jews to manage Christian shame
and culpability.[69] (One might recall that in response to the charge of
anti-Semitism, Gibson removed only the subtitles for the "blood curse"
while leaving the Aramaic, effectively making the curse the hidden truth
of the film.) Few viewers found Gibson's hyperviolent film amusing. Yet
to approach the film, as did so many critics, as *either* a serious, authentic testament to Christ's suffering *or* a hateful, vicious piece of anti-
Semitic propaganda is, like its own writer and director, to overlook its
sheer absurdity. In soliciting evidence of Christ's suffering, Gibson, like
Wilton, translates Christian into Jewish culpability, denying the divine
comedy of the passion narrative in which the monstrous Christ-killer is
revealed to be none other than the Christian subject who needs Christ
to die in order for salvation to be possible. This failure of Christians to
recognize themselves in the Jews grotesquely perpetuates the abjection
for which — at least according to René Girard — Christ died.[70] Come-
dian Sarah Silverman's joke about the crucifixion realizes the Girardian
absurdity of this perpetuation: "Everybody blames the Jews for killing
Christ. And then the Jews try to pass it off on the Romans. I'm one of
the few people that believe it was the blacks."[71]

As Joan Pong Linton remarks, *The Unfortunate Traveller* seems designed to engage us "in the critique of dominant discourses, inviting us to devise our own means to responsibility."[72] It succeeds in this design by collapsing the looks of the reader and the protagonist. Following his trick on the cider merchant, Wilton first invites the reader to share in his enjoyment: "Gentle readers (look you be gentle now, since I have called you so), as freely as my knavery was mine own, it shall be yours to use in the way of honesty" (262). The banished English earl who saves Wilton from hanging on the charge of Heraclide's rape more or less repeats this invitation when advising Wilton to return to England:

> What is here [abroad] but we may read in books, and a great deal more too, without stirring our feet out of a warm study? . . . So let others tell you strange accidents, treasons, poisonings, close packings in France, Spain, and Italy: it is no harm for you to hear of them, but come not near them. (343–44)

Wilton does not heed the loquacious earl, making an excuse to escape and immediately regretting it when he falls into Zadoch's cellar: "God plagued me for deriding such a grave fatherly advertiser" (347). Yet the earl's advice, like Wilton's invitation to the reader, elides another lesson of Heraclide's blush: that to play spectator to another's suffering is no inoculation against the harm of the self. Throughout *The Unfortunate Traveller,* spectatorship facilitates a sadomasochistic anal enjoyment that simply brings one too near the scene of the crime to escape with the eye of one's honesty intact. One escapes only by refusing to recognize one's own role in the narrative striptease, by denying the same enjoyment that motivates one to keep reading. In Wilton's case, such denial contributes to the unfortunate creation of the excremental Jew who figures "what is common to both sexes" and therein defines what the Christian male is not. Accordingly, a competing detranslation of the Jew as a fundamentally comic figure — as the figure for the anal eroticism at the heart of obscene comedy — allows for perhaps the only happy ending that any reading of *The Unfortunate Traveller* might have.

5

The Pardoner's Dirty Breeches

Cynicism and Kynicism in *The Canterbury Tales*

> Goodness only knows how obscure such a pretension
> as the achievement of genital objecthood remains,
> along with what is so imprudently linked to it, namely,
> adjustment to reality.
>
> — Jacques Lacan, *The Ethics of Psychoanalysis*

ODERNITY IS THE AGE OF CYNICISM, OR SO WE HAVE BEEN told by more than a few modernists. Attacking fascism in all its guises, including the psychoanalytic, Gilles Deleuze and Félix Guattari declare that the triumph of capitalism has ushered in an "age of cynicism."[1] Max Horkheimer and Theodor W. Adorno likewise argue that Enlightenment subjects have submitted to a totalitarian logic of capitalist commodification that the subjects themselves "recognize as false."[2] Cynicism, these modernists suggest, entails more than an ability to scoff at platitudes: to be cynical is to submit fully to an ideological structure despite knowing better. Slavoj Žižek further contends that cynicism has thoroughly exhausted the forces of Marxist ideology critique. "We are not aware of this, nevertheless we do it" ("Sie wissen das nicht, aber sie tun es"), Marx famously pronounces in *Capital,* referring to the way we evaluate the different kinds of human labor in the exchange of products of equal value. These words have long served as the motto for "false consciousness" — the veil of ignorance that shrouds the true motives and consequences of human action, the veil whose lifting will out "the secret of our own social products" and, in a move that seems the inevitable consequence of allying knowledge with power, effect a revolution of both base and superstructure.[3] But as Žižek argues, cynics are aware of what they do, *and they do it anyway.* Thus, cynics exploit the connection between ideology and reality that traditional Marxism fails to identify: "the fundamental level of ideological fantasy, the level on which ideology structures the social reality itself."[4]

So described, cynicism is not merely the brainchild of nineteenth- and twentieth-century capitalism. It has a history both philosophical and cultural, a history charted by the work upon which Žižek's argument relies: Peter Sloterdijk's *Critique of Cynical Reason.*[5] Sloterdijk roots this history in antiquity (in the Greek *kynikos*), traces cynicism's flourishing against the Enlightenment, and culminates his study with an extensive analysis of the cynicism that bore its deadliest fruits in Weimar Germany. Though Sloterdijk posits a teleological narrative of the Enlightenment's rise and fall, he nonetheless makes a powerful demand on pre- and early modernists to analyze the operations of cynical ideology as symptoms of the epistemic shifts that have come to define the modern consciousness. This last chapter accordingly turns back from the Renaissance to the late fourteenth century in order to argue that one of Chaucer's more critically worked pilgrims champions a cynical coming-to-consciousness. In what could be a description of the Pardoner with his deceptive but transparent "Oure Lady veyl" (I.695), Žižek writes, "The cynical subject is quite aware of the distance between the ideological mask and the social reality, but he nonetheless insists upon the mask."[6] By inviting the pilgrims to kiss relics he freely admits are fraudulent, the Pardoner does not try to bring the pilgrims out from beneath the veil of false consciousness. To the contrary, as a harbinger of "enlightened false consciousness," he encourages their cynical subscription to a spiritual ideology that he knows is impoverished.[7]

While a cynic is a type of social person, it is not an identity in the sense of what Chaucerians have long tried to pin on the Pardoner.[8] Nor is it entirely correlative to the familiar critical representation of the Pardoner as a fragmented subject in search of his own subjective reconstitution, for cynics (no optimistic ego psychologists among them) are acutely aware of the impossibility of such a find.[9] His cynicism attaches more to what recent critics, wrestling with the Pardoner's signifying excesses, consider to be his queerness. According to Robert S. Sturges, the problem with reading the Pardoner is not "that Chaucer provides too little information. . . . Rather, he provides too much: the Pardoner's gender identity signifies in too many ways."[10] To take perhaps the most well-known example of this excess, the narrator famously "trowe[s]" that the Pardoner is either a "geldyng or a mare" (I.691), an insult that *The Riverside Chaucer* glosses as "a eunuch or a homosexual." Yet considering that, from a purely historicist perspective, there technically were no homosexuals in the Middle Ages, the latter of these equine terms is far more indeterminate than the "staggeringly confident" gloss implies.[11] Furthermore, the Host's wish to cut off the Pardoner's "coillons" (VI.952), as well as the Pardoner's bragging about having "a joly wenche in every toun" (VI.453), suggests that the Pardoner may indeed have testicles, and that he may be quite heterosexually virile.[12] The critical turn to embrace rather than resolve such incoherency has corrected for past analyses that, in Glenn Burger's phrase, try to locate the Pardoner's "true identity."[13] Burger explains, "Neither some unnatural monster absolutely other to us, nor some symbolic entity of nonmeaning, 'he,' the Pardoner, is both of these things and more, a nexus of intermingling discourses about the subject and its meaning. . . ."[14] Carolyn Dinshaw makes a similar claim:

> [T]he queer, *always* playing a role (and thereby revealing that others do), eliminating any idea of essence, obviates all questions of originality, sincerity, even truth. . . . The queer empties out the natural, the essential (those conventional foundations of representation and identity), shakes the heterosexual edifice."[15]

As the monstrous child of the Middle Ages and modernity, the queer Pardoner (a)historically destabilizes naturalized binaries of gender and sexuality to reveal their construction within both medieval and modern sign systems.

Such descriptions of the Pardoner's queerness go a long way toward accounting for what semiotically troubles both the Pardoner's readers and his fellow pilgrims. As Dinshaw further shows, his queerness is even more troubling given that his erotic indeterminacies also destabilize the boundary between orthodox and Lollard identity.[16] Yet I want to argue that the political utility of the Pardoner's (a)historical queerness — which for Dinshaw affords queer historians an "affective, even tactile relation to the past" — needs to be further assessed alongside the Pardoner's cynicism.[17] My question, put simply, is this: how queer can the Pardoner be when he guards an ideological system he does not believe in? While Dinshaw's queer is a proud social rebel, a superhero who "shakes the heterosexual edifice," the Pardoner actually functions as if the edifice he shakes were still stable. Cynically, the Pardoner performs as if his own performance does not pose the queer challenge that it does. How then does he, or any queer for that matter, contest ideology? When ideology critique no longer works, what disposition does an effective contest require?

In the previous chapter, I suggested that one might effectively critique ideology through laughter. I explore this possibility in further detail toward the end of this chapter when I analyze the pilgrims' laughter at the feud between the Host and the Pardoner. To understand what's at stake in this laughter, however, it is first necessary to reckon with the anal erotic implications of the Host equating the Pardoner's relics with the products of the Pardoner's "fundement" (VI.950) and conjuring the image of the Pardoner's testicles "shryned in an hogges toord" (VI.955). Prompted by the Host's curse as much as by the Pardoner's description in the General Prologue, decades of critical wondering about the Pardoner's sexuality have pivoted around the suspicion that his erotic pleasures are not securely phallic, or not normative in the psychoanalytic sense of genital heterosexuality. My own reasons for calling him an anal erotic are not at all based on my suspicions of what (if anything) he does in bed, but on the way he embodies the anal erotic motivation of the pilgrimage itself. In both its orthodox and criminal practices, pardoning, like pilgrimage, depends on the infusion of "excremental" objects with spiritual power through the process of sublimation. I claim that nothing incites the Host's anger and threatens the pilgrimage so much as the Pardoner's cynical attitude toward sublimation. Without trying to exhaust everything there is to say about cynicism or anal eroticism in *The Canterbury Tales*, I want to suggest that this moment of crisis necessitates a comic resistance to the forces of cynical reason and their antisocial effects. For contemporary queers, in turn, *The Canterbury Tales* offers an important political lesson on the dangers of taking one's self too seriously.

The Solid, Materialist Basis

The thesis of Paul Strohm's *Hochon's Arrow* — that some "lie[s] might as well be true" — identifies the cynicism present in many fourteenth-century texts.[18] While proof of one's consciousness of falsehood is often hard to establish, we have no such problem with outspoken cynics like the Pardoner. Cynics know that they are lying, yet they act as if their lie were the truth. While I will focus mostly on the cynicism directed toward spiritual institutions and ideologies of late fourteenth- and early fifteenth-century England, we should be aware that other realms of Chaucer's culture were inundated with cynical reason. (Strohm demonstrates, for instance, how Chaucer's "Complaint to His Purse" becomes part of the Lancastrian propaganda machine that overtakes the poet's authorial intent in rewriting Richard II as a despot.[19]) Furthermore, we should beware of locating all of Chaucer's works in a false binary between cynicism and idealism. A third position is that of the so-called laughing cynic, the kynical Diogenes, whose philosophical influence can be felt across *The Canterbury Tales.*

As Sloterdijk portrays him, Diogenes "smells the swindle of the idealist abstractions and the schizoid staleness of thinking limited to the head. Thus he creates, as the last archaic Sophist and the first in the tradition of satirical resistance, an uncivil enlightenment."[20] Diogenes is Plato's arch-nemesis. He farts in response to the sage's theory of Forms and masturbates to the theory of Eros. When Plato defines the human as a biped without feathers, Diogenes tears the feathers from a rooster and pronounces it human. Žižek surmises that kynics "confront the pathetic phrases of the ruling official ideology — its solemn, grave tonality — with everyday banality and . . . hold them up to ridicule, thus exposing behind the sublime *noblesse* of the ideological phrases the egotistical interests, the violence, the brutal claims to power."[21] And Sloterdijk emphasizes that such confrontations often involve more than an exchange of words: "kynicism gives a new twist to the question of how to *say* the truth" by utilizing "a second, speechless language," a language of the body, often bawdy, outside the verbal register.[22] Kynics "speak" through the gestures of the mouth, the direction and movement of the eyes, the exposure of the breasts and genitals, and especially the exposure of and expulsions from the rear. "The arse," Sloterdijk writes, "is the plebian, the grass-roots democrat, and the cosmopolitan among the parts of the body — in a word, the elementary kynical organ. It provides the solid, material-ist basis."[23] Through the rhetorical gestures of farting, defecating, and mooning, the arse generates laughter that has the power to deflate the highest pretensions, secular and spiritual, right and left.

Thomas's fart in The Summoner's Tale exemplifies kynical wit, for it speaks volumes in rebuffing an avaricious friar who is himself full of hot air. While the gift that Thomas keeps "hyd in pryvetee" (III.2143) parodies most obviously the Holy Ghost's Pentecostal descent upon the twelve disciples, Peter Travis notes that "many things may be said at once about this lower order speech act."[24] Scholars have argued that the fart sounds a blow against ecclesiastical materialism and the feudal economy of gift-giving, the voice of the rebels in the 1381 revolt, and a Boethian lesson in how a good may be distributed without diminishing in worth. The Miller's Tale is no less kynical. In this fabliau rejoinder to the Knight's idealist romance, Alison's "naked ers" (I.3734) rebuffs a par-ish priest who puts on courtly airs. The tale's kynical energies then turn against Nicholas as he tries to one-up the jest by farting in Absolon's face. When Absolon stabs him in the ass with a hot poker, the tale emblem-atically collapses homosocial competition, as previously valorized by the Knight, into sodomy.[25] Furthermore, Nicholas's fart — "[a]s greet as it had been a thonder-dent" (I.3807) — sets off a chain reaction: it prompts the stabbing, which prompts Nicholas's cry for "Water" (I.3815), which prompts John to wake up, cut the ropes to the tubs, and come crash-ing to the ground.[26] At one and the same time a parody of The Knight's Tale, the nativity, and Noah's flood, The Miller's Tale uses Nicholas's fart and Alison's "nether ye" (I.3852) to illustrate why, according to the Miller, a man should not be "inquisityf / Of Goddes pryvetee, nor of his wife" (I.3163–64). This famously equivocal moral, to which I will return below, equates the protection of God's privacy with a willful ignorance of cuck-oldry, while the tale itself kynically detranslates male competition over access to God and women into buggery.

Of course, the Pardoner is no kynic. The kynic speaks (always in scare quotes) blasphemous truths through the material body, but the Pardoner equates truth with appearance underwritten equally by naïve belief and cynical practice. The kynic speaks truth to power, but the cynical Pardoner acts as if truth and power were allies, exploiting his audience's belief in — or desire to believe in — the reality of his relics. He scandalizes because he states as much so baldly: he freely attests that his relics are counterfeit, describing his sales-pitch as "an hundred false japes" (VI.394) and his aim in preaching to be "nat but for to wynne, / And nothyng for correccioun of synne" (VI.403–4). And though he surely does not admit as much in front of his regular audience of "lewed peple" (VI.437), his "confession" to his fellow pilgrims signals his keen awareness of the role both naïve *and* willful misperception plays in a religious practice that trades in material goods. The Pardoner believes in nothing if not the ability of belief to transform nothing into something, the material into the spiritual. He fills his pockets with the profits of this transformation, and in doing so he conjures the specter of sodomy — of illegitimate reproduction — that trails him throughout the text and its criticism. The Canon's Yeoman pointedly echoes the moral of The Pardoner's Tale, "*Radix malorum est Cupiditas*" (VI.334), when he describes the alchemist's attempt to generate money from nothing as the "roote of alle cursednesse" (VIII.1301). Yet whereas the Canon's Yeoman decries creation *ex nihilo* as the practice of a (perhaps) self-deceived and wicked man, the Pardoner cynically and sodomitically exploits creation *ex nihilo* for his own material benefit.

The specter of sodomy also haunts the Pardoner's death-driven tale of three rioters. As Elizabeth Fowler notes, the tale's "concluding image — a tree with gold at its roots and the strange fruit of dead rioters beneath its branches — memorializes the *radix malorum* theme of the preceding sermon."[27] Though in medieval Christian theology sodomy may connote "the pure essence of the erotic without connection to reproduction," in Mark Jordan's phrase, it also connotes, as we have seen, dishonest procreativity — or here, paradoxically, fruitful death.[28] The Pardoner's relationship with the Summoner is likewise symptomatically fertile. The two pilgrims are joined together in song: to the Pardoner's "Come hider, love, to me" (I.672), the Summoner "bar . . . a stif burdoun" (I.673). The possible phallic pun on "stif burdoun" marks the two pilgrims as erotically distinct from the ideally nonsodomitical Christian pilgrim body.[29] Yet another possible pun on *burdoun* as *pregnancy* suggests that their relationship may not simply be one of sterile expenditure.[30] We might hear a description of the Summoner as the Pardoner's pregnant wife, a description that testifies to sodomy's paradoxically perverse existence within the "natural" order of procreation. In psychoanalytic terms, the pun demonstrates how sodomy is "extimate" to the Symbolic order of sexuality that defines and distinguishes it — and how sodomy is likewise extimate to the same order's religious orthodoxy.

Within the standard psychoanalytic paradigm that stresses, in Freud's words, the "similarity between the process of civilization and the libidinal impulse of the individual," the naturalized achievement of "reality" as an ideological fantasy quilted through the metaphor of the phallus requires the repressive disjunction of the anus from desire and/or the sublimation of anal eroticism into the living ends of economic and aesthetic production.[31] On this Freudian level, the Pardoner figures the anal eroticism of the civilized order. But the Pardoner also more pointedly exemplifies Lacan's particular claim, quoted as the epigraph to this chapter, that "genital objecthood" and "adjustment to reality" are "imprudently linked."[32] Reality (as opposed to the Lacanian Real) is not an objective "thing" to which one must conform, but a fantasy shaped by the organization of desire. The Pardoner has therefore not simply failed to adjust to the reality of speaking in front of a pilgrim audience who already knows him to be dishonest; were this the case, his fellow pilgrims and his readers could comfortably dismiss his performance. The Host's outraged response to the Pardoner's invitation to come forward and kiss his relics suggests instead that the Pardoner has touched a collective nerve:

> "Nay, nay!" quod he, "thanne have I Cristes curs!
> Lat be," quod he, "it shal nat be, so theech!
> Thou woldest make me kisse thyn olde breech,
> And swere it were a relyk of a seint
> Though it were with thy fundement depeint!
> But, by the croys which that Seint Eleyne fond,
> I wolde I hadde thy coillons in myn hond
> In stide of relikes or of seintuarie.
> Lat kutte hem of, I wol thee helpe hem carie;
> They shul be shryned in an hogges toord!" (VI.946–55)

Interrupting The Tale of Sir Thopas, the Host similarly curses Chaucer with being an incompetent narrator, a foul wordsmith whose rhyming "is nat worth a toord!" (VII.930). Perhaps Harry Bailly is even harsher with the Pardoner—accusing him of trying to pass off his shit-stained breeches for authentic relics and threatening him with castration—because the Pardoner proves himself a competent wordsmith whose performance imbues excremental objects with spiritual value.

This suggestion presumes that the Host falls under the sway of this performance, but he need only do so insofar as the Pardoner's performance exploits the orthodox relationship between the material and spiritual worlds. Even critics whose readings of the Pardoner differ profoundly share this sense that his performance somehow calls into question the structure of faith underwriting the pilgrimage itself. In Canterbury, after all, the pilgrims will acquire indulgences, hear sermons, and see the "true" relics of Thomas à Becket—his breeches foremost among them. Lee Patterson aptly remarks that, in cursing the Pardoner, the Host "unwittingly reveals how easy it is to imagine St. Thomas's holy breeches as fouled garments. Once the underwriting spiritual presence has been called into question, is it relics we kiss, or feces?"[33] Late fourteenth-century church reformers acknowledge no difference at all; they make no distinction between true and false relics, as once did Guibert of Nogent, who complains in his twelfth-century *Treatise on Relics* about those who turn authentic salvational aids into the "mere excrement of their money-bags."[34]

Glenn Burger further contends that pardoning was often linked in late fourteenth-century England to the foreign exportation of wealth: as English resentment towards papal authority increased, the repudiation of pardoning and the "magic" of relics served as the avenue for a national, civilized consolidation of gentlefolk.[35] The status of both relics and pardoning as foreign elements in need of purging from an English body politic therefore arguably underwrites the Host's association of the Pardoner's relics with his soiled breeches. Yet Burger also suggestively positions the nationalistic repudiation of pardoning against the lines in the General Prologue that describe the pilgrims going to Canterbury "The hooly blisful martir for to seke, / That hem hath holpen whan that they were seeke" (I.17–18). These lines suggest that "everyone expects some real return from this pilgrimage, that its spiritual reward will be materially signified — whether by a physical cure or by release from time in purgatory."[36] This expectation aligns the ostensibly orthodox pilgrims with the evocatively heretical Pardoner underneath the contractual umbrella of the "penance 'industry.'" For Burger, in short, the abjection of the Pardoner results not from his totalizing difference from the pilgrims but rather from the fact that he constitutes the "open secret" of the pilgrimage: his materialism is "transgressive and dangerous precisely because it is congruent with the desires of the rest of the company."[37] The Pardoner thus breaches the distinction between the ideal fantasy of Christian pilgrimage — that it is, in essence, an entirely different, *truer* economy than that of the corrupt pardon market — and the reality of the desires that fuel it.

The Host's curse further indicates that this breach is both spiritually and erotically traumatic: to kiss the Pardoner's relics/soiled breeches is to come face-to-face with the solid material foundation of the orthodox economy of pilgrimage. Needless to say, the Pardoner's possible testicular lack has long been correlated with his spiritual "castration" — with his status as a sinner, and even perhaps an irredeemably lost soul. I am suggesting, however, that we might better apprehend his spiritual *potency* — his disruptive, affective force — by focusing less on the question of his phallic lack and more on the Host's symptomatic recourse to scatological invective.[38] Of considerable help in making this focal shift is Georges Bataille's distinction between a homogeneous economy and its heterogeneous materials. The sanitized pilgrimage fits Bataille's description of homogeneity: it operates on the presumption of "commensurability" between spiritual and material registers, each answering to the other as prayers are exchanged for cures and pilgrimages are exchanged for less time in purgatory.[39] In confessing his crimes to the pilgrims and then preaching to them, the Pardoner is not confused and forgetful; he rather exploits the fact that this orthodox religious economy trades in material objects that have no guarantee of commensurate spiritual value. The Pardoner's open secret is this operational truth, and accordingly he and his wares appear within this homogeneous economy as its heterogeneous materials. The result of "*unproductive* expenditure," these materials include "properly sacred things," "waste products of the human body," and "parts of the body, persons, words, or acts having a suggestive erotic value." The security of a homogeneous religious economy depends on sustaining the semblance of commensurability — the fiction of wasteless expenditure. Thus, according to Bataille, heterogeneous materials provoke "affective reactions of varying intensity... sometimes attraction, sometimes repulsion."[40] The Host's curse suggests that this paradoxically perverse pilgrim threatens the pilgrimage insofar as he and his "false" relics constitute the disavowed heterogeneous products of this orthodox economy. Moreover, his cynical performance shatters the illusion of commensurability in ways that make him an object of both intense critical attraction and *homophobic* repulsion.

Privy Theology

The extent to which the Pardoner encodes Chaucer's challenge to the church and orthodox theology has long been a point of critical debate. The portraits of the Clerk and the Parson arguably underscore Chaucer's commitment to the church as the structural support of faith, but this commitment clearly did not foreclose Chaucer's contemplation of reformist arguments.[41] Lee Patterson points out that the Pardoner evokes the reformist condemnation of simony, "a materialism that took the literal for the spiritual, the sign for the signified."[42] I submit that the Pardoner more scandalously reveals that simony is actually endemic to faith, which enables the connection between word and thing.[43] Faith binds, or makes commensurate, the material and spiritual worlds, and nothing less than faith is at stake in the Pardoner's exposure of their incommensurability. The scatological content of the Host's curse therefore illuminates the very *matter* of faith — what is left after the exchanges of this homogeneous economy have been exposed as incommensurable. Put simply, unless the secret of incommensurability is kept, or guarded by faith, everything turns to shit.

Faith's conjunction of base matter and divine spirit also evokes Lacan's meditation, in his seventh seminar, on the sublime object, or the object raised "to the dignity of the Thing."[44] Money is perhaps the paradigmatic example of a sublime object, insofar as money has not simply a material body (paper, metal, etc.) but also a spiritual body, an "'indestructible and immutable' body which persists beyond the corruption

of the body physical."[45] The Pardoner's relics, like St. Helen's cross and
St. Thomas's breeches, are similarly sublime objects that materialize
divinity, the "beyond-of-the-signified."[46] When the Host refuses the
relics' transcendence by equating them with the Pardoner's own soiled
breeches, he unwittingly reveals how easy it is to desublimate the relics
that await the pilgrims at the end of their journey. Indeed, the image of
the Pardoner's stained breeches and turd-enshrined testicles further suggests the Host's possession of what Norman O. Brown calls modernity's
"excremental vision" of human being. Brown famously looks to Martin
Luther for the foundation of this excremental vision, as does Lacan:

> [Luther] renewed the very basis of Christian teaching when he sought
> to express our dereliction, our fall in a world where we let ourselves
> go. . . . Luther says literally, "You are that waste matter which falls into
> the world from the devil's anus." . . . One finds articulated here precisely
> the essential turning point of a crisis from which emerged our whole
> modern immersion in the world.[47]

The digestive troping of the demonic is common enough in medieval and
early modern iconography, as we saw in chapter 1, and Chaucer's Summoner relies on the trope for his joke about friars in hell. Yet Lacan's
Luther distinctively extends this trope into a "literal" statement about
modern embodiment. In the excremental vision of both Lutheran and
psychoanalytic theology, the "crisis" of our "modern immersion" stems
from our resistance to the excremental materiality of our being. These
visions differ only on the nature of this immersion: what is for Luther the
consequence of mankind's fall into sin becomes in the Lacanian narrative
the consequence of the subject's fall into the Symbolic order of language.

Žižek's translation of the subject's immersion into modernity evokes
Shakespeare's *Hamlet:* "Modern subjectivity emerges when the subject
perceives himself as 'out of joint.' . . . There is not subjectivity without
the reduction of the subject's positive-substantial being to a disposable
piece of shit."[48] Any claim for Chaucer's anticipation of this formulation
in the Host's curse must perforce throw time even further out of joint,
displacing the origins of modernity from Shakespeare's Renaissance to
Chaucer's late fourteenth century. My claim is thus that debates about
the origins of modern subjectivity prove only that modern subjectivity

is itself out of joint, perpetually subject to reformation and refounda-
tion in the always-anachronistic terrain of the literary.[49] Within this terrain, The Pardoner's Prologue and Tale can evince Lutheran subjectivity
before its time, and do so in a way that further develops Lacan's own
Lutheranism.

As Brown demonstrates at length, Luther relentlessly insists on the
base materiality of subjectivity, the Pauline flesh. He makes faith alone
the instrument of sublimation that unites the soul to Christ. At the same
time, he maintains that nothing imperils sublimation/faith so much as
the reality of embodiment, the soul's imprisonment by the flesh in a life
the subject is forbidden to take.[50] We find in Luther's account of the soul's
lifelong struggle against the flesh what psychoanalysis describes as the
loop of the death drive, and for an example of life in this loop we need
look no further than the old man of The Pardoner's Tale. Unable to find
a youth with whom to exchange his age, but unable also to die, the old
man "equivocates," in Elizabeth Fowler's words, "ever more wildly and
abstractly between carnality and spirituality."[51] He therein obscenely figures, as I read him, the function of faith at the heart of both the Pardoner's performance and the pilgrimage. For the embodied subject, faith
is not merely the vehicle of sublimation. Faith also sustains the subject
at a relevant distance from the object of the death drive — the traumatic
Thing, or what Lacan calls *das Ding*. In this way, faith operates much like
the pleasure principle, which "governs the search for the object and
imposes detours which maintain the distance in relation to its end."[52]
Faith sustains the lifelong (and in this sense endless) desire for a true
union between the spiritual and the material.

The Lacanian dictum that "truth has the structure of fiction" means
that the reality one perceives or believes to be true takes shape around
das Ding — this Symbolic void that, like Bataille's heterogeneous materials, upsets appearances. Richard Halpern argues in his own study of
the relationship between sodomy and sublimation that Lacan develops
his concept of *das Ding* from Heidegger, but that Lacan distinctly uses
the anus as its metaphor, Lacan's Thing being an empty vase *(la vase)*
as opposed to Heidegger's libation jug *(der Krug)*. Halpern adds that
"the essentially veiled nature of the Thing precludes any imposing of
definitional contours." Thus, *das Ding* no more "'is' the anus than it 'is'

the vagina, or the mother, or the neighbor . . . or any of the other objects that come to occupy its space."[53] But keeping in mind Lacan's Lutheranism, as well as fourteenth-century church reformers' radical disjunction of the material from the spiritual, I would like to suggest that this particular semiotic connection between the anus and *das Ding* makes itself felt in *The Canterbury Tales* around issues of unrepresentable sacred secrecy and divine privacy. Although anxieties about public and private spirituality surface throughout the *Tales,* we can focus most immediately on two tales that I have already indicated share some relation to the Pardoner and his tale. The Miller's Tale and The Canon's Yeoman's Tale both pivot around a shrouded, private center of spiritual truth — God's secret realm — into which men best not pry.[54]

The Canon's Yeoman frequently employs the words *pryvetee* (VIII.1052, 1138) and *pryvely* (VIII.1178, 1323) in his exposure of alchemical deceptions, and he ends his tale by repudiating the search for the philosopher's "privee stoon" (VIII.1452). Because God has kept the location of this particular sublime object a secret, he argues, we best "lete it goon" (VIII.1475), or we run the risk of making God our "adversarie" (VIII.1476). The Yeoman neurotically couples an insistence on the limits of human knowledge with a passionate enforcement of these limits. He inveighs against human breaching of the knowledge barrier while he simultaneously maintains that this barrier cannot be breached. Yet the Yeoman (who rides up to the pilgrims) was not around to hear the Miller earlier equate the protection of divine secrecy with a will-to-ignorance regarding cuckoldry:

> An housbonde shal nat been inquisityf
> Of Goddes pryvetee, nor of his wyf.
> So he may fynde Goddes foyson there,
> Of the remenant nedeth nat enquere. (I.3163–66)

As The Miller's Tale demonstrates, prying too hard into "Goddes pryvetee" does not merely raise God's ire. More devastatingly, it risks bringing the whole theological edifice crashing to the ground. The Miller would seem to imply in his anticipatory rejoinder to the Canon's Yeoman that to keep the faith, one must not seek too hard to know the truth. The pleasures of faith, like the pleasures of marriage, reside precisely in the perpetual suspension of knowledge regarding the truth of one's "spouse."

Of course, the Miller also genders God's secrets by eliding them with female private parts: feminine *pryvetees* underwrite the marital and spiritual economies that the Miller conflates. The Miller is a remarkably curious anatomist, however, and his tale turns on a "confusion of orifices" culminating in the notoriously ambiguous reference to Alison's "nether ye" (I.3852).[55] Elaine Tuttle Hansen argues that The Miller's Tale "effects the conventional association of (female) genital and anal functions, of woman's sex (or sex with a woman) as dirt, decay, and dissolution."[56] I would add that the tale likewise effects the long historical association of female sexuality with divinity. Numerous critics have explored how Lacan's own meditation on these associations — what he calls the introduction of "the feminine object . . . through the door of *privation* or of inaccessibility" — turns on the literature of courtly love relations in the Middle Ages.[57] Lacan focuses particularly on a twelfth-century *langue d'oc* lyric by Arnaut Daniel in which a group of men discuss the impropriety of one Lady Ena's request that her suitor, Bernart, prove his fidelity by putting "his mouth to her trumpet."[58] The men provide a grotesque description of Lady Ena's "rough, ugly and hairy" trumpet, her "funnel between spine and mount pubic, there where rust colored substances proceed."[59] In lines that recall Nicholas's thunderous, blinding fart and scalded "toute" (I.3811), they dwell at some length on the blinding heat of the trumpet's "smoke" and its "stench . . . worse than dung in a garden."[60] Lacan puts the case mildly when he states that the lyric "breaches the boundaries of pornography to the point of scatology":

> The idealized woman, the Lady, who is in the position of the Other and of the object, finds herself suddenly and brutally positing, in a place knowingly constructed out of the most refined of signifiers, the emptiness of a thing in all its crudity, a thing that reveals itself in its nudity to be the thing, her thing, the one that is to be found at her very heart in its cruel emptiness. That Thing, whose function certain of you perceived in the relation to sublimation, is in a way unveiled with a cruel and insistent power.[61]

Chaucer's Alison finds herself in a similar situation as her "nether ye" focuses the Miller's kynical detranslation of the Knight's homosocial romance. Some scatological *thing* surfaces there too as the traumatic void of desire below the fantasy of the courtly love relation. In *Lacan's Medievalism,* Erin Felicia Labbie remarks that Daniel presents Lady Ena's request as a "limit-case" for fidelity and that, from his perspective, Bernart should refrain from honoring it.[62] In doing so, Daniel delimits the boundaries of courtly love for the purpose of male self-preservation, whereas the Miller's fabliau exposes the ease with which these boundaries collapse. Given Lacan's return to courtly love in his late, controversial seminar on female sexuality, however, both Daniel's lyric and The Miller's Tale may also be understood as stark demonstrations of Lacan's argument in that seminar that the sexual relation — the relationship of mutual subjective completion between "man" and "woman" — does not exist.[63] Psychoanalysts and feminist critics have long debated the implications of this argument, but they have done so, I think, largely at the expense of its status as a theological claim. As Lacan theorizes it in his lecture on "God and [Barred] Woman's Jouissance," the sexual relation is also the relation between the human and the divine, between the subject of the signifier (man/human) and what is beyond the signifier (Woman/God).

When Lacan declares that Woman does not exist, he says the same thing of God: both are idealizations that aid man in avoiding the traumatic emptiness of *das Ding.* Both are fantastical beings whose distance is imposed as a way of "making up for the absence of the sexual relation." At the same time, Lacan contends that God and Woman *do* exist insofar as they figure an enjoyment "beyond the phallus" — an impossible enjoyment that cannot signify in a Symbolic order where the phallus alone determines sexual difference. "There is a *jouissance* that is hers," Lacan states, "that belongs to that 'she' that doesn't exist and doesn't signify anything."[64] This theology of desire seems to me distinctly Chaucerian. In their joint fixation on privation, Lacan and Chaucer circle around the same masculine anxieties: that fidelity to Woman, like fidelity to God, is fidelity to an impossible being that simultaneously promises *jouissance* and withholds it, a being whose appearance within the Symbolic order is scatalogically obscene. As the Miller advises, it is therefore best not to pry into the *pryvetee,* lest one discover that Woman, God, and Woman-as-God do not exist — or, what amounts to the same thing, that they only exist outside of signification as figures for the Real.

Neither simply orthodox nor heretical, masculine nor feminine, human nor nonhuman, the cynical Pardoner does not *believe* in what I now want to call "privy theology" — a theology predicated on the preservation of secrecy, or what Karma Lochrie terms "the economy of coverture."[65] Perhaps the only devout believer is the Yeoman. The Pardoner believes only in the ability of his words to bring him material reward. There is no mystery to his God, no secrets that must be kept, no remnants after which one must not inquire. Yet the fact that he operates as if religious transactions were nonetheless mysterious makes him more threatening to the pilgrimage than the Miller, whose kynical defamation of privy theology pleases the other pilgrims:

> Whan folk hadde laughen at this nyce cas
> Of Absolon and hende Nicholas
> Diverse folk diversely they seyde
> But for the moore part they loughe and pleyde. (I.3855–58)

The Prioress offers her own controversial apology for privy theology with a sentimental tale of Christian martyrdom in the "privee place" (VII.568). When the young boy, murdered by Jews, begins to sing from his grave, the privy becomes the productive site of spiritual evidence for an anti-Semitic Christianity and its sanctification of Mary as the exemplar of impossible Womanhood.[66] The Prioress materializes the "pryvetee" as a privy — as the place where God works his mysteries — and in doing so she protects the economy of coverture while simultaneously returning it to its base site of transaction. Because she is herself ambiguously pious and blasphemous, seemingly devout yet materialistic, erotic, and worldly-wise, the mysterious Prioress might well be nominated the priestess of privy theology. Unlike the Pardoner, who cynically empties belief of sincerity, the Prioress's ability to disturb modern readers derives from the possibility that, as otherwise hypocritical as she may be, she may indeed believe in the murderous version of Christianity her tale promotes.

To the extent that the portraits of the pilgrims all take shape within an economy of coverture, the Pardoner joins the Prioress as one of Chaucer's most accomplished case studies in antihermeneutics. Perhaps only the Wife of Bath — who bears the birthmark of masculinity, the "Martes

mark" (III.619), both on her face and "in another privee place" (III.620) —
rivals them as enigmas. Like the mystery of the Wife's birthmark, the
mystery of the Pardoner's *coillons* is one of presence and manifestation —
a mystery of how material, immanent, bodily things denote gender. I
have been perhaps covertly suggesting throughout this chapter that to
dwell on this testicular mystery, to try and make sense of the Pardoner
with appeal to the phallus as the master signifier of identity, betrays his
fundamental queerness. More pointedly, it overlooks the Host's revelation
that, in Tim Dean's words, the "phallus is simply a turd in disguise."[67] The
Pardoner is most potently queer when we look beyond the question of
his genitalia, when we allow his anality to (a)historically confound the sex
and gender identities (homosexual, sodomite, and eunuch) delineated by
the phallocentric orders of both the Middle Ages and modernity. For it
is in this capacity as an anal erotic that the Pardoner brings the pilgrimage to its Lacanian crisis, the moment when "we find the whole texture
of appearance has been rent apart, . . . [and] the whole thing might just
disappear."[68]

Queer Play

The following remarks from Lacan immediately precede those about the
physiology of psychoanalytic fundamentals that I quoted in the Introduction, and so return this book, at its end, to the eroticized connection
between comedy and scatology in psychoanalytic discourse:

> But if the truth of the subject, even when he is in the position of mas-
> ter, does not reside in himself, but, as analysis shows, in an object that
> is, of its nature, concealed, to bring this object out into the light of day
> is really and truly the essence of comedy.[69]

If the identification of the material object as the "truth of the subject"
constitutes the "essence of comedy," then The Pardoner's Prologue and
Tale is a comedy par excellence: one that reduces the subject to a disposable piece of shit. At the same time, I have suggested, the Pardoner is no
queer hero. Although he rips apart the texture of appearance, he offers
no effective ideological critique; he only admits his personal investment
in the ideological status quo. In this respect, his cynicism corresponds
with his sin of "avarice" (VI.428) as he exploits an ideological fantasy to

his own material benefit. The problem for both his critics and his fellow pilgrims lies in responding to him in a way that neither shares in his cynicism nor resorts to naïve idealism. This problem is all the more pronounced for queer critics, myself included, who (a)historically orient ourselves and our politics within figures of the past. In concluding this book, I would like to return to what I described as one of its structural principles and consider the pilgrims' laughter at the quarrel between the Pardoner and the Host as the sound of a new foundation for queer politics — a politics of play. A politics of play is neither idealistic nor cynical; rather, it facilitates the creation of expanding social relations while continuously calling attention to the contingency of society's foundations. Put another way, a politics of play is not antisocial; rather, it promiscuously seeks after relations with others while avoiding any predetermination about who those others might be.[70]

The Host's response to the Pardoner is instructive for its failure to negotiate successfully between idealism and cynicism. By making explicit in his curse what the Pardoner has achieved — the reduction of the sublime object to its most material foundation — the Host paradoxically profanes for the salvation of the sacred. As Žižek observes, sometimes "the only way to sustain the (Sacred) Place is to fill it up with trash, with an excremental abject."[71] The excremental abject calls attention to the sacred *as sacred* — as a place, quite literally, not to be shit upon. In these terms, by equating a shrine with a turd, the Host enacts a "desperate strategy to ascertain that the Sacred Place is still there."[72] And once he has made this desperate gesture, he tries to preempt any further ideological threats that may arise from these pilgrim games: "'Now,' quod oure Hoost, 'I wol no lenger pleye / With thee, ne with noon oother angry man'" (VI.958–59). Through his effort to preserve his authority and the pilgrimage itself from the corrosive implications of the Pardoner's cynicism, the Host seems well on his way to becoming cynical himself.

To be sure, a brooding Harry Bailly now looks much like the Pardoner, who is also so angry that "no word ne wolde he seye" (VI.957). Moreover, whereas the Pardoner's cynicism was previously pronounced, his disbelief "confessed," both men now look remarkably like Sloterdijk's modern cynic, who "has withdrawn into a mournful detachment that internalizes its knowledge as though it were something to be ashamed of."[73] The Pardoner's own anger at the Host's rebuke, together with the Host's shock at the Pardoner's solicitation, leads to their dual withdrawal from the "felaweshipe" (I.32) as they bury their knowledge beneath the level of speech. But the tale does not end here, forecasting a modernity of isolated, melancholic individuals. When the other pilgrims begin to "lough"(VI.961), and the Knight orders the Host to kiss the Pardoner, the pilgrims open a middle path between cynicism and idealism that allows them to continue on their merry way:

> But right anon the worthy Knyght bigan,
> Whan that he saugh that al the peple lough,
> "Namoore of this, for it is right ynough!
> Sire Pardoner, be glad and myrie of cheere;
> And ye, sire Hoost, that been to me so deere,
> I prey yow that ye kisse the Pardoner.
> And Pardoner, I prey thee, drawe thee neer,
> And, as we diden, lat us laughe and pleye."
> Anon they kiste, and ryden forth hir weye. (VI.960–68)

The pilgrims direct their laughter at *both* the Pardoner and the Host, as the Knight perceives before he intervenes. Theirs is a group response, one that circumvents our ability to gauge the effects of the Pardoner's performance on each pilgrim, but one that joins the pilgrims together in opposition to both men's anger. Despite whatever individual beliefs and degrees of investment they may have in the smooth operation of a homogeneous spiritual economy (the Miller and the Prioress, for instance, differ considerably in this regard), their laughter registers at least in part as kynical — as taking aim at "the ego itself, which had taken things so seriously."[74] At issue here is not whether the pilgrims can any longer subscribe to the ideological structure of pilgrimage — certainly they can and do, and therefore it is crucial to note the difference between the potential cynicism of this subscription and the Pardoner's fallacious attempt to exploit that cynicism for his own individual benefit — but whether they will take their (dis)beliefs so seriously as to destroy their fellowship. At least momentarily, their laughter unites the pilgrims across estate and gender boundaries, sounding unity within difference by opposing the isolating effects of both idealistic belief and the cynical internalization of disbelief.[75]

The Knight's intervention then routes this kynical energy back into the pilgrimage itself. The kiss he orders is not itself kynical, but the gesture is certainly of no small queer significance given the Host's refusal to kiss the Pardoner's relics. Whether it queers only the Host (because he alone must kiss the Pardoner) or the pilgrimage itself (because the kiss brings the Pardoner back into the fellowship), the kiss potentially registers as the ultimate cynical gesture that subordinates knowledge to silence and social grace as the price of order.[76] Glenn Burger, for one, resists such overt cynicism, arguing that "the Pardoner must be constructed, in some form at least, as a worthy, normal male agent of the church." Yet he goes on to express his misgivings: "[C]an we really laugh and play 'as we diden' when this action marries the supposedly normal with the perverse . . . ?"[77] Carolyn Dinshaw shares Burger's qualms, and she suggests that the pilgrims themselves refuse the queerness of the kiss: the fact that they ride onward signals their attempt to dismiss the "uncomfortable uncertainties" that the Pardoner raises about gender, sexual, and religious identity.[78] As inspiring as these readings have been in my own thinking about the Pardoner, their shared characterization of the pilgrims as cynical homophobes seems ultimately to elide the overall queer value of their play. The kiss restores the textual and social space of this play — a boundless space of inquiry (*sentence*) and pleasure (*solas*) wherein the pilgrims explore the limitations, truth claims, and consequences of ideology. Only by having the Host kiss the Pardoner, and only by riding onward, are social relations restored, and the possibilities for communication and relationality reopened. Far from a disavowal of the Pardoner and all the uncertainties he represents, the pilgrims' return to their game may far more queerly signal their recognition that the cynical and idealist sin of taking things so seriously — the sin of ideological severity — destroys communal foundations that must remain contingent in order for the pilgrims to accommodate the economic, social, theological, and political shifts that produce such a diverse bunch as themselves.[79]

In making this claim, I do not simply want to celebrate the pilgrims' fellowship, even though this fellowship seems to me a more ethical model of comic community than the Freudian one predicated upon scape-goating. I rather want to emphasize that in the midst of celebrating the queer's potential to disrupt social regimes of the normal and the natural, Chaucer's queer critics have perhaps too easily lost sight of the queer sociality that is always a part of the pilgrims' world-making play.[80] This play joins the fragmented *Canterbury Tales* into an unfinished whole, and keeps Chaucer, who lays a famous claim to "unkonnynge" (X.1081), from seeming like a cynic or an idealist himself. This play also keeps the pil-grims, including the Pardoner, from falling out of the fellowship and affords the continuous redrawing of social and temporal boundaries. I further want to emphasize that what matters most in *The Canterbury Tales,* ideologically speaking, is never simply the end, or even the forward narrative progression, but the back and forth between the pilgrims that registers within and between each tale. As Jeffrey Jerome Cohen states in his own Deleuzo-Guattarian analysis of the structure of the *Tales,* "*The Canterbury Tales* could not be finished by Chaucer because it aspires to no totality."[81] These playful exchanges repeatedly place *The Canterbury Tales* at the contested foreground of early modernity. They also demonstrate that the Symbolic is mutable and pluralistic, always open to contests of signification and translation that recalibrate reality itself. Though quite queer, the Pardoner acts as if his cynical confession does not generate the contest that it does, as if the ideologies that shape reality itself were not themselves amenable to change. Especially in our present political climate, where much homophobic rhetoric is so absurd as to raise the question of belief, it is key to not becoming similarly cynical that we who identify as queer refuse the same assumption of immutability, and that we do not relinquish the ability to speak—and why not kynically?—truth to power.

ℐ𝓸𝓽𝑒𝓼

Introduction

1. Jacques Lacan, "Desire and the Interpretation of Desire in *Hamlet*," in *Literature and Psychoanalysis, The Question of Reading: Otherwise,* ed. Shoshana Felman (Baltimore: The Johns Hopkins University Press, 1982), 12.

2. Ibid., 23. All citations from Shakespeare's plays refer to *The Norton Shakespeare,* 2nd ed., ed. Stephen Greenblatt, Walter Cohen, Jean E. Howard, and Katharine Eisaman Maus (New York: Norton, 2008).

3. Ibid., 33.

4. Ibid., 34.

5. Ibid.

6. On the conflation of the play and its protagonist, see Margreta de Grazia, *"Hamlet" without Hamlet* (Cambridge: Cambridge University Press, 2007). Lacan's restriction of Hamlet's lost object, the object *a,* to the phallus elides all the other forms that the object *a* takes in Lacan's own work, including the gaze, the voice, the breast, and feces. In *Beyond Sexuality* (Chicago: University of Chicago Press, 2000), Tim Dean argues for resituating the phallus as a "provisional rather than foundational concept" with respect to the object *a* (45). Dean writes, "Whereas the phallus implies a univocal model of desire (insofar as all desiring positions are mapped in relation to a single term), object *a* implies multiple, heterogeneous possibilities for desire, especially since object *a* bears no discernable relationship to gender" (250).

7. For example, in his essay on the play's recursive temporality, "Telmah," in *Shakespeare and the Question of Theory,* ed. Patricia Parker and Geoffrey Hartman,

310–32 (New York: Methuen, 1985), Terence Hawkes cautions against "try[ing] to reconcile, to bring peace to, to *appease* a text whose vitality resides precisely in its plurality: in the fact that it contradicts itself and strenuously resists our attempts to resolve, to domesticate that contradiction" (330).

8. Paul Ricouer, *Freud and Philosophy: An Essay on Interpretation,* trans. Denis Savage (New Haven, Conn.: Yale University Press, 1970), 32–34.

9. Jean Laplanche, "Psychoanalysis as Anti-Hermeneutics," *Radical Philosophy* 79 (1996): 8. See also Jean Laplanche, "Sexuality and the Vital Order in Psychical Conflict," in *Life and Death in Psychoanalysis,* trans. Jeffrey Mehlman (Baltimore: The Johns Hopkins University Press, 1985), 25–47; and Laplanche's critique of Ricouer in "Interpreting (with) Freud," *Psychoanalysis, Culture & Society* 11 (2006): 171–84.

10. Eve Kosofsky Sedgwick, "Paranoid Reading and Reparative Reading; or, You're So Paranoid, You Probably Think This Introduction Is About You," in *Novel Gazing: Queer Readings in Fiction,* ed. Eve Kosofsky Sedgwick (Durham, N.C.: Duke University Press, 1997), 11 (original emphasis). In "Art as Symptom: Žižek and the Ethics of Psychoanalytic Criticism," *Diacritics* 33, no. 2 (2002): 21–41, Tim Dean suggests that antihermeneutic psychoanalysis may be the only truly *ethical* mode of criticism. Critiquing Slavoj Žižek's tendency to turn every text he encounters into evidence for his own interpretation of Lacan, Dean ends his essay with a provocative challenge to the assumption that interpretation is even the primary work of psychoanalytic criticism: "If psychoanalysis has a future that consists in more than merely repeating itself in ever varying contexts à la Žižek, then interpretation may prove negligible to what we want to say next about art" (41).

11. Jonathan Goldberg and Madhavi Menon, "Queering History," *PMLA* 120, no. 5 (2005): 1609. On queer temporality, see also José Esteban Muñoz, *Cruising Utopia: The Then and There of Queer Futurity* (New York: New York University Press, 2009); Madhavi Menon, *Unhistorical Shakespeare: Queer Theory in Shakespearean Literature and Film* (New York: Palgrave Macmillan, 2008); "Theorizing Queer Temporalities: A Roundtable Discussion," *GLQ: A Journal of Lesbian and Gay Studies* 13, nos. 2–3 (2007): 177–95; Heather Love, *Feeling Backward: Loss and the Politics of Queer History* (Cambridge, Mass.: Harvard University Press, 2007); Valerie Rohy, "Ahistorical," *GLQ* 12, no. 1 (2006): 61–83; Judith Halberstam, *In a Queer Time and Place: Transgender Bodies, Subcultural Lives* (New York: New York University Press, 2005); Lee Edelman, *No Future: Queer Theory and the Death Drive* (Durham, N.C.: Duke University Press, 2004); and Paul Morrison, "End Pleasure," *GLQ* 1, no. 1 (1993): 53–78.

12. Jean Laplanche, *Essays on Otherness* (New York: Routledge, 1999), 265. Laplanche describes this temporal progression using the neologism "afterwardsness," from Freud's *Nachträglichkeit*.

13. Carla Freccero, *Queer/Early/Modern* (Durham, N.C.: Duke University Press, 2005), 4.

14. Graham L. Hammill, *Sexuality and Form: Caravaggio, Marlowe, and Bacon* (Chicago: University of Chicago Press, 2000), 3.

15. Carla Mazzio and Douglas Trevor, "Dreams of History: An Introduction," in *Historicism, Psychoanalysis, and Early Modern Culture*, ed. Mazzio and Trevor, 1–18, (New York: Routledge, 2000), 1. Throughout this book, I cite and discuss many other works on the relationship between psychoanalysis and historicism. Besides these works, I am also indebted to Barbara Freedman, *Staging the Gaze: Postmodernism, Psychoanalysis, and Shakespearean Comedy* (Ithaca, N.Y.: Cornell University Press, 1991); Elizabeth J. Bellamy, *Translations of Power: Narcissism and the Unconscious in Epic History* (Ithaca, N.Y.: Cornell University Press, 1992); Juliana Schiesari, *The Gendering of Melancholia: Feminism, Psychoanalysis, and the Symbolics of Loss in Renaissance Literature* (Ithaca, N.Y.: Cornell University Press, 1992); Teresa Brennan, *History after Lacan* (New York: Routledge, 1993); Meredith Skura, "Understanding the Living and Talking to the Dead: The Historicity of Psychoanalysis," *Modern Language Quarterly* 54, no. 1 (1993): 77–89; Gayle Margherita, *The Romance of Origins: Language and Sexual Difference in Middle English Literature* (Philadelphia: University of Pennsylvania Press, 1994); Timothy Murray and Alan K. Smith, eds., *Repossessions: Psychoanalysis and the Phantasms of Early Modern Culture* (Minneapolis: University of Minnesota Press, 1999); Christopher Pye, *The Vanishing: Shakespeare, the Subject, and Early Modern Culture* (Durham, N.C.: Duke University Press, 2000); Philip Armstrong, *Shakespeare's Visual Regime: Tragedy, Psychoanalysis, and the Gaze* (New York: Palgrave Macmillan, 2001); and Elizabeth Scala, "Historicists and Their Discontents: Reading Psychoanalytically in Medieval Studies," *Texas Studies in Literature and Language* 41, no. 1 (2002): 108–31.

16. Sigmund Freud, *The Standard Edition of the Complete Psychological Works of Sigmund Freud*, 24 vols., ed. and trans. James Stratchey (London: Hogarth, 1953–74), 16:315.

17. I see more universal potential in Lacan's abstraction of the anal stage away from a single moment in infantile development: "The passage from the oral to the anal drive can be produced not by a process of maturation," he states, "but by the intervention, the overthrow, of the demand of the Other." See *The Four Fundamental Concepts of Psychoanalysis: The Seminar of Jacques Lacan, Book XI*, ed. Jacques-Alain Miller, trans. Alan Sheridan (New York: Norton, 1981), 180.

18. I am reiterating Shoshana Felman's call in "To Open the Question," in *Literature and Psychoanalysis,* ed. Felman, for a "real *dialogue* between literature and psychoanalysis, as between two different bodies of language and between two different modes of knowledge" (6). On Shakespeare's particular importance in the development of psychoanalytic thought, see Julia Reinhard Lupton and Kenneth Reinhard, *After Oedipus: Shakespeare in Psychoanalysis* (Ithaca, N.Y.: Cornell University Press, 1993); and Philip Armstrong, *Shakespeare in Psychoanalysis* (New York: Routledge, 2001).

19. David Hillman, *Shakespeare's Entrails: Belief, Skepticism, and the Interior of the Body* (New York: Palgrave Macmillan, 2007); Cynthia Marshall, *The Shattering of the Self: Violence, Subjectivity, and Early Modern Texts* (Baltimore: The Johns Hopkins University Press, 2002); and Michael C. Schoenfeldt, *Bodies and Selves in Early Modern England: Physiology and Inwardness in Spenser, Shakespeare, Herbert, and Milton* (Cambridge: Cambridge University Press, 1999).

20. Schoenfeldt, *Bodies and Selves in Early Modern England,* 15.

21. Susan Signe Morrison, *Excrement in the Late Middle Ages: Sacred Filth and Chaucer's Fecopoetics* (New York: Palgrave Macmillan, 2008), 139.

22. Norbert Elias, *The Civilizing Process,* ed. Eric Dunning, Johan Groudsblum, and Stephen Mennell, trans. Edmund Jephcott (1994; repr. Oxford: Blackwell Publishing, 2000); Mary Douglas, *Purity and Danger: An Analysis of Concepts of Pollution and Taboo* (1966; repr. New York: Routledge, 2002); Mikhail Bakhtin, *Rabelais and His World,* trans. Hélène Iswolsky (Bloomington: Indiana University Press, 1984); Julia Kristeva, *Powers of Horror: An Essay on Abjection,* trans. Leon S. Roudiez (New York: Columbia University Press, 1982); and Martha Nussbaum, *Hiding From Humanity: Shame, Disgust, and the Law* (Princeton, N.J.: Princeton University Press, 2004).

23. Besides the works by Gail Kern Paster, Bruce Boehrer, Jonathan Gil Harris, and others that I reference at greater length later in this book, see also Peter Stallybrass and Allon White, *The Politics and Poetics of Transgression* (Ithaca, N.Y.: Cornell University Press, 1986); Jeff Persels and Russell Ganim, eds., *Fecal Matters in Early Modern Literature and Art: Studies in Scatology* (Burlington, Vt.: Ashgate, 2004); and Emily Cockayne, *Hubbub: Filth, Noise, and Stench in England, 1600–1770* (New Haven, Conn.: Yale University Press, 2007).

24. Leo Bersani, "Is the Rectum a Grave?" in *AIDS: Cultural Analysis, Cultural Activism,* ed. Douglas Crimp (Cambridge, Mass.: MIT Press, 1988), 222. Bersani's work on queer sexuality and the psychoanalytic body is itself inspired by Jean Laplanche's account of the origins of sexuality in the infantile ego's pleasurable experience of its violated boundaries; see Leo Bersani, *The Freudian Body: Psychoanalysis and Art* (New York: Columbia University Press, 1986). Bersani's work has

also recently gained some prominence in early modern sexuality studies thanks to the work of Cynthia Marshall and Daniel Juan Gil. In *The Shattering of the Self,* Marshall draws on Bersani to explore the pleasure Renaissance readers take in violent spectacles, a subject I discuss at greater length myself in chapter 4. In *Before Intimacy: Asocial Sexuality in Early Modern England* (Minneapolis: University of Minnesota Press, 2006), Gil "transpose[s] Bersani's model of sexuality as a failure of a well-fashioned self into an account of sexuality as a historically conditioned failure of the functional social ties upon which selves depend" (xiii).

25. Bersani, "Is the Rectum a Grave?" 211.

26. Jeffrey Masten, "Is the Fundament a Grave?" in *The Body in Parts: Fantasies of Corporeality in Early Modern Europe,* ed. David Hillman and Carla Mazzio (New York: Routledge, 1997), 132. On the preposterous, see Patricia Parker, *Shakespeare from the Margins: Language, Culture, Context* (Chicago: University of Chicago Press, 1996), 26–27; and Jonathan Goldberg, *Sodometries: Renaissance Texts, Modern Sexualities* (Stanford, Calif.: Stanford University Press, 1992), 4.

27. Masten, "Is the Fundament a Grave?" 134.

28. Ibid., 135. See also Guy Hocquenghem, *Homosexual Desire,* trans. Daniella Dangoor (Durham, N.C.: Duke University Press, 1993), 100, 107. For similar critiques of the psychoanalytic construction of homosexuality as degeneracy, see Jonathan Goldberg, "The Anus in *Coriolanus,*" *Historicism, Psychoanalysis, and Early Modern Culture,* ed. Mazzio and Trevor, 260–71; and Eve Kosofsky Sedgwick, "Is the Rectum Straight? Identification and Identity in *The Wings of the Dove,*" in *Tendencies,* 73–103 (Durham, N.C.: Duke University Press, 1993).

29. Masten, "Is the Fundament a Grave?" 138.

30. For an extensive defense of antihomophobic practices of psychoanalysis, see Tim Dean and Christopher Lane's introduction to their *Homosexuality and Psychoanalysis,* 1–42 (Chicago: University of Chicago Press, 2001).

31. Lacan, *The Four Fundamental Concepts of Psychoanalysis,* 5 (original emphasis). In context, Lacan also links the fundamentals of psychoanalysis to the essence of comedy: both expose the object that constitutes the "truth of the subject." I return to this connection in chapter 5.

32. Celia R. Daileader, "Back Door Sex: Renaissance Gynosodomy, Aretino, and the Exotic," *ELH* 69, no. 2 (2002): 317. On this point, Daileader cites Valerie Traub, who observes in *The Renaissance of Lesbianism in Early Modern England* (Cambridge: Cambridge University Press, 2002) that "scatological disgust seethes from descriptions of female genitals across the early modern period" (104).

33. Michel Foucault, *The History of Sexuality, Volume I: An Introduction,* trans. Robert Hurley (New York: Random House, 1990), 101.

34. Valerie Traub, "The Psychomorphology of the Clitoris; or, the Reemergence of the Tribade in English Culture," in *The Renaissance of Lesbianism in Early Modern England*, 188–228.

35. On the sodomitical and anal confusion of sexual difference, see also Jonathan Goldberg, "Romeo and Juliet's Open Rs," in *Queering the Renaissance* (Durham, N.C.: Duke University Press: 1994), 218–35.

36. Douglas, *Purity and Danger*, 3. Valerie Rohy makes a similar claim: "[S]traight hegemony must represent anachronism as deviance in order to displace the burden of the ahistorical onto others — queers and people of color, each differently stigmatized as 'primitive' — and to claim for itself the role of truth, not falsification, the path of progress, not regression" ("Ahistorical," 68). On the relationship between queerness and filth in contemporary American politics, see Nussbaum's, *Hiding From Humanity* and, more recently, *From Disgust to Humanity: Sexual Orientation and Constitutional Law* (Oxford: Oxford University Press, 2010).

37. Beyond this Lacanian usage, "play" is of course an important concept in psychoanalysis. Melanie Klein's development of play therapy perhaps comes to mind first. See also D. W. Winnicott, *Playing and Reality* (1971; repr., New York: Routledge, 1991), which emphasizes play's creativity.

38. This particular reader was Ellen MacKay.

39. On the modern divide, see Linda Charnes, "The Fetish of 'the Modern,'" in *Hamlet's Heirs: Shakespeare and the Politics of a New Millennium* (New York: Routledge, 2006), 13–25; and Margreta de Grazia "The Modern Divide: From Either Side," *Journal of Medieval and Early Modern Studies* 37, no. 3 (2007): 453–67. Patricia Clare Ingham offers an incisive meditation on Renaissance novelty and medievalism in "Making All Things New: Past, Progress, and the Promise of Utopia," *Journal for Medieval and Early Modern Studies* 36, no. 3 (2006): 479–92. See also David Aers, "A Whisper in the Ear of Early Modernists; or, Reflections on Literary Critics Writing the 'History of the Subject,'" in *Culture and History 1350–1600*, ed. David Aers, 177–202 (Detroit, Mich.: Wayne State University Press, 1992); and Lee Patterson, "On the Margin: Postmodernism, Ironic History, and Medieval Studies," *Speculum* 65 (1990): 87–108.

40. Ewan Fernie, "Shakespeare and the Prospect of Presentism," *Shakespeare Survey* 58 (2005): 169.

41. Terence Hawkes, *Shakespeare in the Present* (New York: Routledge, 2002), 5.

42. I have argued at greater length for the expansion of presentism's purview in "Reading Like a Sodomite: Deleuze, Donne, Eliot, Presentism, and the Modern Renaissance," *Rhizomes: Cultural Studies in Emerging Knowledge* 17 (2008): www.rhizomes.net/issue17/stockton.html.

43. Michel Foucault, "The Confession of the Flesh," *Power/Knowledge: Selected Interviews and Other Writings, 1972–1977,* ed. Colin Gordon (New York: Pantheon Books, 1980), 209.

44. Ibid., 211.

45. Ibid., 213–14 (emphasis added).

46. Jean Baudrillard, *Forget Foucault* (Cambridge, Mass.: MIT Press, 2007).

1. The Wandering Anus

1. David Riggs, *Ben Jonson: A Life* (Cambridge, Mass.: Harvard, 1989), 241.

2. Ibid., 240–41.

3. Ibid., 241.

4. All quotations from Jonson's works are drawn from *Ben Jonson,* ed. C. H. Herford, Percy Simpson, and Evelyn Simpson, 11 vols. (Oxford: Clarendon Press, 1925–52).

5. Riggs, *Ben Jonson,* 243.

6. Ibid.

7. As I am using it, the concept of the grotesque feminine derives from Mikhail Bakhtin's distinction between grotesque and classical bodies in *Rabelais and His World.* Whereas the classical body is contained and proportioned, the grotesque body "discloses its essence as a principle of growth which exceeds its own limits in copulation, pregnancy, childbirth, the throes of death, eating, drinking, or defecation" (26). In "Patriarchal Territories: The Body Enclosed," in *Rewriting the Renaissance: The Discourses of Sexual Difference in Early Modern Europe,* ed. Margaret W. Ferguson, Maureen Quilligan, and Nancy J. Vickers, 123–42 (Chicago: University of Chicago Press, 1986), Peter Stallybrass argues that the difference between classical and grotesque bodies is also a difference in gender, where the female body is imagined as naturally grotesque — loquacious and sexually promiscuous. This argument has been significantly developed by Gail Kern Paster's study of women as "leaky vessels" in *The Body Embarrassed: Drama and the Disciplines of Shame in Early Modern England* (Ithaca, N.Y.: Cornell University Press, 1993), 23–63; and Jonathan Gil Harris's exploration of early modern England's gendered plumbing in "This Is Not a Pipe: Water Supply, Incontinent Sources, and the Leaky Body Politic," in *Enclosure Acts: Sexuality, Property, and Culture in Early Modern England,* ed. Richard Burt and John Michael Archer, 203–28 (Ithaca, N.Y.: Cornell University Press, 1994).

8. Edmund Wilson, "Morose Ben Jonson," in *The Triple Thinkers: Twelve Essays on Literary Subjects* (New York: Oxford University Press, 1948), 213–32.

9. Freud makes his classic statement of anal erotic character traits in "Character and Anal Eroticism," in *Standard Edition,* 9:169–75. See also Ernst Jones,

"Anal-Erotic Character Traits," in *Papers on Psycho-analysis* (London: Baillière, Tindall, and Cox, 1950), 413–37.

10. E. Pearlman, "Ben Jonson: An Anatomy," *English Literary Renaissance* 9 (1979): 366; also quoted in Bruce Boehrer, *The Fury of Men's Gullets: Ben Jonson and the Digestive Canal* (Philadelphia: University of Pennsylvania Press, 1997), 9.

11. Boehrer, *The Fury of Men's Gullets,* 9

12. Riggs, *Ben Jonson,* 31. See also Boehrer, *The Fury of Men's Gullets,* 9–10.

13. Boehrer, *The Fury of Men's Gullets,* 11.

14. Ibid., 12. See also 168–69.

15. Norman O. Brown, *Life against Death: The Psychoanalytical Meaning of History* (Middletown, Conn.: Wesleyan University Press, 1959), 3–10. See also Freud, *Civilization and Its Discontents,* in *Standard Edition,* 21:57–145.

16. Boehrer, *The Fury of Men's Gullets,* 12–13.

17. Freud, *Standard Edition,* 21:96–97.

18. Brown, *Life against Death,* 6.

19. Riggs, *Ben Jonson,* 243–44.

20. Joan Copjec, *Read My Desire: Lacan against the Historicists* (Cambridge, Mass.: MIT Press, 1994), 14 (original emphasis).

21. Bruce R. Smith, *Homosexual Desire in Shakespeare's England: A Cultural Poetics* (Chicago: University of Chicago Press, 1993), 12.

22. In other words, I want neither to evade nor to dwell on the differences between psychoanalysis and historicism. Rather, I agree with Jeffrey Jerome Cohen that historicism is not "a monolithic practice — and there is no 'other' to it: meaning that historicism has to be part of any critical encounter with the past. It is the *sine qua non* that enables other, potentially unhistorical modes." See "Time out of Memory," in *The Post-Historical Middle Ages,* ed. Elizaebth Scala and Sylvia Frederico (New York: Palgrave Macmillan, 2009), 61 n37.

23. Foucault, *The History of Sexuality,* 81–82.

24. In "The Experience of the Outside: Foucault and Psychoanalysis," in *Lacan in America,* ed. Jean-Michel Rabaté, 309–47 (New York: Other Press, 2000), Christopher Lane cites this passage as an example of Foucault's "obvious debt to Lacan" (323 n27), but there remains a difference in Lacan's method of relating desire and the law, as I will argue. On Foucault's ambivalent relationship to psychoanalysis more generally, see also Jacques Derrida, "'To Do Justice to Freud': The History of Madness in the Age of Psychoanalysis," trans. Pascale-Anne Brault and Michel Naas, *Critical Inquiry* 20, no. 2 (1994): 227–66; and Jacques-Alain Miller, "Michel Foucault and Psychoanalysis," *Michel Foucault, Philosopher,* ed. Timothy J. Armstrong, 58–64 (London: Harvester Wheatsheaf, 1992).

25. Slavoj Žižek, *The Sublime Object of Ideology* (New York: Routledge, 1989), 74–75.

26. Copjec, *Read My Desire,* 24–25 (original emphasis).

27. For the original French, see Michel Foucault, *Histoire de la sexualité: La volonté de savoir* (Paris: Gallimard, 1976), 108.

28. Copjec, *Read My Desire,* 25.

29. Freud, *Standard Edition,* 8:101.

30. Laplanche, "Psychoanalysis as Anti-hermeneutics," 11.

31. Alan Stewart, *Close Readers: Humanism and Sodomy in Early Modern England* (Princeton, N.J.: Princeton University Press, 1997), xx.

32. Jonson, *Ben Jonson,* 8:615–16.

33. Stephen Guy-Bray considers alternative uses of the reproductive metaphor in *Against Reproduction: Where Renaissance Texts Come From* (Toronto: University of Toronto Press, 2010). He argues that many writers in the Renaissance queerly manipulate the metaphor, resisting the justification of art through social and political utility (symbolized and achieved through reproduction). Although doing so is outside the scope of this chapter, Guy-Bray's thesis would be interesting to measure against Jonson's own use of the reproductive metaphor and his own insistence on his art's worth and value.

34. Jonson, *Ben Jonson,* 8:587–88.

35. Ibid., 8:585.

36. Dominique Laporte, *History of Shit,* trans. Nadia Benabid and Rodolphe el-Khoury (Cambridge: MIT Press, 2002), 1–7.

37. See Ben Saunders, "Iago's Clyster: Purgation, Anality, and the Civilizing Process," *Shakespeare Quarterly* 55, no. 2 (2004): 161–62; and Henry Jephson, *The Sanitary Evolution of London* (London: T. Fisher Unwin, 1907). For a history of sanitation in modern Europe, see David Inglis, *A Sociological History of Excretory Experience: Defecatory Manners and Toiletry Technologies* (Lewiston, Maine: Edwin Mellen, 2001).

38. Laporte, *History of Shit,* 13.

39. Ibid., 7.

40. Jonson, *Ben Jonson,* 8:588.

41. Laporte, *History of Shit,* 14. I cite Laporte on these points, but much of this chapter was actually inspired by Samuel Delany's book on the effort to "clean up" New York City's Times Square in the late 1990s. See *Times Square Red, Times Square Blue* (New York: NYU Press, 1999).

42. Richard Helgerson, "Ben Jonson," *The Cambridge Companion to English Poetry: Donne to Marvell,* ed. Thomas Corns (Cambridge: Cambridge University Press, 1996), 152.

43. Besides Boehrer's analysis of the poem in *The Fury of Men's Gullets,* 161–66, see also his essay "Horatian Satire in Jonson's 'On the Famous Voyage,'" *Criticism* 44, no. 1 (2002): 9–26; Andrew McRae, "'On the Famous Voyage': Ben Jonson and Civic Space," *Early Modern Literary Studies* 3 (September 1998), http://purl .oclc.org/emls/04-2/mcraonth.htm; Sara van den Berg, *The Action of Ben Jonson's Poetry* (Newark: University of Delaware Press, 1987), 103–8; and Peter E. Medine, "Object and Intent in Jonson's 'Famous Voyage,'" *Studies in English Literature* 15 (1975): 97–110.

44. For a discussion of the sink of the body with reference to the period's gynecological and midwifery treatises, see Traub, *The Renaissance of Lesbianism in Early Modern England,* 104–7.

45. Boehrer, *The Fury of Men's Gullets,* 162.

46. Laporte, *History of Shit,* 14.

47. Ibid., 12–13.

48. Sir John Harington, *A New Discourse on a Stale Subject, Called the Metamorphosis of Ajax,* ed. Elizabeth Story Donno (New York: Columbia University Press, 1962), 21. Subsequent references to this text will be noted parenthetically.

49. Gilles Deleuze and Félix Guattari, *Anti-Oedipus: Capitalism and Schizophrenia,* trans. Brian Massumi (Minneapolis: University of Minnesota Press, 1987), 143.

50. Gail Kern Paster, "The Epistemology of the Water Closet: John Harington's *Metamorphosis of Ajax* and Elizabethan Technologies of Shame," in *Material Culture and Cultural Materialism in the Middle Ages and Renaissance,* ed. Curtis Perry (Turhout, Belgium: Brepolis, 2001), 152, 142.

51. Ibid., 152.

52. Ibid., 154.

53. On Jonson's alimentary metaphors for composition, see Bruce Boehrer, "A Well-Digested Work," in *The Fury of Men's Gullets,* 112–46; and Joseph Lowenstein, "The Jonsonian Corpulence, or The Poet as Mouthpiece," *ELH* 53 (1986): 491–518.

54. Besides Paster's and Boehrer's work, see Julian Yates, "Under the Sign of (A)jax; or, The Smell of History," in *Error, Misuse, Failure: Object Lessons from the English Renaissance* (Minneapolis: University of Minnesota Press, 2003), 67–100; and Jason Scott-Warren, "Privy Politics," in *Sir John Harington and the Book as Gift* (Oxford: Oxford University Press, 2001), 56–80.

55. Paster, "The Epistemology of the Water Closet," 140.

56. Harington actually appends to *The Metamorphosis* a lengthy apology in which he imagines being indicted "at a privie Sessions" (209) by a group of Rabelaisians. At first the Rabelaisians are delighted with the text: "they sayd it was scurrill, base, shallow, sordidous; the dittie, the dirge, the etymologie, the

pictures, gave matter of jest, of scorne, of derision, of contempt. . . . [T]hey were so pleased with it, they were readie to untrusse, and thought to have gone to it presently." Only when they discover the meaning of Misacmos ("Hater of Filth") do they realize Harington's actual agenda: "It was such a jerke, that they were halfe out of countenance with it; swounds saith one of them, this fellow is an enemie to us, for we are counted but filthie fellowes among the grave gray-beardes" (208).

57. Boehrer, *The Fury of Men's Gullets,* 167.

58. Paster offers a similar interpretation: "To find defecation more pleasurable than sex is the happiness of finding erotic satisfactions within the physiological circuits of one's own body — the pleasures of an anal eroticism that in Freudian etiology is undifferentiated by gender but that here, unusually, seems specific to the male and to the heterosexually credentialled [sic] male at that ("The Epistemology of the Water Closet," 150).

59. Yates, *Error, Misuse, Failure,* 91. On the laws of urinary segregation, see Jacques Lacan, "The Instance of the Letter in the Unconscious, or Reason since Freud," in *Écrits: A Selection,* trans. Bruce Fink (New York: Norton, 2002), 143.

60. Paster, "The Epistemology of the Water Closet," 145.

61. Freud, *Standard Edition,* 8:100.

62. Paster, "The Epistemology of the Water Closet," 146.

63. Juliet Mitchell, *Mad Men and Medusas: Reclaiming Hysteria* (New York: Basic Books, 2000), 19.

64. Wayne Koestenbaum, *Double Talk: The Erotics of Male Literary Collaboration* (New York: Routledge, 1989), 18. On the reproductive homoerotics of literary collaboration in the Renaissance, see Jeffrey Masten, *Textual Intercourse: Collaboration, Authorship, and Sexualities in Renaissance Drama* (Cambridge: Cambridge University Press, 1997).

65. Koestenbaum, *Double Talk,* 19.

2. Shakespeare's Ass

1. Patricia Parker, *Literary Fat Ladies: Rhetoric, Gender, Property* (London: Methuen, 1987); and *Shakespeare from the Margins: Language, Culture, Context,* especially chapter four, "'Illegitimate Construction': Translation, Adultery, and Mechanical Reproduction in *The Merry Wives of Windsor,*" 116–48. In "Once More into the Preech: The Merry Wives' English Pedagogy," *Shakespeare Quarterly* 55, no. 4 (2004): 420–49, David Landreth builds on Parker's work to suggest a correlation between linguistic and sexual discipline that one might also perceive in my own argument about *Merry Wives.* For another wide-ranging discussion of the poetics of translation in the Renaissance, see Judith H. Anderson, *Translating*

Investments: Metaphor and the Dynamic of Cultural Change in Tudor-Stuart England (New York: Fordham University Press, 2005).

2. See Frank Whigham, "Reading Social Conflict in the Alimentary Tract: More on the Body in Renaissance Drama," *ELH* 55, no. 2 (1988): 333–50.

3. "ass, *n2*," *The Oxford English Dictionary Online:* http://dictionary.oed.com. All *OED Online* references were verified in October 2008.

4. Gordon Williams, *A Dictionary of Sexual Language and Imagery in Shakespearean and Stuart Literature,* 3 vols. (London: Athlone, 1994).

5. Paster, *The Body Embarrassed,* 126n.

6. Deborah Baker Wyrick, "The Ass Motif in *The Comedy of Errors* and *A Midsummer Night's Dream*," *Shakespeare Quarterly* 33, no. 3 (1982): 432–48.

7. Frankie Rubenstein, *A Dictionary of Shakespeare's Sexual Puns and Their Significance* (London: Macmillan, 1989), 17.

8. Annabel Patterson, *Shakespeare and the Popular Voice* (Cambridge: Basil Blackwell, 1989), 66.

9. Mario DiGangi, *The Homoerotics of Early Modern Drama* (Cambridge: Cambridge University Press, 1997), 64–65.

10. "butt, *n4*," *OED Online.* The *OED* cites Beaumont and Fletcher's *Custom of the Country* (1616) as the first use of *butt* to refer to "an object at which ridicule, scorn, or abuse, is aimed."

11. Susan Purdie, *Comedy: The Mastery of Discourse* (Toronto: University of Toronto Press, 1993), 59.

12. For a Bakhtinian reading of Falstaff's body, see Jonathan Hall, "The Evacuations of Falstaff *(The Merry Wives of Windsor),*" in *Shakespeare and Carnival: After Bakhtin,* ed. Rowland Knowles, 123–51 (New York: St. Martin's Press, 1998). My ability to think Falstaff's body in relation to the body politic also owes much to Valerie Traub, "Prince Hal's Falstaff: Positioning Psychoanalysis and the Female Reproductive Body," in *Desire and Anxiety: Circulations of Sexuality in Shakespearean Drama,* 50–70 (New York: Routledge, 1992).

13. See Margreta de Grazia, "Homonyms before and after Lexical Standardization," *Deutsche Shakespeare-Gesellschaft West Jahrbuch* (1990): 143–56; and Mary Bly, *Queer Virgins and Virgin Queans on the Early Modern Stage* (Oxford: Oxford University Press, 2000), 11–12.

14. Michael Moon and Eve Kosofsky Sedgwick, "Divinity: A Dossier, a Performance Piece, a Little Understood Emotion," *Discourse* 13, no. 1 (1990–91): 27 (original emphasis).

15. Purdie, *Comedy,* 59 (original emphasis).

16. On the wives' empowerment within the gendered space of the household, see Wendy Wall, *Staging Domesticity: Household Work and English Identity in*

Early Modern Drama (Oxford: Oxford University Press, 2002), 90–93 and 112–26; and Nastasha Korda, "'Judicious oeillades': Supervising Marital Property in *The Merry Wives of Windsor*," in *Marxist Shakespeares,* ed. Jean E. Howard and Scott Cutler Shershow, 82–103 (New York: Routledge, 2001). To this equation of domesticity and power, Pamela Allen Brown adds that *Merry Wives* may appeal to female spectators through its demonstration of the power of women to jest; see "Near Neighbors, Women's Wars, and Merry Wives," in *Better a Shrew Than a Sheep: Women, Drama, and the Culture of Jest in Early Modern England* (Ithaca, N.Y.: Cornell University Press, 2003), 33–55.

17. Thomas Nashe mentions Gillian of Brentford and her will once in Will Summer's prologue to *Summer's Last Will and Testament* and once in a letter to William Cotton; see Thomas Nashe, *The Works of Thomas Nashe,* ed. Ronald B. McKerrow, 5 vols. (Oxford: Basil Blackwell, 1958), 3:235 and 5:195. For further speculation on Gillian of Brentford and her significance in the play, see Mary Ellen Lamb, *The Popular Culture of Shakespeare, Spenser, and Jonson* (New York: Routledge, 2007), 141–43.

18. "prat, *n3,*" *OED.* The first definition for the noun *prat* is slang for *buttocks.* A 1567 text provides the first recorded evidence of this usage.

19. On Ford's anxieties, see Nancy Cotton, "Castrating (W)itches: Impotence and Magic in *The Merry Wives of Windsor*," *Shakespeare Quarterly* 38, no. 3 (1987): 320–26.

20. In *Sodometries,* Jonathan Goldberg warns against the potential misogyny and homophobia of reductively reading Falstaff as feminine (172).

21. Rosemary Kegl, *The Rhetoric of Concealment: Figuring Class and Gender in Renaissance Literature* (Ithaca, N.Y.: Cornell University Press, 1994), 79, 78.

22. Ibid., 85.

23. Stanley Wells and Gary Taylor, *William Shakespeare: A Textual Companion* (New York: Norton, 1997), 343.

24. Rubenstein's often wild *Dictionary of Shakespeare's Sexual Puns* offers the most complete treatment of possible scatological puns on names in *Merry Wives.* See the following entries from which I have drawn the etymology of the puns offered here: *Anne* (10), *Caius* (43), and *colour/choler/collier* (52–53).

25. This recognition is itself attributable to Patricia Parker's analysis of the play, particularly her focus on Mistress Quickly's obscene misconstructions of Latin words in 4.1 ("'Illegitimate Construction,'" 116–18).

26. A. C. Bradley, *Oxford Lectures on Poetry* (London: Macmillan, 1959), 248. In the 1980s, some critics do try to account for Falstaff's (mis)treatment in both theoretical and genre terms. In "Falstaff's Punishment: Buffoonery as Defensive Posture in *The Merry Wives of Windsor*," *Shakespeare Studies* 14 (1981): 163–74,

Barbara Freedman makes the psychoanalytically influenced argument that Falstaff, as the play's clown, actually solicits his own abuse. In "Falstaff and the Comic Community," in *Shakespeare's "Rough Magic": Essays in Honor of C. L. Barber,* ed. Peter Erickson and Coppélia Kahn, 131–48 (Newark: University of Delaware Press, 1985), Anne Barton argues that Falstaff is a properly historical character who Shakespeare misplaces in a comedy. For a critical history of the play prior to the 1980s, see Jeanne Addison Roberts, *Shakespeare's English Comedy: "The Merry Wives of Windsor" in Context* (Lincoln: University of Nebraska Press, 1979), 84–118.

27. Walter Cohen, "Introduction to *The Merry Wives of Windsor*," in *The Norton Shakespeare,* ed. Greenblatt et al., 1261.

28. Ibid. This misgiving was more pronounced in the first edition of the Norton, published in 1997. There Cohen wrote of the "dubious decision by the Fords and Pages to subject Falstaff to one more round of abuse, even though they are confident that he no longer poses a threat" (1231).

29. Jerry Aline Flieger, *The Purloined Punch Line: Freud's Comic Theory and the Postmodern Text* (Baltimore: The Johns Hopkins University Press, 1991), 77. Flieger is developing Freud's claim that the "urge to tell the joke to someone is inextricably bound up with the joke-work: indeed, this urge is so strong that it often is carried through with serious misgivings. A joke *must* be told to someone else" (*Standard Edition,* 8:143).

30. Richard Helgerson, "Language Lessons: Linguistic Colonialism, Linguistic Postcolonialism, and the Early Modern English Nation," *The Yale Journal of Criticism* 11, no. 1 (1998): 289–99.

31. On the Garter Ceremony, see Peter Erickson, "The Order of the Garter, the Cult of Elizabeth, and Class–Gender Tension in *The Merry Wives of Windsor*," in *Shakespeare Reproduced: The Text in History and Ideology,* ed. Jean E. Howard, 116–40 (London: Methuen, 1987); and Cohen, "Introduction to *The Merry Wives of Windsor*," 1257.

32. Kegl, *The Rhetoric of Concealment,* 79 (original emphasis).

33. This distinction belongs to Erickson, "The Order of the Garter," 124.

34. Cohen, "Introduction to *The Merry Wives of Windsor*," 1261.

35. In "*The Merry Wives of Windsor:* Domestic Nationalism and the Refuse of the Realm," in *The Popular Culture of Shakespeare, Spenser, and Jonson,* 124–59, Mary Ellen Lamb offers a wonderful analysis of the way these figures of the prodigal gentry double the vagrant poor as "refuse of the realm," yet her analysis proceeds largely with reference to the cultural poetics of economic consumption rather than to the play's scatology.

36. After Falstaff admits that he has been "made an ass," Ford adds "Ay, and an ox too. Both proofs are extant" (5.5.116). Vin Nardizzi reminds me that Falstaff

is also a "woodman" (5.5.24–25) — not simply a womanizing hunter but more literally *timber.* See his essay "Felling Falstaff in Windsor Park," in *Ecocritical Shakespeare,* ed. Dan Brayton and Lynn Bruckner (Burlington, Vt.: Ashgate: 2011).

37. Lacan, *The Four Fundamental Concepts of Psychoanalysis,* 178.

38. Ibid., 180.

3. Happy Endings

1. David Fountain, "Why Was It Worth it?" Exodus International, http://exodus.to/content/view/555/149/. All citations from the Exodus Web site were current as of September 2010.

2. Exodus International, "Policy Statements," http://exodus.to/content/view/34/118/. Of course, a "Godly single life" is presumably a celibate life and thus not a sexually satisfied one, and one's ability to sustain a "lifelong and healthy marriage" can really only be determined after one has died. As visual indicators of transformation, both single celibacy and lifelong marital commitment seem particularly superficial.

3. Tanya Erzen, *Straight to Jesus: Sexual and Christian Conversion in the Ex-Gay Movement* (Berkeley and Los Angeles: University of California Press, 2006), 14. On Exodus International, see 42–51.

4. Ibid., 14.

5. Ibid., 3.

6. Smith, *Homosexual Desire in Shakespeare's England,* 11 (original emphasis). See also Alan Bray, *Homosexuality in Renaissance England* (New York: Columbia University Press, 1995), 16–17.

7. Exodus International, "Policy Statements."

8. On essentializing and minoritizing discourses of sexual identity, see Eve Kosofsky Sedgwick, *The Epistemology of the Closet* (Berkeley and Los Angeles: University of California Press, 1990), 40–44.

9. On the historicity of heterosexuality, see Jonathan Ned Katz, *The Invention of Heterosexuality* (New York: Dutton, 1995); Karma Lochrie, *Heterosyncrasies: Female Sexuality When Normal Wasn't* (Minneapolis: University of Minnesota Press, 2005); James A. Shultz, *Courtly Love, the History of Courtliness, and the History of Sexuality* (Chicago: University of Chicago Press, 2006); and Rebecca Ann Bach, *Shakespeare and Renaissance Literature before Heterosexuality* (New York: Palgrave Macmillan, 2007).

10. I follow Lars Engle, "Shakespearean Normativity in *All's Well That Ends Well,*" *Shakespeare International Yearbook* 4 (2004): 264–78, in using the term *norm* to describe a contestable moral proscription. Engle argues that *All's Well* encourages a skeptical discussion of norms of military behavior and chastity. For a

critique of the statistical basis of norms that underwrites most uses of the term *heteronormative*, see Lochrie, *Heterosyncrasies.*

11. See, for instance, Alan Bray's work on eighteenth-century mollies as prototypical male homosexuals ("Molly," in *Homosexuality in Renaissance England,* 81–114); and Mary Bly, *Queer Virgins and Virgin Queens,* on the queer community of the First Whitefriar's theater in Renaissance London. Some Renaissance historians also explicitly acknowledge their desire to shape the early modern past through the lens of modern homosexual identification. Thus, Bruce Smith writes of his "attempt to consolidate gay identity in the last decade of the twentieth century, to help men whose sexual desire is turned towards other men realize that they have not only a present community but a past history" (*Homosexual Desire in Shakespeare's England,* 27). Likewise, in *The Renaissance of Lesbianism in Early Modern England,* Valerie Traub strategically employs the anachronistic term *lesbian* in order to forge a genealogy of lesbian desire that "begins" in the Renaissance.

12. On *Troilus and Cressida,* see Jonathan Gil Harris, "Canker/Serpego and Value: Gerard Malynes, *Troilus and Cressida,*" in *Sick Economies: Drama, Mercantilism, and Disease in Shakespeare's England* (Philadelphia: University of Pennsylvania Press, 2004), 83–107; and Linda Charnes, "'So Unsecret to Ourselves': Notorious Identity and the Material Subject in *Troilus and Cressida,*" in *Notorious Identity: Materializing the Subject in Shakespeare* (Cambridge, Mass.: Harvard University Press, 1993), 70–102. On *Measure for Measure,* see Catherine Cox, "'Lord Have Mercy Upon Us': The King, the Pestilence, and Shakespeare's *Measure for Measure,*" *Exemplaria* 20, no. 4 (2008): 430–57.

13. David Scott Kastan, "*All's Well That Ends Well* and the Limits of Comedy," *ELH* 52, no. 3 (1985): 579. On the problem of ending in *All's Well,* see also Ian Donaldson, "*All's Well That Ends Well:* Shakespeare's Play of Endings," *Essays in Criticism* 27 (1977): 34–55; and Susan Snyder "'The king's not here': Displacement and Deferral in *All's Well That Ends Well,*" *Shakespeare Quarterly* 43, no. 1 (1992): 20–32.

14. I follow the Norton in using the name Helen rather than Helena.

15. Parker, *Shakespeare from the Margins,* 211–15.

16. On sodomy's unnatural productivity and its connection to usury, see Will Fisher, "Queer Money," *ELH* 66, no. 1 (1999): 1–23.

17. Without making the connection to sodomy, Michael D. Friedman argues this point in "Service is no heritage': Bertram and the Ideology of Procreation," *Studies in Philology* 92 (1995): 80–101.

18. Garret A. Sullivan Jr., *Memory and Forgetting in English Renaissance Drama: Shakespeare, Marlowe, Webster* (Cambridge: Cambridge University Press, 2005), 57.

19. Goldberg, *Sodometries,* 19 (emphasis mine).

20. Jonathan Dollimore, *Sexual Dissidence: Augustine to Wilde, Freud to Foucault* (Oxford: Oxford University Press, 1991), 121.

21. For the classic discussion of women's time, see Julia Kristeva, "Women's Time," trans. Alice Jardine and Harry Blake, *The Kristeva Reader,* ed. Toril Moi, 188–213 (New York: Columbia University Press, 1986). See also Patricia Parker on temporality and pregnancy, inflation and narrative dilation, in her discussion of *All's Well* in *Shakespeare from the Margins,* 185–218.

22. We can also cast the question of whether Helen receives her due in terms of the temporal conflicts endemic to the Lacanian drives. Because the attainment of one's due is a structural impossibility — because the attainment of one's object of desire can only be achieved through the fictional stop-gap of a happy ending — the coming hour is forever, and constitutively, delayed. The temporal structure of the drives forms the basis for Lee Edelman's antisocial and apolitical formation of queerness in *No Future.* See also Adrian Johnston, *Time Driven: Metapsychology and the Splitting of the Drive* (Evanston, Ill.: Northwestern University Press, 2005).

23. Halberstam, *In a Queer Time and Place,* 153.

24. See Richard P. Wheeler, *Shakespeare's Development and the Problem Comedies: Turn and Counter-Turn* (Berkeley and Los Angeles: University of California Press, 1981), 35–45; and Janet Adelman, *Suffocating Mothers: Fantasies of Maternal Origin in Shakespeare's Plays, "Hamlet" to "The Tempest"* (New York: Routledge, 1992), 76–86.

25. On war and sodomy, see Smith, *Homosexual Desire in Shakespeare's England,* 59–61; Gregory W. Bredbeck, *Sodomy and Interpretation: Marlowe to Milton* (Ithaca, N.Y.: Cornell University Press, 1991), 33–48; and Jonathan Goldberg, "The Anus in *Coriolanus.*" While it is possible to read horses as mediating male homoerotic desires, it is also quite possible that they are not simply, as it were, the middle men. Consider Hostpur's punning retort to his wife in *1 Henry IV:* "Come, wilt thou see my ride? / And when I am a-horseback, I will swear / I love thee infinitely" (2.4.92–94); and the conversation between the constable, Rambures, Orléans, and Bourbon in *Henry V* (3.7).

26. D. A. Miller, "Anal *Rope,*" in *Inside/Out: Lesbian Theories, Gay Theories,* ed. Diana Fuss (New York: Routledge, 1991), 134. See also Lee Edelman, "*Rear Window* 's Glasshole," in *Out Takes: Essays on Queer Theory and Film,* ed. Ellis Hanson, 72–96 (Durham, N.C.: Duke University Press, 1999); and Kathryn Bond Stockton, "When Are Dirty Details and Scenes Compelling? Tucked in the Cuts of Interracial Anal Rape," in *Beautiful Bottom, Beautiful Shame: When "Black" Meets "Queer"* (Durham, N.C.: Duke University Press, 2006), 101–47.

27. Miller, "Anal *Rope,*" 134.

28. Ibid., 130 (original emphasis).

29. David McCandless, "Helena's Bed-trick: Gender and Performance in *All's Well That Ends Well*," *Shakespeare Quarterly* 45, no. 4 (1994): 450.

30. Both this chapter and the next draw comparisons between early modern and film media. For a substantive discussion of the theoretical basis for such comparisons, see Richard Burt, *Medieval and Early Modern Film and Media* (New York: Palgrave Macmillan, 2008).

31. See Bruce Thomas Boehrer, "The Privy and Its Double: Scatology and Satire in Shakespeare's Theater," in *A Companion to Shakespeare's Works: Volume IV: The Poems, Problem Comedies, Late Plays,* ed. Richard Dutton and Jean E. Howard (New York: Blackwell, 2003), 83–85; Sujata Iyengar, "'Handling Soft the Hurts': Sexual Healing and Manual Contact in *Orlando Furioso, The Faerie Queene,* and *All's Well That Ends Well*," in *Sensible Flesh: On Touch in Early Modern Culture,* ed. Elizabeth D. Harvey (Philadelphia: University of Pennsylvania Press, 2003), 53; Bard C. Cosman, "*All's Well That Ends Well:* Shakespeare's Treatment of Anal Fistulas," *Upstart Crow* 19 (1999): 78–97; and Whigham, "Reading Social Conflict in the Alimentary Tract," 337–38.

32. Andrew Boorde, *The Breuiary of Healthe* (London, 1542), confirms that fistulas are "most commonlye ... in a man's foundament" (H1), as does the author of *An Account of the Causes of Some Particular Rebellious Distempers* (London, 1547), fol. 58. Both sources are quoted in Iyengar, "'Handling Soft the Hurts,'" 53. If, as Iyengar reports, anal fistulas were a common consequence of horseback riding, and a cause of concern for men in war, the king's might be understood to manifest the consequences of Paroles's own call to war. In *Shakespeare from the Margins,* Patricia Parker also argues for Paroles's association with the fistula through the proverbial association of loquacity with mental leakage (195).

33. In "'Doctor She': Healing and Sex in *All's Well That Ends Well*," in *A Companion to Shakespeare's Works: Volume IV,* ed. Dutton and Howard, 333–46, Barbara Howard Traister offers a compelling discussion of Helen as an empiric, or an unlicensed physician, whose ministrations the king likens to those of a prostitute: "I say we must not / So stain our judgment or corrupt our hope / To prostitute our past-cure malady / To empirics" (2.1.117–20). Also contributing to the erotic overtones of Helen's cure is Lefeu's likening of himself to "Cressid's uncle" (2.1.96).

34. Wendy Wall, "Tending to Bodies and Boys: Queer Physic in *The Knight of the Burning Pestle,*" in *Staging Domesticity,* 161–88.

35. See John Arderne, *Treatises of Fistula in Ano, Haemorrhoids, and Clysters,* ed. D'Arcy Power (Oxford: Oxford University Press, 1968). As Jeffrey Masten observes, in Arderne's text "the fundament is assuredly not a grave[;] ... it

becomes the foundation or seat of knowledge, which is *set* forth and *set* down (as foundation, basis, groundwork), and, following the cure, the foundation of a castle of health for its patients" ("Is the Fundament a Grave?" 137 [original emphasis]). In Shakespeare's play, by contrast, the fistula promises death, and its cure is constructed as a miracle rather than something that can be explained.

36. Kiernan Ryan, "'Where hope is coldest': *All's Well That Ends Well*," in *Spiritual Shakespeares,* ed. Ewan Fernie, 28–49 (New York: Routledge, 2005). See also Helen Wilcox, "Shakespeare's Miracle Play? Religion in *All's Well, That Ends Well*," in *All's Well, That Ends Well: New Critical Essays,* ed. Gary Waller, 191–214 (New York: Routledge, 2006).

37. Jonathan Gil Harris, "All Swell That End Swell: Dropsy, Phantom Pregnancy, and the Sound of Deconception in *All's Well That Ends Well*," *Renaissance Drama* 35 (2006): 181–82.

38. On the anus as an "improper vessel" for semen, see Richard Halpern, *Shakespeare's Perfume: Sodomy and Sublimation in the Sonnets, Wilde, Freud, and Lacan* (Philadelphia: University of Pennsylvania Press, 2002), 20–21.

39. Stanley Wells, *Looking for Sex in Shakespeare* (Cambridge: Cambridge University Press, 2004), 69. Wells characterizes a lewd interpreter as one whose sexual interpretations "proceed from what once would have been considered 'dirty minds,' rather than from the imaginations of the dramatist and of his early audiences" (2). Besides the obviously different suppositions with which Wells and I go looking for sex in Shakespeare, I find it curious that Wells borrows the phrase "lewd interpreters" from *The Merchant of Venice*'s Portia, one of Shakespeare's master manipulators of sexual signifiers. For more on lewd interpretation, see chapter 1 of this book.

40. Harris, "All Swell That End Swell," 184. On the soundscapes of the early modern theater, see also Bruce R. Smith, *The Acoustic World of Early Modern England: Attending to the O-Factor* (Chicago: University of Chicago Press, 1999).

41. Snyder, "'The king's not here,'" 23.

42. Stephen Orgel, *Impersonations: The Performance of Gender in Shakespeare's England* (Cambridge: Cambridge University Press, 1996), 76.

43. Daileader, "Back Door Sex."

44. In "'Twas mine, 'twas Helen's': Rings of Desire in *All's Well, That Ends Well*," in *All's Well, That Ends Well: New Critical Essays,* ed. Waller, 255–76, Nicholas Ray also reads the rings as anal signifiers that mediate male homoerotic and homosocial desires. I am more interested, however, in the way the rings also work to trope the vagina as anal.

45. Samuel Johnson, *Notes to Shakespeare,* ed. Arthur Sherbo, Augustan Reprint Society 60 (Los Angeles: Augustan Reprint Society, 1956), 114–15.

46. To further the comparison with *Merchant*, it seems significant that Portia excuses herself from Belmont under the pretense of going to a monastery (3.4.26–32).

47. Natalie Zemon Davis, *Society and Culture in Early Modern France* (Stanford, Calif.: Stanford University Press, 1975), 130. On *Merchant*'s Portia as a woman on top, see Karen Newman, "Portia's Ring: Unruly Women and Structures of Exchange in *The Merchant of Venice*," *Shakespeare Quarterly* 38, no. 1 (1987): 19–33. On the much-discussed problem of Helen's feminist agency, see especially McCandless, "Helena's Bed-trick"; and Kathryn Schwarz, "'My intents are fix'd': Constant Will in *All's Well That Ends Well*," *Shakespeare Quarterly* 58, no. 2 (2007): 200–27.

48. On the difference in male and female "waters," see Gail Kern Paster's discussion of Thomas Middleton's *A Chaste Maid in Cheapside* in *The Body Embarrassed*, 57.

49. Madhavi Menon, *Wanton Words: Rhetoric and Sexuality in English Renaissance Drama* (Toronto: University of Toronto Press, 2004), 86.

50. Ibid.

51. Ibid. Menon actually uses the name Helena.

52. Ibid., 89.

53. Henri Bergson, *Laughter: An Essay in the Meaning of the Comic* (London: Macmillan, 1911), 96.

54. On Helen's approximation of Mary, see McCandless, "Helena's Bed-trick," 456; and Harris, "All Swell That End Swell," 172.

55. Kastan, "*All's Well That Ends Well* and the Limits of Comedy," 586.

56. Erzen, *Straight to Jesus*, 229.

4. Happy Endings II

1. By the "primal scene" of the obscene joke, I mean the joke's basic libidinal structure. Freud speaks only of the joke's primary "conditions." In Freud's taxonomy, a joke that is not "innocent," or "is not an aim in itself," is either "a *hostile* joke (serving the purpose of aggressiveness, satire, or defense) or an *obscene* joke (serving the purpose of exposure)" (*Standard Edition*, 8:96–97).

2. Freud, *Standard Edition*, 8:100.

3. Ibid., 8:97–98.

4. Ibid., 8:97.

5. Copjec, *Read My Desire*, 34.

6. Linda Williams, *Hard Core: Power, Pleasure, and the "Frenzy of the Visible"* (1989; repr. Berkeley and Los Angeles: University of California Press, 1999), 50.

7. This thesis places me at odds with Ian Fredrick Moulton's in *Before Pornography: Erotic Writing in Early Modern England* (Oxford: Oxford University Press, 2000). As his title indicates, Moulton differentiates pornography (which is principally visual, as its etymology suggests) from early modern erotic writing.

8. I want to be explicit about the fact that I am concerned here with "heterosexual" pornography's representation of sexual difference *qua* orificial difference. The pornographic representation of female pleasures that Williams so brilliantly analyzes are distinctly vaginal and/or clitoral pleasures. She is largely unconcerned with gay porns, which are themselves comparatively unconcerned with sexual difference, though they are guided by different kinds of representational imperatives. In *Unlimited Intimacy: Reflections on the Subculture of Barebacking* (Chicago: University of Chicago Press, 2010), Tim Dean argues that heterosexual anal porn and gay male bareback porn, both of which frequently fetishize the dilated anus, emphasize not sexual difference but rather the difference between the body's exterior and its interior. He rightly notes that "only in a heterosexist imagination does sexual difference constitute the primary, structuring difference" between bodies (111).

9. John Donne, *The Complete English Poems of John Donne,* ed. C. A. Patrides. (London: Dent, 1985).

10. Jonathan Sawday, *The Body Emblazoned: Dissection and the Human Body in Renaissance Culture* (New York: Routledge, 1995), 206.

11. Kaja Silverman, *Male Subjectivity at the Margins* (New York: Routledge, 1992), 144.

12. *Happy Endings,* directed by Don Roos (Lions Gate Films, 2005).

13. Roland Barthes, *The Pleasure of the Text,* trans. Richard Miller (New York: Hill and Wang, 1979), 9–10.

14. Harris, "All Swell That End Swell," 169–70.

15. Edelman, *No Future.*

16. In "Tom Nashe and Jack Wilton: Personality as Structure in *The Unfortunate Traveler,*" *Studies in Short Fiction* 3 (1967), 201–16, Richard A. Lanham writes, "Literary analysis is helpless" to account for Nashe's violence (214). In *Thomas Nashe and the Scandal of Authorship* (Baltimore: The Johns Hopkins University Press, 1982), Jonathan Crewe similarly remarks on the "nonsignifying excess of violence that repeatedly confronts readers of *The Unfortunate Traveller* " (75).

17. Steven R. Mentz, "The Heroine as Courtesan: Dishonesty, Romance, and the Sense of an Ending in *The Unfortunate Traveler,*" *Studies in Philology* 98 (2001): 343–44. Mentz reproduces part of this essay as "Dishonest Romance: Greene and Nashe," in *Romance for Sale in Early Modern England: The Rise of Prose Fiction*

(Burlington, Vt.: Ashgate, 2006), 173–206. See also Frank Kermode, *The Sense of an Ending: Studies in the Theory of Fiction* (1966; repr., Oxford: Oxford University Press, 2000), 6.

18. Critics who view *The Unfortunate Traveller* as generically incoherent include G. R. Hibbard, *Thomas Nashe: A Critical Introduction* (Cambridge, Mass.: Harvard University Press, 1962); David Kaula, "The Low Style in Nashe's *Unfortunate Traveller*," *Studies in English Literature* 6 (1966): 43–57; and Alexander Leggat, "Artistic Coherence in *The Unfortunate Traveller*," *Studies in English Literature* 14 (1974): 31–46. Stanley Wells, *Thomas Nashe* (London: Arnold, 1964), holds a similar view on the work's genres, though he emphasizes Nashe's aim to provide a "variety of mirth" (8). For further discussion of attempts to classify *The Unfortunate Traveller*, see Ann Rosalind Jones, "Inside the Outside: Nashe's *Unfortunate Traveller* and Bakhtin's Polyphonic Novel," *ELH* 50, no. 1 (1983): 63; Louise Simons, "Rerouting *The Unfortunate Traveler*: Strategies for Coherence and Direction," *Studies in English Literature* 28 (1988): 18–23; and Wendy Hyman, "Authorial Self-Consciousness in Nashe's *The Vnfortunate Traveller*," *Studies in English Literature* 45, no. 1 (2005): 23–25. Though not about *The Unfortunate Traveller* per se, see also Lorna Hutson's essay on the difference between Elizabethan prose fiction and plot-driven novels: "Fortunate Travelers: Reading for the Plot in Sixteenth-Century England," *Representations* 41 (1993): 83–103.

19. Mentz, "The Heroine as Courtesan," 342.

20. As Mentz notes, the scholarship on Nashe's skepticism is considerable ("The Heroine as Courtesan," 340 n4), but see in particular Arthur F. Kinney, "Thomas Nashe and the Revival of the Second Sophistic," in *Humanist Poetics: Thought, Rhetoric, and Fiction in Sixteen-Century England* (Amherst: University of Massachusetts Press, 1986), 304–62.

21. Margaret Ferguson, "Nashe's *Unfortunate Traveller*: The 'Newes of the Maker' Game," *ELH* 11 (1981): 167.

22. Mentz, "The Heroine as Courtesan," 343.

23. All quotes from *The Unfortunate Traveller* are drawn from Thomas Nashe, *The Unfortunate Traveller and Other Works,* ed. J. B. Steane (New York: Penguin, 1982).

24. The phrase "spectacle of the scaffold" belongs to Michel Foucault, *Discipline and Punish: The Birth of the Prison,* trans. Alan Sheridan (New York: Random House, 1995).

25. On the sadomasochistic pleasures of this spectacle, see Marshall, *The Shattering of the Self,* 104–5.

26. In "Film Bodies: Gender, Genre, and Excess," in *Film Genre Reader III,* ed. Barry Keith Grant (Austin: University of Texas Press, 2003), 141–59, Linda

Williams groups horror, pornography, and melodrama together as "body genres." See also Isabel Cristina Pinedo, "The Pleasures of Seeing/Not Seeing the Spectacle of the Wet Death," in *Recreational Terror: Women and the Pleasures of Horror Film Viewing* (Albany: State University of New York Press, 1997), 51–68; and Carol Clover, "Her Body, Himself: Gender in the Slasher Film," *Representations* 20 (1987): 187–288. Clover's focus on the relationship between slasher films and pornography moves to the background in her more extensive consideration of horror cinema, *Men, Women, and Chainsaws: Gender in the Modern Horror Film* (Princeton, N.J.: Princeton University Press, 1993).

27. Sawday, "The Body in the Theater of Desire," in *The Body Emblazoned,* 39–53. On *The Unfortunate Traveller*'s relationship to anatomies, as well as the relationship between anatomies and executions, see also Andrew Fleck, "Anatomizing the Body Politic: The Nation and the Renaissance Body in Thomas Nashe's *Unfortunate Traveller,*" *Modern Philology* 104 (2007): 295–328; and Hillary M. Nunn, *Staging Anatomies: Dissection and Spectacle in Early Stuart Tragedy* (Burlington, Vt.: Ashgate, 2005), 38.

28. Foucault, *Discipline and Punish,* 45.

29. Jonathan Gil Harris, *Foreign Bodies and the Body Politic: Discourses of Social Pathology in Early Modern England* (Cambridge: Cambridge University Press, 1998), 80.

30. Ibid., 88.

31. Whigham, "Reading Social Conflict in the Alimentary Tract," 338.

32. Clover, "Her Body, Himself."

33. Mentz, "The Heroine as Courtesan," 345.

34. Mentz actually treats the prose romance sources of *All's Well* in "Revising the Sources: Novella, Romance, and the Meanings of Fiction in *All's Well, That Ends Well,*" in *All's Well, That Ends Well: New Critical Essays,* ed. Waller, 57–70.

35. René Girard, *The Scapegoat,* trans. Yvonne Freccero (Baltimore: The Johns Hopkins University Press, 1989).

36. Michael Keefer, "Violence and Extremity: Nashe's *Unfortunate Traveller* as an Anatomy of Abjection," in *Critical Approaches to Elizabethan Prose Fiction, 1520–1640,* ed. Donald Beecher (Ottowa: Dovehouse, 1998), 202–3.

37. Lorna Hutson, *Thomas Nashe in Context* (Oxford: Clarendon Press, 1989), 240.

38. Freud, *Standard Edition,* 17:79.

39. Yates, *Error, Misuse, Failure,* 132.

40. Ibid.

41. On Nashe's admiration for and identification with Aretino, see Moulton, *Before Pornography,* 159–68.

42. Yates, *Error, Misuse, Failure*, 131–32.

43. Ibid., 133. See also Barbara J. Baines, *Representing Rape in the English Early Modern Period* (Lewiston, N.Y.: Edwin Mellen Press, 2003), 120–26.

44. More accurately, as Constance C. Relihan observes in "Rhetoric, Gender, and Audience Construction in Thomas Nashe's *The Unfortunate Traveller,*" in *Framing Elizabethan Fiction: Contemporary Approaches to Early Modern Narrative Prose,* ed. Constance C. Relihan, 141–52 (Kent, Ohio: Kent State University Press, 1996), Wilton is both the orator and writer of his tale, and his audience comprises both listeners and readers.

45. In *Shakespeare's Entrails,* David Hillman offers a pertinent discussion of the similarity between Nashe's and Freud's theories of dreams. Both Nashe and Freud maintain that dreams are the products of bodily stimuli, including indigestion, and translated experiences (24). As Hillman further points out, Freud tropes the untranslatable content of a dream as its "navel." I would argue that in Wilton's representation of Heraclide's rape, including the description of Heraclide's husband awakening "as out of a dream," Nashe also forges this "implicit link between dreams, guts, and unknowability" (25).

46. Freud, *Standard Edition,* 8:101.

47. Matthew Biberman, *Masculinity, Anti-Semitism, and Early Modern English Literature: From the Satanic to the Effeminate Jew* (Burlington, Vt.: Ashgate, 2004), 19.

48. Slavoj Žižek, "Neighbors and Other Monsters: A Plea for Ethical Violence," in *The Neighbor: Three Inquiries in Political Theology,* Slavoj Žižek, Eric L. Santner, and Kenneth Reinhard (Chicago: University of Chicago Press, 2006), 147.

49. See Jean Laplanche, "Notes on Afterwardsness," in *Essays on Otherness,* 260–65.

50. Freud, *Standard Edition,* 17:245.

51. Ibid., 13:144.

52. Slavoj Žižek, *Enjoy Your Symptom! Jacques Lacan in Hollywood and Out* (New York: Routledge, 1992), 125.

53. Jacques Lacan, *The Ethics of Psychoanalysis, 1959–1960: The Seminar of Jacques Lacan, Book VII,* ed. Jacques-Alain Miller, trans. Dennis Porter (New York: Norton, 1986), 97.

54. Ferguson, "Nashe's *Unfortunate Traveller,*" 165. See also Mihoko Suzuki, "'Signiorie ouer the Pages': The Crisis of Authority in Nashe's *The Unfortunate Traveller,*" *Studies in Philology* 81 (1984): 348–71.

55. Joan Pong Linton, "Counterfeiting Sovereignty, Mocking Mastery: Trickster Poetics and the Critique of Romance in Nashe's *Unfortunate Traveller,*" in *Early Modern Prose Fiction: The Cultural Politics of Reading,* ed. Naomi Conn Liebler (New York: Routledge, 2006), 131.

56. My reading of this scene is greatly indebted to Yates, *Error, Misuse, Failure,* 116–23.

57. Stephen Greenblatt, "Filthy Rites," in *Learning to Curse: Essays in Early Modern Culture* (New York: Routledge, 1990), 70.

58. Ibid., 68.

59. Ibid.

60. I owe the details about the Duke of Burbon and the Field of the Cloth of Gold to J. B. Steane's notes to *The Unfortunate Traveller.* See, respectively, 358 n330 and 370 n347.

61. Michael Keefer picks up on the comedy of such remarks by arguing that they constitute a travesty of apocalyptic discourse — "a discourse, literally, of unveiling, which reveals the structures, causality and purposes of human time in a manner analogous to that in which the anatomist's flaying of a corpse exposes the hidden structures, organs and functioning of the human body" ("Violence and Extremity," 196).

62. Following David Hillman's work in *Shakespeare's Entrails,* one could locate *The Unfortunate Traveller* in the context of Protestantism's "de-corporealisation of belief" (40), which lends itself to skepticism about the relationship between the somatic and sacred.

63. For this analysis of the banquet house, see Yates, *Error, Misuse, Failure,* 125–30.

64. Žižek, "Neighbors and Other Monsters," 162–63.

65. Thomas Hobbes, *Leviathan,* ed. Edwin Curley (Indianapolis: Hackett, 1994), 32.

66. Bergson, *Laughter,* 4.

67. Copjec, *Read My Desire,* 43

68. The accusation of "bad taste" belongs to J. B. Steane, editor of the Penguin edition of *The Unfortunate Traveller* (32). I am also thinking of C. S. Lewis's oft-quoted sentiment, with its possible pun on "nothing": "In a certain sense of the verb 'say,' if asked what Nashe 'says,' we should have to reply, 'Nothing.'" See C. S. Lewis, *English Literature in the Sixteenth Century Excluding Drama* (Oxford: Clarendon Press, 1954), 416.

69. As Susan Bordo argues of Gibson's earlier film *Braveheart,* Gibson valorizes a masculine body that proves its worth through sustaining absurd amounts of torture. I would argue in this vein that *The Passion of the Christ* exemplifies the way anti-Semitism continues to discipline Christian masculinity. Jack Wilton could even provide the film's tagline: "[T]here's no such ready way to make a man a true Christian as to persuade himself he is taken up for an anatomy" (349). See Susan Bordo, "*Braveheart, Babe,* and the Contemporary Body," in *Twilight Zones:*

The Hidden Life of Cultural Images from Plato to O. J. (Berkeley and Los Angeles: University of California Press, 1997), 27–65.

70. I am inspired here by Alenka Zupančič's discussion of comedy as a "short circuit" between the universal and the concrete, in this case the Christian order of salvation and the Jews who founded that order. See *The Odd One In: On Comedy* (Cambridge, Mass.: The MIT Press, 2008).

71. Sarah Silverman tells this joke in her film *Jesus Is Magic,* directed by Liam Lynch (Black Gold Films, 2005).

72. Linton, "Counterfeiting Sovereignty, Mocking Mastery," 132.

5. The Pardoner's Dirty Breeches

1. Deleuze and Guattari, *Anti-Oedipus,* 225.

2. Max Horkheimer and Theodor W. Adorno, *Dialectic of Enlightenment,* trans. Edmund Jephcott (Stanford, Calif.: Stanford University Press, 2002), 33.

3. Karl Marx and Peter Engels, *The Marx-Engels Reader,* 2nd edition, ed. Robert C. Tucker (New York: Norton, 1978), 322. For the original German, see Karl Marx, *Das Kapital: Kritik der politischen Ökonomie,* in *Marx-Engels Werke,* vol. 23, ed. Institut für Marxismus-Leninusmus beim SK der SED (Berlin: Dietz Verlag, 1962), 88.

4. Žižek, *The Sublime Object of Ideology,* 30. Žižek, it must be said, is trying to rescue Marx from the Marxists. He argues for a more cynically attuned Marx who distinguishes between theory (what we know) and practice (what we do despite what we know).

5. Peter Sloterdijk, *Critique of Cynical Reason,* trans. Michael Eldred (Minneapolis: University of Minnesota Press, 1987).

6. Žižek, *The Sublime Object of Ideology,* 29. All quotes from *The Canterbury Tales* come from *The Riverside Chaucer,* 3rd edition, ed. Larry D. Benson (Boston: Houghton Mifflin, 1987).

7. Žižek, *The Sublime Object of Ideology,* 29. Sloterdijk uses the phrase "enlightened false consciousness" as a synonym for cynicism throughout his book.

8. On the Pardoner's often contradictory evocation of both medieval and modern social persons, see Elizabeth Fowler, "Chaucer and the Habituation of the Reader: The Pardoner's Thought Experiment," in *Literary Character: The Human Figure in Early English Writing* (Ithaca, N.Y.: Cornell University Press, 2003), 32–94.

9. For two such readings, see Lee Patterson, "The Subject of Confession: The Pardoner and the Rhetoric of Penance," in *Chaucer and the Subject of History,* 367–421 (Madison: University of Wisconsin Press, 1991); and Carolyn Dinshaw,

"Eunuch Hermeneutics," in *Chaucer's Sexual Poetics,* 156–84 (Madison: University of Wisconsin Press, 1991).

10. Robert S. Sturges, *Chaucer's Pardoner and Gender Theory: Bodies of Discourse* (New York: St. Martin's Press, 2000), 40.

11. I borrow my characterization of the gloss from Alastair Minnis, "Chaucer and the Queering Eunuch," *New Medieval Literatures* 6 (2003): 125. Monica McAlpine first made the controversial claim for the Pardoner's homosexuality in "The Pardoner's Homosexuality and How it Matters," *PMLA* 95 (1980): 8–22.

12. Richard Firth Green makes this argument in "The Sexual Normalcy of Chaucer's Pardoner," *Mediaevalia* 8 (1982): 351–57.

13. Glenn Burger, *Chaucer's Queer Nation* (Minneapolis: University of Minnesota Press, 2003), 140. Burger's argument in *Chaucer's Queer Nation* is a revision of his earlier, important essay "Kissing the Pardoner," *PMLA* 107 (1992): 1143–56, one of the first markedly queer readings of the Pardoner. See also Steven F. Kruger, "Claiming the Pardoner: Toward a Gay Reading of Chaucer's Pardoner's Tale," *Exemplaria* 6 (1994): 115–39.

14. Burger, *Chaucer's Queer Nation,* 141.

15. Carolyn Dinshaw, *Getting Medieval: Sexualities and Communities, Pre- and Postmodern* (Durham, N.C.: Duke University Press, 1999), 135.

16. Ibid., 115–16. Dinshaw relies on Alan John Fletcher, "The Topical Heresy of Chaucer's Pardoner," *Chaucer Review* 25 (1990): 110–26. See also Lee Patterson, "Chaucer's Pardoner on the Couch: Psyche and Clio in Medieval Literary Studies," *Speculum* 76, no. 3 (2001): 638–80. Although I rely on Patterson's work in what follows, Patterson simultaneously offers in this essay a harsh (if familiar) critique of psychoanalytic approaches to medieval history and literature. While I would hope that a full engagement with Patterson's critique is unnecessary, part of my aim here is to show that the sharp division Patterson imposes between a medieval interpretive context for the Pardoner (the reformist condemnation of simony) and a psychoanalytic context (the Oedipus complex and phallic lack) overlooks what these contexts have in common, and the way this commonality allows us to do exactly what Patterson requests: "to approach [psychoanalysis] with a full awareness of its own historicity" (679).

17. Dinshaw, *Getting Medieval,* 142.

18. Paul Strohm, *Hochon's Arrow: The Social Imagination of Fourteenth-Century Texts* (Princeton, N.J.: Princeton University Press, 1992), 3.

19. Strohm, "Saving the Appearances: Chaucer's 'Purse' and the Fabrication of the Lancastrian Claim," in *Hochon's Arrow,* 75–94.

20. Sloterdijk, *Critique of Cynical Reason,* 102.

21. Žižek, *The Sublime Object of Ideology,* 29.

22. Sloterdijk, *Critique of Cynical Reason,* 104 (original italics), 139.

23. Ibid., 148.

24. Peter W. Travis, "Thirteen Ways of Listening to a Fart: Noise in Chaucer's *Summoner's Tale,*" *Exemplaria* 16, no. 2 (2004): 17. See also Valerie Allen, *On Farting: Language and Laughter in the Middle Ages* (New York: Palgrave Macmillan, 2006), as well as two articles on The Summoner's Tale in particular: Tiffany Beechy, "Devil Take the Hindmost: Chaucer, John Gay, and the Pecuniary Anus," *Chaucer Review* 41, no. 1 (2006): 71–85; and Mary Hayes, "Privy Speech: Sacred Silence, Dirty Secrets in the Summoner's Tale," *Chaucer Review* 40, no. 3 (2006): 263–88. Hayes's reading of Thomas's fart as a parody of liturgical silence echoes the psychoanalytic account of divine secrecy that I develop later in this chapter.

25. On sodomy and The Miller's Tale, see David Lorenzo Boyd, "Seeking 'Goddes pryvetee': Sodomy, Quitting, and Desire in The Miller's Tale," in *Words and Works: Studies in Medieval English Language and Literature in Honour of Fred C. Robinson,* ed. Peter S. Baker and Nicholas Howe, 243–60 (Toronto: University of Toronto Press, 1998).

26. On the Miller's parodies of these Biblical stories, see Beryl Rowland, "Chaucer's Blasphemous Churl: A New Interpretation of the Miller's Tale," in *Chaucer and Middle English Studies in Honor of Rossell Hope Robbins,* ed. Beryl Rowland, 43–55 (Kent: Ohio University Press, 1974); and Laura Kendrick, *Chaucerian Play: Comedy and Control in the Canterbury Tales* (Berkeley and Los Angeles: University of California Press, 1988), 16–19.

27. Fowler, *Literary Character,* 40.

28. Mark Jordan, *The Invention of Sodomy in Christian Theology* (Chicago: University of Chicago Press, 1998), 176.

29. See Sturges, "The Pardoner's Different Erotic Practices," in *Chaucer's Pardoner and Gender Theory,* 47–59; and John M. Bowers, "Queering the Summoner: Same-Sex Union in Chaucer's *Canterbury Tales,*" in *Speaking Images: Essays in Honor of V.A. Kolve,* ed. R. F. Yeager and Charlotte C. Morse, 301–24 (Asheville, N.C.: Pegasus Press, 2001).

30. "burden, burthene, *n,*" *OED Online.* The *OED* cites a 1250 translation of Genesis and Exodus as the first appearance of *burdene* to mean pregnancy.

31. Freud, *Standard Edition,* 21:97.

32. Lacan, *The Ethics of Psychoanalysis,* 293.

33. Patterson, *Chaucer and the Subject of History,* 410. See also William Kamowski, "'Coillions,' Relics, Skepticism, and Faith on Chaucer's Road to Canterbury: An Observation on the Pardoner's and the Host's Confrontation," *English Language Notes* 28 (1991): 5–7; and Morrison, *Excrement in the Late Middle Ages,* 97–101.

34. Guibert de Nogent, "Treatise on Relics," in *Life in the Middle Ages,* vol. 1, ed. C. G. Coulton (New York: Macmillan, 1910), 22.

35. Burger, *Chaucer's Queer Nation,* 152.

36. Ibid.

37. Ibid. Here is where I think both Burger's and Patterson's readings remain more persuasive than Alastair Minnis's more recent assessment of the Pardoner as simply too materialistic to reap the benefits of the spiritual economy of pilgrimage. See Alastair Minnis, "Purchasing Pardon: Material and Spiritual Economies on the Canterbury Pilgrimage," in *Sacred and Secular in Medieval and Early Modern Cultures,* ed. Lawrence Besserman, 63–82 (New York: Palgrave Macmillan, 2006); and "Reclaiming the Pardoners," *Journal of Medieval and Early Modern Studies* 33, no. 2 (2003): 311–34. In the latter essay, Minnis objects to Burger's argument for the "open secret" on the dual grounds that there is no textual evidence for it and that it depends on each pilgrim's knowledge of reformist critiques regarding pardoning and pilgrimage — a knowledge Minnis questions (333 n53 and 334 n60). I would argue that the open secret is less something each pilgrim must know than something that is symptomatically present within and across the text, and between the text and its readers. Likewise, reformist critiques are less something each pilgrim must know than an indisputable cultural influence on the text itself. Maintaining that Chaucer is not a Lollard but one whose fiction makes "gestures of difference" (xvi) that are not necessarily legible as heresy, Minnis explores this influence extensively in a trenchant book that reprints some of the arguments in these essays: *Fallible Authors: Chaucer's Pardoner and the Wife of Bath* (Philadelphia: University of Pennsylvania Press, 2008).

38. In *Castration: An Abbreviated History of Western Manhood* (New York: Routledge, 2002), Gary Taylor observes that testicles were more important than the penis as signifiers of pre- and early modern masculinity. Of course, castration even now technically refers to the removal of the testicles, but this fact is largely lost in the psychoanalytic use of the term to denote phallic lack.

39. Georges Bataille, "The Psychological Structure of Fascism," in *Visions of Excess: Selected Writings, 1927–1939,* trans. Allan Stoekl (Minneapolis: University of Minnesota Press, 1985), 137. I take my cue here from Linda Charnes, who similarly appeals to Bataille in *Notorious Identity: Materializing the Subject in Shakespeare* (Cambridge, Mass.: Harvard University Press, 1993) to argue that Shakespeare's Richard III is the heterogeneous product of the political economy of divine right (48).

40. Bataille, "The Psychological Structure of Fascism," 142 (original italics).

41. Besides Minnis's *Fallible Authors,* see David Aers, "Faith, Ethics, and Chaucer," in *Faith, Ethics, and Church: Writing in England, 1360–1409* (Cambridge: D. S. Brewer, 2000), 25–55.

42. Patterson, "Chaucer's Pardoner on the Couch," 664.

43. As R. A. Shoaf argues in *Dante, Chaucer, and the Currency of the Word: Money, Images, and Reference in Late Medieval Poetry* (Norman, Okla.: Pilgrim Press, 1983), "faith, first and foremost, was faith in the ontological relation between word and thing" (13). Shoaf's Pardoner is a man of faith: "He takes metaphors seriously, and he believes that words are creative" (218).

44. Lacan, *The Ethics of Psychoanalysis*, 112.

45. Žižek, *The Sublime Object of Ideology*, 18.

46. Lacan, *The Ethics of Psychoanalysis*, 54.

47. Ibid., 92–93.

48. Slavoj Žižek, *The Ticklish Subject: The Absent Centre of Political Ontology* (New York: Verso, 1999), 157.

49. Here I echo Valerie Rohy: "As queer theory has turned back to the question of temporality, it has discovered in itself the ageless anachronism whose other name is literariness" ("Ahistorical," 71).

50. See Norman O. Brown, "The Protestant Era," in *Life against Death*, 202–33.

51. Fowler, *Literary Character*, 85.

52. Lacan, *The Ethics of Psychoanalysis*, 58.

53. Halpern, *Shakespeare's Perfume*, 94.

54. Citing Catherine S. Cox, "'Grope wel bihynde': The Subversive Erotics of Chaucer's Summoner," *Exemplaria* 7 (1995): 145–77, Michael O'Rourke develops a related argument apropos of The Summoner's Tale in a post about Chaucerian fisting on the blog *In the Middle*: "Catherine Cox in a discussion of the textual erotics of the Summoner's Tale persuasively argues that when the Friar unadvisedly gropes Thomas's behind, places his hand in Thomas's 'clifte,' and receives the gift of a fart 'amydde his hand,' we are reminded of an earlier scene when the Friar explains how the law was written with God's finger. If one conflates the Friar's glossing with his groping, then one can argue that, as Cox suggests, 'Thomas receives Friar John's finger.' However, I would go even further, and Chaucer's text permits my reading, and say that Thomas's anus is penetrated by the entire hand or fist of the Friar. The Friar penetrates, gropes Thomas enthusiastically; the sexual encounter is, however, invited, not coerced and cannot be recuperated for a reading of eroticized violence and/or rape as other Chaucerian penetrations can. Rather, it charts the possibility for an erotic or social encounter beyond the phallus. The Friar... assumes an aggressive, assertive role and eagerly gropes the 'tuwel' of his 'compeer' (the Summoner gets to grope the Pardoner perhaps?) in search of the unnamed 'thyng' located in his 'pryvetee,' that is to say, inhabiting the zone of secret, private, but also genital territories as David

Lorenzo Boyd has shown in a discussion of the Miller's Tale." See http://jjcohen.blogspot.com/2007/03/fisting-and-other-gifts-for-graduate.html (accessed September 9, 2010).

55. On the Miller's "confusion of orifices," see Karma Lochrie, *Covert Operations: The Medieval Uses of Secrecy* (Philadelphia: University of Pennsylvania Press, 1999), 173; and Louise M. Bishop, "Of Goddes pyvetee nor of his wyf: Confusion of Orifices in Chaucer's Miller's Tale," *Texas Studies in Literature and Language* 44, no. 3 (2002): 231–46.

56. Elaine Tuttle Hansen, *Chaucer and the Fictions of Gender* (Berkeley and Los Angeles: University of California Press, 1992), 230; also quoted in Patterson, "Chaucer's Pardoner on the Couch," 644. Though it is true, as Patterson argues, that Hansen's argument relies on the Freudian interpretation of Oedipus, Hansen knows that Oedipus is no crude universal, but rather a "fiction" that The Miller's Tale "anticipated" (Hansen 230).

57. Lacan, *The Ethics of Psychoanalysis,* 149. See Slavoj Žižek, "Courtly Love, or Woman as Thing," in *The Metastases of Enjoyment: Six Essays on Woman and Causality* (New York: Verso, 1994), 89–112; Sarah Kay, *Courtly Contradictions: The Emergence of the Literary Object in the Twelfth Century* (Stanford, Calif.: Stanford University Press, 2001); L. O. Aranye Fradenburg, *Sacrifice Your Love: Psychoanalysis, Historicism, Chaucer* (Minneapolis: University of Minnesota Press, 2002), 18–24; Bruce Holsinger, *The Premodern Condition: Medievalism and the Making of Theory* (Chicago: University of Chicago Press, 2005), 83–87; and Erin Felicia Labbie, *Lacan's Medievalism* (Minneapolis: University of Minnesota Press, 2006).

58. Quoted in Lacan, *The Ethics of Psychoanalysis,* 162.

59. Ibid.

60. Ibid.

61. Ibid., 161, 163.

62. Labbie, *Lacan's Medievalism,* 98.

63. Jacques Lacan, *On Feminine Sexuality, The Limits of Love and Knowledge, 1972–1973: Encore, The Seminar of Jacques Lacan, Book XX,* ed. Jacques-Alain Miller, trans. Bruce Fink (New York: Norton, 1998), 69.

64. Ibid., 74.

65. Lochrie, *Covert Operations,* 175.

66. On the collapse of the sacred and the filthy in The Prioress's Tale, see Morrison, *Excrement in the Late Middle Ages,* 85–88.

67. Dean, *Beyond Sexuality,* 266.

68. Lacan, *The Ethics of Psychoanalysis,* 122.

69. Lacan, *The Four Fundamental Concepts of Psychoanalysis,* 5.

70. The antisocial strain of queer theory derives in large part from Leo Bersani's conjunction of sexuality with anatomizing, self-shattering *jouissance* in "Is the Rectum a Grave?" but much critical attention has lately focused on Lee Edelman's *No Future*. For Edelman, queerness is synonymous with the death drive: "The death drive names what the queer, in the order of the social, is called forth to figure: the negativity opposed to every form of social viability" (9). Here I emphasize an alternative strain of queer theorizing focused on the importance of developing nonheteronormative forms of sociality: see, among many examples, Leo Bersani, *Homos* (Cambridge, Mass.: Harvard University Press, 1995); Leo Bersani, "Sociality and Sexuality," *Critical Inquiry* 26 (2002): 641–56; Michael Snediker, *Queer Optimism: Lyric Personhood and Other Felicitous Persuasions* (Minneapolis: University of Minnesota Press, 2008); and Muñoz, *Cruising Utopia*.

71. Slavoj Žižek, *The Fragile Absolute or, Why Is the Christian Legacy Worth Fighting For?* (New York: Verso, 2000), 32.

72. Ibid., 31.

73. Sloterdijk, *Critique of Cynical Reason,* 144.

74. Ibid.

75. This claim does not discount the fact that specific tales, the Man of Law's and the Prioress's foremost among them, brutally carve out Christian communities from their Islamic and Jewish others.

76. Tison Pugh argues that the kiss queers the Host in "Queering Harry Bailly: Gendered Carnival, Social Ideologies, and Masculinity under Duress in *The Canterbury Tales,*" *Chaucer Review* 41, no. 1 (2006): 57. Glenn Burger argues that the kiss queers the pilgrimage by reincorporating the Pardoner's perverse body into the body of Christ (*Chaucer's Queer Nation,* 147).

77. Burger, *Chaucer's Queer Nation,* 147.

78. Dinshaw, *Getting Medieval,* 135.

79. Rather late in my work on this chapter, I discovered John M. Hill's complementary thesis in *Chaucerian Belief: The Poetics of Reverence and Delight* (New Haven, Conn.: Yale University Press, 1991). Hill describes Chaucer's "openness of belief" ("not faith") as the author's "way of entertaining seriously whatever comes his way through fictions, especially those truth claims found in old books. This does not commit him to a general relativism or to the emptiness of competing ideas juggled purely in the spirit of play. Rather, Chaucer would gather all kinds of tales as his empirical ground for sorting through various claims about any number of subjects" (6–7).

80. I derive the notion of queer world-making in large part from Lauren Berlant and Michael Warner, "Sex in Public," *Critical Inquiry* 24, no. 2 (1998): 547–66.

"The queer world," they write, "is a space of entrances, exits, unsystematized lines of acquaintance, projected horizons, typifying examples, alternate routes, blockages, incommensurate geographies" (558).

81. Jeffrey Jerome Cohen, *Medieval Identity Machines* (Minneapolis: University of Minnesota Press, 2003), 23. See also Glenn Burger, "Post-ality and the 'End' of *The Canterbury Tales*," in *Chaucer's Queer Nation*, 186–207.

Index

Will Stockton is assistant professor of English at Clemson University.